The Psalms

A Primer for Prayer

WILLIAM BARRICK

WITH ERIC KRESS

Published by:
Kress Biblical Resources
www.kressbiblical.com

NASB: Scripture quotations taken from the New American Standard Bible® (NASB), Copyright © 1960, 1962, 1963, 1968, 1971, 1972, 1973, 1975, 1977, 1995 by The Lockman Foundation. Used by permission. www.Lockman.org

Cover Design: Terry McClain

ISBN: 978-1-934952-61-0

We dedicate this volume on praying the Psalter to a godly and prayer-oriented man, Dr. James E. Rosscup, who entered his Savior's presence on November 5, 2020. By his patient instruction and persistent example, he taught many believers how to pray. May God give to the church men and women of prayer like our beloved mentor, colleague, and friend. A prior James, half-brother of our Lord, also known for his praying, left us a fitting epitaph for Dr. Rosscup:

"The effective prayer of a righteous man
can accomplish much."

James 5:16

Introduction

The very title of the Book of Psalms (*Tehillim*) means "Praises" or "Prayers." The Psalter is a collection of prayers, just as the composer of Books 1 and 2 indicates in the closing appended to Solomon's psalm: "The prayers of David the son of Jesse are ended" (Ps. 72:20). Such an ending implies Solomon's hand in compiling the final form of Books 1 and 2, even though David himself might have chosen most of their contents. The five different books or divisions of the Psalter reflect various stages of its compilation (similar to what we see in the book of Proverbs—see Prov. 25:1). David had written many psalms, so most of the books within the Psalter include some of his works. Some of the psalms are titled as "a prayer" (Pss. 17, 86, 90, 102, 142); others indicate that the psalmist is praying, speaking of his prayer, or exhorting others to pray (for example, Pss. 4:1; 5:2; 6:9; 17:1; 32:6; 35:13; 39:12). Therefore, it behooves God's people to take this book of prayer (the Psalter) in their hands to read, into their mouths to repeat, and into their hearts to pray. Thus we increase our own prayer life and, by example and teaching, encourage others to begin to pray more both privately and publicly.

Two specific spheres of prayer claim our attention as we pray through the Psalter: (1) The prayers of God's people as displayed in the individual psalms, and (2) the consideration of how Jesus Himself might have prayed these prayers. The first arises out of the variety of circumstances and petitioners involved in the production of the individual psalms. Some psalms remain anonymous—perhaps purposefully to engage believers as though the prayers were their very own expression. The second seeks to replicate the way Jesus prayed certain psalms during His ministry (for example, His praying Ps. 22:1 on the cross, Matt. 27:47).

Jesus Himself gave us an example of prayer and its significance. He withdrew to a mountain or to a wilderness area (Mark 1:35; Luke 5:16) away from people so He might pray—sometimes all night (cf. Matt 14:23; Mark 6:46; Luke 6:12; 9:28). We encounter Him praying at His baptism (Luke 3:21–22), thanking God for providing food for thousands (Matt. 15:36; Mark 8:6; John 6:11), praying to the Father at the raising of Lazarus from the dead (John 11:41–42), praying that the Father would send His Spirit for the disciples (John 14:16), interceding for His disciples and the fruit of their labors in the gospel (John 17), praying at the institution of the Lord's Supper (Matt. 26:26–27), praying for Peter (Luke 22:32), praying fervently in the Garden of Gethsemane (Luke 22:41–46), and calling out to the Father on the cross (Luke 22:34). When He taught His disciples how to pray (the "Lord's Prayer" in Matt. 6:7–13), Jesus, as the greater Son of David, uses the general pattern of David's prayer in 1 Chronicles 29:10–18, thus showing His disciples how to adapt and reword a prayer from prior Scripture when they pray. Since David contributed more psalms (or, prayers) to the Psalter than any other individual, we might expect the greater Son of David to echo those same prayers—and He does. His prayers are often either saturated with Scripture or with scriptural concepts, many of which occur in the Psalter. His own devotional life would have been saturated with reading and singing the psalms.

When the 70 disciples return to Jesus (Luke 10:17–22), Jesus gives thanks to the Father (10:21). His prayer paraphrases the prayer of thanks in Psalm 7:17, using the same Greek verb as the Septuagint and changing "LORD Most High" to "Lord of heaven and earth." As Jesus prepared to raise Lazarus (John 11:41–42), He paraphrased Psalm 118:21. His high priestly prayer in John 17:11–12 echoes Psalms 9:10 and 71:22. In Gethsemane (Matthew 26:38) Jesus seems to associate His own feelings with Psalms 42:5, 11 and 43:5. As He prays in Matthew 26:39, He echoes Psalms 40:8; 51:12; 116:4; and 143:10. He does not quote these psalms directly, but selects concepts from them that He applies in His prayer.

Jesus' disciples (including the apostles) also paraphrase prayers in the Psalter. Before they replace Judas with Matthias, they refer to God as the one who knows their hearts (Acts 1:24; Ps. 44:21). When Peter and John were released from prison, they praised God with an adaption of Psalm 146:6.

To Whom should we pray? Normally, we pray to the Father, just as Jesus instructed His disciples and in accordance with His own example (Matt. 6:6, 9; 11:25; John 17:1). However, prayer involves all three persons of the Godhead. We are familiar with their individual roles and describe prayer in the Trinitarian view as to the Father, in the name of Jesus, and with the help of the Holy Spirit (John 14:13–14; Rom. 8:26–27). Many believers ask whether they should ever pray directly to the Holy Spirit. When we pray, we speak to God and God involves all three persons of the Trinity. What we say to the Father, we also say to the Son and to the Spirit—all three hear our prayers. In order for the Spirit to intercede for us and help us in our praying, He must hear and know what we are praying. Indeed, every believer should be praying "in the Spirit" (Eph. 6:18; Jude 20; cp. Eph. 2:18). Jesus sent the Holy Spirit to teach us (John 14:26; 1 John 2:27). We abound in hope by the power of the Holy Spirit (Rom. 15:13), we are led by the Spirit (Gal. 5:18), and God commands us not to grieve the Spirit (Eph. 4:30). Therefore, nothing should be more natural than prayers like the following:

> Holy Spirit, help me to pray and make the thoughts of my heart clear.
> Spirit of God, teach me and give me a correct understanding of Your Word.
> Increase my hope—make it abound more and more, O Spirit of God.
> Dear Spirit, I'm so confused and desire to do my Father's will to the glory of His Son. Please lead me to do that which is right.
> I am sorry, Holy Spirit, that I have grieved You by how I have sinned.

The focus on Jesus Christ in this current guide to praying the Psalter arises out of our Savior's own use of the Psalter as well as the Psalter's testimony to Messiah. The Bible does not contain any prayers by the Spirit of God, but we do have the very words of a number of prayers Jesus addressed to His Father. Scripture is also quite clear that God's people may pray to Jesus specifically, not just to the Father. Believers may pray to Jesus because He is God and prayer to Him is one of the ways by which we testify to His deity. In the Gospel of John we learn how Jesus taught His followers to pray to Him (John 14:14; 15:16; 16:23–24). In Acts 1:24–25 we learn that His disciples prayed to Him at the time they chose a man to replace Judas Iscariot among Christ's apostles. Evidence of this prayer to Christ includes the fact that "chosen" is the same word Jesus Himself used in verse 2 and that Peter had just referred to Jesus as "Lord" in verse 21. Stephen, while he was being stoned to death, prayed to Jesus: "Lord Jesus, receive my spirit" and "Lord, do not hold this sin against them" (Acts 7:59, 60). Ananias told the newly born again Saul to be baptized and to pray by calling on Jesus' name (Acts 22:16). Indeed, when it comes to an individual's salvation, Paul taught that "everyone who calls on the name of the Lord will be saved" (Rom. 10:13; see 1 Cor. 1:2). Paul himself practiced praying to Christ when he asked Him to remove the "messenger of Satan" (2 Cor. 12:7–8). As the entire New Testament reaches its conclusion, we hear again a prayer to Jesus that we should be bringing before Him ourselves, "Come, Lord Jesus!" (Rev. 22:20–21).

As believers we constantly speak of what Jesus did for us in the past: He came to earth for us, He died for our sins, He rose again from the dead, and He ascended back into heaven. Prayer, however, focuses on His present work. We experience in prayer what Jesus is doing for us today. He intercedes for us. Indeed, all three persons of the Trinity engage in this present work: the Father hears and answers our prayers, the Son intercedes for us, and the Spirit also intercedes for us. Today, beloved, They work on our behalf while we pray! *Why would we through our prayerlessness risk missing out on Their present work?*

The ultimate worship of Christ Jesus must include our acknowledging His love for us (cf. John 17:23–25). His intercession for us exhibits one aspect of His love for us (Rom. 8:34). As we read the Psalter and pray individual psalms, let's also remind ourselves that Jesus Himself is interceding for us simultaneously (Heb. 7:25). When we pray, we come with hearts that are not always pure (Jas. 4:3), but Jesus comes before the Father without sin as our holy and pure High Priest (Heb. 4:14–15). Jesus asked the Father to send the Holy Spirit to minister to Jesus' disciples (John 14:16) and promised Peter He would pray for him (Luke 22:32). He, our Savior, fulfills His role as our Advocate before the Father (1 John 2:1). Andrew Murray reminds us,

> Because He prays, we pray too. As the disciples, when they saw Jesus pray, asked Him to make them partakers of what He knew of prayer, so we, now we see Him as intercessor on the throne, know that He makes us participate with Himself in the life of prayer.*

---

*   Andrew Murray, *With Christ in the School of Prayer: Thoughts on Our Training for the Ministry of Intercession* (Philadelphia: Rodgers Company, n.d.), 210.

We learn how to pray as He prayed and is now praying. We cannot hear His present intercessions, but we can reasonably deduce how He might be praying by learning from His prayers recorded in the Gospels. Therefore, this volume leading our prayer life in the Psalter provides potential prayers of Jesus Himself based upon His recorded prayers, teachings, and example. Such awareness and consideration should cause our love for Him, our trust in Him, and our praying alongside Him to abound all the more. As we grow in the knowledge of His love and care for us, we grow in our love and care for others, stimulated by interceding for them in prayer.

How to Use This Book of Prayer

1. Read each psalm in its entirety before letting the psalm guide your praying.
2. Start again at the beginning of each psalm. Read a verse. If there is a prayer in this book for that verse or its section, read it next. That prayer is merely one potential way of praying that text.
3. Now put the words of the verse and the suggested prayer into your own words—personalize them, if possible. Do not force the personalizing. Some verses or the suggested prayers might not apply to you or to your situation. Record prayers in the book's white spaces.
4. As you get the idea of personalizing a psalm's prayer in your own words, begin with reading the verse, pray your prayer, then look at the suggested prayer.
5. View the psalms in the Psalter as catalysts for prayer.
6. Lastly, read the potential intercessory prayer of your Savior at the conclusion of each psalm. Read the Bible references supporting different parts of that intercessory prayer. Meditate on those verses and dwell upon the fact that Christ is praying for you even at that moment. We cannot know exactly what He is praying, but we do know that He is. We also know that His prayers will always be in keeping with the Word. Periodically, read Jesus' high priestly prayer in John 17 and meditate on how you yourself are included in His prayer.

The following expressions occur often in the Psalms:

Selah May mean *Pause, Crescendo* or *Musical Interlude*
Maskil Possibly, *Contemplative,* or *Didactic,* or *Skillful Psalm*
Mikhtam Possibly, *Epigrammatic Poem,* or *Atonement Psalm*
Sheol The nether world

Book 1

Psalm 1

The Righteous and the Wicked Contrasted.

1   How blessed is the man who does not walk in the counsel of
       the wicked,
    Nor stand in the path of sinners,
    Nor sit in the seat of scoffers!
2   But his delight is in the law of the LORD,
    And in His law he meditates day and night.
3   He will be like a tree *firmly* planted by streams of water,
    Which yields its fruit in its season
    And its leaf does not wither;
    And in whatever he does, he prospers.

4   The wicked are not so,
    But they are like chaff which the wind drives away.
5   Therefore the wicked will not stand in the judgment,
    Nor sinners in the assembly of the righteous.
6   For the LORD knows the way of the righteous,
    But the way of the wicked will perish.

Praying Psalm 1

The preamble to the Psalter introducing Israel's (and the Church's) prayer book.

Blessed are You O God—the One Who blesses! You are the source of every blessing. Thank You for revealing the way of true satisfaction for mankind (v. 1).

Keep me from acting on sin, associating with sin, or even taking sin lightly. I need You, Lord (v. 1).

Spirit, please increase my delight in Your Word—the Word that You inspired and which exalts the Son (v. 2; cf. 2 Pet. 1:20–21; John 16:14).

I believe, Lord. But sometimes I feel the drought all around me closing in. I will wait for the fruitful season of Your promise (v. 3).

Father, Your judgment is just and good. Bring the unrighteous to judgment in Your time and Your way (vv. 4–5).

I praise You as the God of all grace, Who chooses to have a relationship with me—and all those who are right with You by faith in Your righteous Son, Jesus Christ (v. 6; cf. Rom. 4:5; 2 Cor. 5:21).

Thank You, Lord Jesus that though You are God, You humbled Yourself and lived as a man here with us. You always turned away from sin—and as a man, You fulfilled all righteousness for me. You too had to learn to live by faith and follow the blessed path revealed here in Psalm 1 (cf. Phil. 2:6–10; Heb. 2:14, 17–18; 4:15; 5:7–9).

How Jesus could be interceding for you: Father, bless Your people (Matt. 5:6; Luke 11:28); produce holiness and righteousness in them (John 17:17, 19).

Psalm 2

The Reign of the LORD's Anointed.

1   Why are the nations in an uproar
     And the peoples devising a vain thing?
2   The kings of the earth take their stand
     And the rulers take counsel together
     Against the LORD and against His Anointed, saying,
3   "Let us tear their fetters apart
     And cast away their cords from us!"

4   He who sits in the heavens laughs,
     The Lord scoffs at them.
5   Then He will speak to them in His anger
     And terrify them in His fury, saying,
6   "But as for Me, I have installed My King
     Upon Zion, My holy mountain."

7   "I will surely tell of the decree of the LORD:
     He said to Me, 'You are My Son,
     Today I have begotten You.
8   'Ask of Me, and I will surely give the nations as Your inheritance,
     And the *very* ends of the earth as Your possession.
9   'You shall break them with a rod of iron,
     You shall shatter them like earthenware.'"
10   Now therefore, O kings, show discernment;
     Take warning, O judges of the earth.
11   Worship the LORD with reverence
     And rejoice with trembling.
12   Do homage to the Son, that He not become angry, and you
          perish *in* the way,
     For His wrath may soon be kindled.
     How blessed are all who take refuge in Him!

Praying Psalm 2

Close of the Psalter's introduction by focusing on the Son of God, Messiah.

Your Word is true, Lord. Most of the world and the rulers of this world don't want to acknowledge You or submit to You (vv. 1–3).

Lord, put down rebellion—even in my own heart (vv. 1–3).

How foolish we are in our rebellion. O God, have mercy on us. Have mercy on this foolish world (vv. 4–5).

Thank You for Christ the King and His coming Kingdom (v. 6).

Come, Lord Jesus—rule over us in righteousness (vv. 7–9).

Father, teach presidents, kings, rulers, governors, legislators, dictators, mayors, and all people to worship You through Your Son (vv. 10–12).

Help me serve You, Lord, with reverential awe and rejoicing (v. 11).

I take refuge in You, Jesus, to save me, protect me, and guide me (v. 12).

I will delight in Your Word, Father, and trust in Your Son—I love You both. Thank You for Your blessing and the path of true satisfaction (Pss. 1:1; 2:12).

———

How Jesus could be interceding for you: Father, may Your Kingdom come through Me and may Your people remain alert for My coming (Luke 12:37) and experience all the blessings of My Kingdom (Matt. 6:10; 25:34; Luke 14:15).

Psalm 3

Morning Prayer of Trust in God.

A Psalm of David, when he fled from Absalom his son.

1   O Lord, how my adversaries have increased!
     Many are rising up against me.
2   Many are saying of my soul,
     "There is no deliverance for him in God."   *Selah.*

3   But You, O Lord, are a shield about me,
     My glory, and the One who lifts my head.
4   I was crying to the Lord with my voice,
     And He answered me from His holy mountain.   *Selah.*
5   I lay down and slept;
     I awoke, for the Lord sustains me.
6   I will not be afraid of ten thousands of people
     Who have set themselves against me round about.

7   Arise, O Lord; save me, O my God!
     For You have smitten all my enemies on the cheek;
     ou have shattered the teeth of the wicked.
8   Salvation belongs to the Lord;
     Your blessing *be* upon Your people!   *Selah.*

Praying Psalm 3

A prayer of David as he faces severe family problems.

God, only You can use the betrayal of a child to benefit Your children. David's prayer in the midst of his pain is now my blessing as I read and pray through this psalm (cf. 2 Sam. 15–18).

Help me to see my pain—even if it involves betrayal by a loved one, or partially the consequences of my own sin—as an opportunity to worship and trust you (vv. 1–2).

Dear God, even if my sin has contributed to my desperate situation, there is always deliverance in You—no matter what others may say (v. 2).

Many may be against me, but if You alone are for me, O God—I am safe. You are my shield, the One I hope in, and the One who gives me hope (v. 3).

You hear, Lord. I believe. You hear when I cry (v. 4).

I'm not David, nor am I Jesus. Your covenant promises guaranteed their ultimate victory. But I am Your child through faith in Christ. David was victorious, but lost his son Absalom. Jesus was victorious, but first lost His life. Victory came in His resurrection. I will trust You, Lord, with what my victory looks like here on earth and in eternity (vv. 5–8).

Father, give me a restful sleep as I trust myself into Your care (v. 5).

Remove my fears and give me Your peace, Lord (v. 6).

Salvation belongs to Yahweh. Jesus, Your name means "Yahweh saves." Thank You for saving me (v. 8). Praise the name of Jesus! There is salvation in no one else (cf. Acts 4:12).

How Jesus could be interceding for you: Father, You gave Your people eternal life through My death and resurrection (John 17:2–3). I came to deliver them through My suffering (John 12:27), therefore keep them and preserve them in this world of pain and suffering (John 17:11) and reward them in heaven (Matt. 5:11–12).

Psalm 4

Evening Prayer of Trust in God.

For the choir director; on stringed instruments.
A Psalm of David.

1 Answer me when I call, O God of my righteousness!
   You have relieved me in my distress;
   Be gracious to me and hear my prayer.

2 O sons of men, how long will my honor become a reproach?
   How long will you love what is worthless and aim
      at deception?   *Selah.*

3 But know that the LORD has set apart the godly man for
      Himself;
   The LORD hears when I call to Him.

4 Tremble, and do not sin;
   Meditate in your heart upon your bed, and be still.   *Selah.*

5 Offer the sacrifices of righteousness,
   And trust in the LORD.

6 Many are saying, "Who will show us *any* good?"
   Lift up the light of Your countenance upon us, O LORD!

7 You have put gladness in my heart,
   More than when their grain and new wine abound.

8 In peace I will both lie down and sleep,
   For You alone, O LORD, make me to dwell in safety.

Praying Psalm 4

A prayer of David while under severe stress.

Thank You, Jesus, for being my righteousness and the One who ultimately vindicates me. You have been gracious in the past, please hear me now in my distress (v. 1).

O Father, people can be so ruthless (v. 2).

You sanctify those who love You, Lord. You know I love you. I know You will hear my prayer (v. 3).

Many want to act in anger, Father—but men need faith and forgiveness rather than fury (vv. 4–5).

Fill my mind and my heart with Your Word when I am going to sleep (v. 4).

So many around me doubt You, Lord Jesus—but You have given me joy in my heart, which far exceeds temporal blessings (vv. 6–7).

Increase the gladness in my heart for all the good You've given to me (v. 7).

I will rest in You. You, O God, are my confidence (v. 8).

How Jesus could be interceding for you: Father, sanctify Your people through Your Word (John 17:17) and make their joy full and complete no matter their circumstances (John 14:27; 17:13). Father, forgive those who sin against You and against Your people (Luke 23:34; cf. Ps. 109:4).

Psalm 5

Prayer for Protection from the Wicked.

For the choir director; for flute
accompaniment. A Psalm of David.

1   Give ear to my words, O LORD,
     Consider my groaning.
2   Heed the sound of my cry for help, my King and my God,
     For to You I pray.
3   In the morning, O LORD, You will hear my voice;
     In the morning I will order *my prayer* to You and *eagerly* watch.

4   For You are not a God who takes pleasure in wickedness;
     No evil dwells with You.
5   The boastful shall not stand before Your eyes;
     You hate all who do iniquity.
6   You destroy those who speak falsehood;
     The LORD abhors the man of bloodshed and deceit.
7   But as for me, by Your abundant lovingkindness I will
          enter Your house,
     At Your holy temple I will bow in reverence for You.

8   O LORD, lead me in Your righteousness because
          of my foes;
     Make Your way straight before me.
9   There is nothing reliable in what they say;
     Their inward part is destruction *itself.*
     Their throat is an open grave;
     They flatter with their tongue.
10   Hold them guilty, O God;
     By their own devices let them fall!
     In the multitude of their transgressions thrust them out,
     For they are rebellious against You.
11   But let all who take refuge in You be glad,
     Let them ever sing for joy;
     And may You shelter them,
     That those who love Your name may exult in You.
12   For it is You who blesses the righteous man, O LORD,
     You surround him with favor as with a shield.

Praying Psalm 5

King David depends upon a far greater King—God Himself.

Here I am again, Lord. I need You. You are my King and my God. Please hear me (vv. 1–2).

Father, I bring my case to You. I will watch and wait rather than struggle to vindicate myself (v. 4).

Praise be to You, the living God. You are good—infinitely and eternally good. Therefore, You hate sin and take no pleasure in wickedness and You will rightly destroy that which is evil (vv. 4–6).

Lord, keep me from speaking falsehood (v. 6).

It is by grace alone that I worship You in holiness (v. 7).

Lord, show me the right way to go. Those who don't know Your grace seek to destroy those who worship You—don't let them succeed. Destroy their plans to destroy, and deal with them in justice (vv. 8–10).

Jesus, how You must have prayed this psalm in the days when the religious leaders were seeking to destroy You! Your Father heard. I am Yours and You are His. He will hear me. Praise God!

My joy is in You, O Lord! You are my refuge. A mighty fortress is our God. Hidden in Your Son, I am surrounded by Your favor (vv. 11–12).

How Jesus could be interceding for you: Father, deliver this believer from wicked behavior and from those who are evil (Matt. 6:13). Lead him/her in a path of righteousness (Ps. 23:3) and reveal Your favor when he/she endures suffering (1 Pet. 2:20).

Psalm 6

Prayer for Mercy in Time of Trouble.

*For the choir director; with stringed instruments,
upon an eight-string lyre. A Psalm of David.*

1 O LORD, do not rebuke me in Your anger,
Nor chasten me in Your wrath.
2 Be gracious to me, O LORD, for I *am* pining away;
Heal me, O LORD, for my bones are dismayed.
3 And my soul is greatly dismayed;
But You, O LORD—how long?

4 Return, O LORD, rescue my soul;
Save me because of Your lovingkindness.
5 For there is no mention of You in death;
In Sheol who will give You thanks?

6 I am weary with my sighing;
Every night I make my bed swim,
I dissolve my couch with my tears.
7 My eye has wasted away with grief;
It has become old because of all my adversaries.

8 Depart from me, all you who do iniquity,
For the LORD has heard the voice of my weeping.
9 The LORD has heard my supplication,
The LORD receives my prayer.
10 All my enemies will be ashamed and greatly dismayed;
They shall turn back, they will suddenly be ashamed.

Praying Psalm 6

A prayer of David when joy has gone, perhaps due to sin.

Lord, please be merciful as You correct me and remember kindness as You discipline (v. 1).

Father, help me. I'm weak, scared, and overwhelmed (vv. 2–3).

Rescue my soul and save me in Your love (v. 4).

Don't let me die like this, Lord. See my tears and my grief and those who want to see a believer fail (vv. 5–8).

Lord, hear my prayer and behold my tears (vv. 8–9).

Vindicate my faith, Lord—let all those who want to see me fall from grace be ashamed and depart. Let them know You have heard my prayers (vv. 9–10).

Lord, shame those who are my enemies, so they might understand their sin and turn to You (v. 10).

Messiah Jesus, I am sorry that You knew this kind of sorrow over everyone's sin (though You are sinless) at the prospect of bearing God's wrath for my iniquities. You were faithful. The Father heard your prayers. Thank you (cf. Heb. 5:7).

How Jesus could be interceding for you: Father of all comfort (2 Cor. 1:3), comfort Your children. I suffered and died that We might show them mercy and deliver them from fear (Heb. 2:14–18).

Psalm 7

The L ord Implored to Defend the Psalmist against the Wicked.

*A Shiggaion of David, which he sang to the L ord
concerning Cush, a Benjamite.*

1 O L ord my God, in You I have taken refuge;
    Save me from all those who pursue me, and deliver me,
2 Or he will tear my soul like a lion,
    Dragging me away, while there is none to deliver.

3 O L ord my God, if I have done this,
    If there is injustice in my hands,
4 If I have rewarded evil to my friend,
    Or have plundered him who without cause was my adversary,
5 Let the enemy pursue my soul and overtake *it;*
    And let him trample my life down to the ground
    And lay my glory in the dust.   *Selah.*

6 Arise, O L ord, in Your anger;
    Lift up Yourself against the rage of my adversaries,
    And arouse Yourself for me; You have appointed judgment.
7 Let the assembly of the peoples encompass You,
    And over them return on high.
8 The L ord judges the peoples;
    Vindicate me, O L ord, according to my righteousness and my integrity
        that is in me.
9 O let the evil of the wicked come to an end, but establish the righteous;
    For the righteous God tries the hearts and minds.
10 My shield is with God,
    Who saves the upright in heart.
11 God is a righteous judge,
    And a God who has indignation every day.
12 If a man does not repent, He will sharpen His sword;
    He has bent His bow and made it ready.
13 He has also prepared for Himself deadly weapons;
    He makes His arrows fiery shafts.
14 Behold, he travails with wickedness,
    And he conceives mischief and brings forth falsehood.

Praying Psalm 7

A troubled prayer when David faces personal opposition.

I have run to You—the living God—for refuge. Save me. I feel like I'm being hunted by a roaring lion (vv. 1–2; 1 Pet. 5:8; Eph. 6:11–12).

Lord, save me from those who would persecute me (v. 1).

Lord, you know my heart. I don't believe I am going through this because of some sin in my life (vv. 3–6).

I'm seeking to do what's right. Rise up, Father. Defend me. You know I really do love You. I'm not walking in hypocrisy. Vindicate me, Lord Jesus (vv. 7–8).

Father, examine my life and help me to live with integrity (v. 8).

You are a righteous judge, O Lord. Judge evil and bring an end to those who practice it. Save those who trust in You (vv. 9–11).

Dear Savior, grant me repentance in whatever area I may need it (v. 12).

Train my lips, Holy Spirit, to tell others of the coming judgment and the salvation that is found in Christ (v. 12).

Hold them guilty who will not repent (vv. 12–16).

15 He has dug a pit and hollowed it out,
    And has fallen into the hole which he made.
16 His mischief will return upon his own head,
    And his violence will descend upon his own pate.
17 I will give thanks to the LORD according to His righteousness
    And will sing praise to the name of the LORD Most High.

Thank You, my righteous Savior. Praise belongs to God Most High (v. 17).

How Jesus could be interceding for you: Righteous Father (John 17:25), I too experienced being torn as though by wild beasts (Ps. 22:12–16) and You delivered Me (Ps. 22:19–21). Deliver Your children from the evil one (John 17:15).

Psalm 8

The Lord's Glory and Man's Dignity.

For the choir director; on the Gittith. A Psalm of David.

1   O Lord, our Lord,
     How majestic is Your name in all the earth,
     Who have displayed Your splendor above the heavens!
2   From the mouth of infants and nursing babes You have established
          strength
     Because of Your adversaries,
     To make the enemy and the revengeful cease.

3   When I consider Your heavens, the work of Your fingers,
     The moon and the stars, which You have ordained;
4   What is man that You take thought of him,
     And the son of man that You care for him?
5   Yet You have made him a little lower than God,
     And You crown him with glory and majesty!
6   You make him to rule over the works of Your hands;
     You have put all things under his feet,
7   All sheep and oxen,
     And also the beasts of the field,
8   The birds of the heavens and the fish of the sea,
     Whatever passes through the paths of the seas.

9   O Lord, our Lord,
     How majestic is Your name in all the earth!

Praying Psalm 8

A joyful hymn of praise and adoration.

Yahweh, Master, Your majesty indeed covers the heavens and exceeds them (v. 1).

Lord, fill my mouth with Your praises (v. 2).

Your wisdom, O Lord, is foolishness to the world, and Your foolishness is wiser than men (1 Cor. 1). The babbling of babies and the simple songs of children can shut the mouths of the learned who will not trust You (v. 2; cf. Matt. 21:15–16).

Father, give me the faith of a small child (v. 2).

Father, your plans for man are glorious beyond comprehension. I'm sorry for my sin and the sins of men that have corrupted creation in so many ways. Lord Jesus, You are the man Who fulfills redemption and restoration. Praise be to the God-man, Jesus Christ—ruler over all things (vv. 3–8).

How beautiful and marvelous is Your creation (v. 3)!

Thank You, Lord, for making me and caring for me (v. 4).

Thank You, Father, for sending Jesus Christ as the "second Adam" (vv. 5–6; 1 Cor. 15:45, 47).

O Lord, our Lord, how majestic is Your name in all the earth (v. 9)!

How Jesus could be interceding for you: Holy Father (John 17:11), thank You for the name (Heb. 1:4) and the glory You have given Me for Your children to see (John 17:24). As the Son of Man, I desire to return without delay in Your glory (Matt. 16:27), so they may be with Us where We are (John 17:23–24).

Psalm 9

A Psalm of Thanksgiving for God's Justice.

For the choir director; on Muth-labben. A Psalm of David.

1   I will give thanks to the LORD with all my heart;
     I will tell of all Your wonders.
2   I will be glad and exult in You;
     I will sing praise to Your name, O Most High.

3   When my enemies turn back,
     They stumble and perish before You.
4   For You have maintained my just cause;
     You have sat on the throne judging righteously.
5   You have rebuked the nations, You have destroyed the wicked;
     You have blotted out their name forever and ever.
6   The enemy has come to an end in perpetual ruins,
     And You have uprooted the cities;
     The very memory of them has perished.

7   But the LORD abides forever;
     He has established His throne for judgment,
8   And He will judge the world in righteousness;
     He will execute judgment for the peoples with equity.
9   The LORD also will be a stronghold for the oppressed,
     A stronghold in times of trouble;
10   And those who know Your name will put their trust in You,
     For You, O LORD, have not forsaken those who seek You.
11   Sing praises to the LORD, who dwells in Zion;
     Declare among the peoples His deeds.
12   For He who requires blood remembers them;
     He does not forget the cry of the afflicted.
13   Be gracious to me, O LORD;
     See my affliction from those who hate me,
     You who lift me up from the gates of death,
14   That I may tell of all Your praises,
     That in the gates of the daughter of Zion
     I may rejoice in Your salvation.

Praying Psalm 9

Part One of David's prayer to God from out of a fallen world.

You're worthy, Lord. You are my best song and my joy (vv. 1–2).

꧁꧂

Lord, let me praise You, and You alone (vv. 1–2).

꧁꧂

Father, I praise You for allowing King David to experience in a very minimal fashion what You promised to a far greater extent to his Greater Son, Jesus Christ— the judgment and defeat of wickedness and the establishment of righteousness (vv. 3–9).

꧁꧂

Lord, bring judgment upon wicked and unbelieving nations, so that Your will might be done on earth as it is in heaven (v. 8; Matt. 6:10).

꧁꧂

Father, be a refuge to those who are in need (v. 9).

꧁꧂

Praise You for your loyalty and faithfulness to those who have taken refuge in Your name—who You are in all your character and attributes. The Living One will never forsake those who seek Him. Lord, I need You (v. 10).

꧁꧂

Fill my heart with Your wondrous love and compassion that I may sing and tell the nations (v. 11).

꧁꧂

Lord, I need Your grace to see me through this troubled life. Help me to believe and rejoice in Your salvation (vv. 13–14).

꧁꧂

May Your Kingdom come, Lord Jesus. May You right every wrong. May justice and grace work together in perfect harmony (vv. 11–18).

꧁꧂

15   The nations have sunk down in the pit which they have made;
      In the net which they hid, their own foot has been caught.
16   The LORD has made Himself known;
      He has executed judgment.
      In the work of his own hands the wicked is snared.   *Higgaion Selah.*
17   The wicked will return to Sheol,
      Even all the nations who forget God.
18   For the needy will not always be forgotten,
      Nor the hope of the afflicted perish forever.
19   Arise, O LORD, do not let man prevail;
      Let the nations be judged before You.
20   Put them in fear, O LORD;
      Let the nations know that they are but men.   *Selah.*

Lord, take action that will make all mankind realize they are mere mortals in need of Your salvation (v. 20).

Arise, O Lord! Thy Kingdom come . . . (vv. 19–20).

How Jesus could be interceding for you: Father, even as I taught Your people to pray, may Your Kingdom come (Matt. 6:10). Send me back to the earth quickly in answer to their prayers (Rev. 22:17, 20).

Psalm 10

A Prayer for the Overthrow of the Wicked.

1 Why do You stand afar off, O LORD?
   Why do You hide *Yourself* in times of trouble?
2 In pride the wicked hotly pursue the afflicted;
   Let them be caught in the plots which they have devised.

3 For the wicked boasts of his heart's desire,
   And the greedy man curses *and* spurns the LORD.
4 The wicked, in the haughtiness of his countenance, does not seek *Him.*
   All his thoughts are, "There is no God."

5 His ways prosper at all times;
   Your judgments are on high, out of his sight;
   As for all his adversaries, he snorts at them.
6 He says to himself, "I will not be moved;
   Throughout all generations I will not be in adversity."
7 His mouth is full of curses and deceit and oppression;
   Under his tongue is mischief and wickedness.
8 He sits in the lurking places of the villages;
   In the hiding places he kills the innocent;
   His eyes stealthily watch for the unfortunate.
9 He lurks in a hiding place as a lion in his lair;
   He lurks to catch the afflicted;
   He catches the afflicted when he draws him into his net.
10 He crouches, he bows down,
   And the unfortunate fall by his mighty ones.
11 He says to himself, "God has forgotten;
   He has hidden His face; He will never see it."
12 Arise, O LORD; O God, lift up Your hand.
   Do not forget the afflicted.
13 Why has the wicked spurned God?
   He has said to himself, "You will not require *it.*"
14 You have seen *it,* for You have beheld mischief and vexation to take it into
      Your hand.
   The unfortunate commits *himself* to You;
   You have been the helper of the orphan.

Praying Psalm 10

Part Two of David's prayer to God from out of a fallen world.

Father, do not hide Your face from my troubles (v. 1).

Why do those who ignore and even despise You, O God—why do they seem to prosper and get away with their arrogant rebellion (vv. 1–2)?

They boast, but Your people suffer at their hands. Believers are kidnapped, murdered, imprisoned for Your name's sake. O God, listen to what their captors and murderers say: "There is no God" and "God has forgotten" (vv. 3–11).

Lord, remove our indifference to evil and immorality (vv. 3–11).

Help, O Lord! Arise and act on behalf of the afflicted who trust in You to deliver them and to judge the wicked (vv. 12–14).

O God, may Your Kingdom come, Your will be done . . . (v. 12; Matt. 6:10).

15 Break the arm of the wicked and the evildoer,
    Seek out his wickedness until You find none.

16 The LORD is King forever and ever;
    Nations have perished from His land.

17 O LORD, You have heard the desire of the humble;
    You will strengthen their heart, You will incline Your ear

18 To vindicate the orphan and the oppressed,
    So that man who is of the earth will no longer cause terror.

Jesus, break the power of the wicked—search out and destroy every last one who opposes You. Lord, on my own I too am arrogant and wicked—forgive me! I come to You in faith. Hide me in Your righteousness, I pray (v. 15).

Lord—You are the King, immortal and eternal. You reign forever and ever—all praise be to You (v. 16).

Jesus, your Kingdom will come and those who trust in You will be vindicated. Praise the Lord (vv. 16–18)!

Thank You, Father, for seeing my troubles and hearing my prayer (v. 17).

How Jesus could be interceding for you: O Father, I know how it feels to experience Your apparent absence and to ask You why You have seemingly forsaken Me (Matt. 27:46). Now, in a time of Your children's trouble and loneliness, let Us help them to know We love them, are one with them, and will protect them (John 17:11, 14–15, 23).

Psalm 11

The Lord a Refuge and Defense.

For the choir director. A Psalm *of David.*

1   In the Lord I take refuge;
     How can you say to my soul, "Flee *as* a bird to your mountain;
2   For, behold, the wicked bend the bow,
     They make ready their arrow upon the string
     To shoot in darkness at the upright in heart.
3   "If the foundations are destroyed,
     What can the righteous do?"

4   The Lord is in His holy temple; the Lord's throne is in heaven;
     His eyes behold, His eyelids test the sons of men.
5   The Lord tests the righteous and the wicked,
     And the one who loves violence His soul hates.
6   Upon the wicked He will rain snares;
     Fire and brimstone and burning wind will be the portion of their cup.
7   For the Lord is righteous, He loves righteousness;
     The upright will behold His face.

Praying Psalm 11

David's prayer when he feels helpless in the midst of an unrighteous world.

Some are calling me to run from the difficulties I face—saying there is no hope. Some may say, "God helps them that help themselves." Lord, You know I'm not being naïve or lazy—I trust in You (vv. 1–3).

Lord, help me to know when to run and when to stay (v. 1).

Give me faith to trust in You, Father (v. 1).

Thank You, Lord, for providing me refuge in You (v. 1).

Father, protect me and my family from the subtle forces of evil that assail us each day (v. 2).

You see everything, Lord. You know the hearts of men. You know those who love You and those who love sin (vv. 4–5).

Test me, Lord. Examine my heart and teach me how to be more upright and godly (v. 5).

You will judge those who reject You with brimstone and burning wind. You are good and right (v. 6).

Father, you have caused me to love Your Son. Jesus, You are my righteousness. Thank You for the promise that the upright will behold Your face (v. 7; 1 John 3:1–3).

How Jesus could be interceding for you: Father, how very often I have desired to gather Your children and give them refuge (Matt. 28:37). I desire to gather My chosen ones without delay (Mark 13:27) and bring judgment upon the wicked and unrighteous (John 5:22, 27–30; 2 Pet. 3:10–12).

Psalm 12

God, a Helper against the Treacherous.

For the choir director; upon an eight-stringed lyre. A Psalm of David.

1   Help, LORD, for the godly man ceases to be,
    For the faithful disappear from among the sons of men.
2   They speak falsehood to one another;
    With flattering lips and with a double heart they speak.
3   May the LORD cut off all flattering lips,
    The tongue that speaks great things;
4   Who have said, "With our tongue we will prevail;
    Our lips are our own; who is lord over us?"
5   "Because of the devastation of the afflicted, because of the groaning of the needy,
    Now I will arise," says the LORD; "I will set him in the safety for which he longs."

6   The words of the LORD are pure words;
    As silver tried in a furnace on the earth, refined seven times.
7   You, O LORD, will keep them;
    You will preserve him from this generation forever.
8   The wicked strut about on every side
    When vileness is exalted among the sons of men.

Praying Psalm 12

A prayer of David traditionally read on the last day of the Feast of Booths.

Lord, help me. Genuine believers seem to be scarcer and scarcer. Sincerity and truth no longer exist (vv. 1–2).

Lord, help me (v. 1)!

Help the godly person to stand and prevail (v. 1).

As the Creator of all, You own everything—even the lips of those who mock You by saying, "Who is lord over us?" (vv. 3–4).

O God, shut the mouths of the wicked (vv. 3–4).

Your people long for You, Father. Arise and rescue those suffering for Your name's sake (v. 5).

Praise be to Yahweh—Your words are pure, perfectly pure and perfect in every way! You will keep them, I know. Make the arrogant to know as well (vv. 6–8).

Thank You, Lord, for Your pure and precious Word (v. 6).

Father, give me a greater desire for Your Word (v. 7).

Cleanse me with Your Word (vv. 6–7).

How Jesus could be interceding for you: Father, draw Your children to Me, so I might relieve their weariness, lift their burdens, and give them the rest You sent Me to bring to them (Matt. 11:28–30; cp. Isa. 40:28–31). Sanctify and cleanse them with Your Word (John 17:17).

Psalm 13

Prayer for Help in Trouble.

For the choir director. A Psalm of David.

1   How long, O LORD? Will You forget me forever?
How long will You hide Your face from me?
2   How long shall I take counsel in my soul,
Having sorrow in my heart all the day?
How long will my enemy be exalted over me?

3   Consider *and* answer me, O LORD my God;
Enlighten my eyes, or I will sleep the *sleep of* death,
4   And my enemy will say, "I have overcome him,"
And my adversaries will rejoice when I am shaken.

5   But I have trusted in Your lovingkindness;
My heart shall rejoice in Your salvation.
6   I will sing to the LORD,
Because He has dealt bountifully with me.

Praying Psalm 13

David's briefest prayer in a time of severe trial.

Savior, how long will it be until You answer? I feel alone, racked with sorrow, and defeated in this world (vv. 1–2).

Lord, how long must I suffer with this pain or this disease (vv. 1–2)?

How long before You answer my prayer (v. 1)?

Answer, O Lord my God—please. Help me to experience Your presence. Don't let the enemy see my faith shaken (vv. 3–4).

Father, give me relief (v. 3).

Lord, help me—give me the strength to remain steadfast in my faith in You (v. 4).

I do trust in Your love. I will rejoice in Your salvation. I will sing to You, the Living Lord, because You have indeed dealt with me, not according to my sins, but according to Your bountiful grace (vv. 5–6).

O God, thank You for my salvation (v. 5).

Lord, let me sing of Your abundant mercies (v. 6).

How Jesus could be interceding for you: Enable Your people to proclaim great things You have done for them, Father—how You have had mercy on them in grievous circumstances (Mark 5:19; Heb. 4:16). Give to them a new song of praise to sing to You (Pss. 40:1–3; 144:1–11).

Psalm 14

Folly and Wickedness of Men.

For the choir director. A Psalm of David.

1   The fool has said in his heart, "There is no God."
They are corrupt, they have committed abominable deeds;
There is no one who does good.
2   The LORD has looked down from heaven upon the sons of men
To see if there are any who understand,
Who seek after God.
3   They have all turned aside, together they have become corrupt;
There is no one who does good, not even one.

4   Do all the workers of wickedness not know,
Who eat up my people *as* they eat bread,
And do not call upon the LORD?
5   There they are in great dread,
For God is with the righteous generation.
6   You would put to shame the counsel of the afflicted,
But the LORD is his refuge.

7   Oh, that the salvation of Israel would come out of Zion!
When the LORD restores His captive people,
Jacob will rejoice, Israel will be glad.

Praying Psalm 14

David's prayer in the context of life among depraved people.

Lord, I am a fool apart from Your saving grace. I praise You that You justify the ungodly who believe in Your Son (vv. 1–3; Rom. 4:4–5).

Lord, keep me from acting or talking like a fool (v. 1).

O God, I am a sinner—there is nothing good in me that I should deserve salvation (vv. 1, 3).

Your judgment is coming, Father. Let me hide myself in You (vv. 4–6).

Thank You, God, for being with the righteous (v. 5).

You are my refuge, Lord (v. 6).

Come, Savior of Israel and bring in Your Kingdom (v. 7).

How Jesus could be interceding for you: Father, give refuge to the righteous living in the midst of a wicked and depraved generation (Mark 8:38; Luke 9:41; Phil. 2:14–15) and who seek You in faith (Matt. 7:7–8).

Psalm 15

Description of a Citizen of Zion.

A Psalm of David.

1 O Lord, who may abide in Your tent?
   Who may dwell on Your holy hill?
2 He who walks with integrity, and works righteousness,
   And speaks truth in his heart.
3 He does not slander with his tongue,
   Nor does evil to his neighbor,
   Nor takes up a reproach against his friend;
4 In whose eyes a reprobate is despised,
   But who honors those who fear the Lord;
   He swears to his own hurt and does not change;
5 He does not put out his money at interest,
   Nor does he take a bribe against the innocent.
   He who does these things will never be shaken.

Praying Psalm 15

David's prayer as he prepares for corporate worship at the Tabernacle.

Lord, hear my prayer before Your heavenly throne (v. 1).

The prospect of dwelling in Your holy presence is both exhilarating and terrifying. Can a man see You face-to-face and not be destroyed (v. 1)?

Integrity, righteousness, truth—no slander, no evil, no reproach—hating sin, loving others. These are my heart's desires. But Lord, only Jesus has lived these perfectly. Teach me to pursue holiness and trust in Jesus alone and I will never be shaken (vv. 2–5).

Help me to pursue honesty in all I say and do (v. 2).

Father, keep me from lying—even to myself (v. 2).

Jesus, give me a sincere love for others (v. 3).

Help me control my mouth (vv. 3–4).

Father, remove greed and materialism from my heart (v. 5).

How Jesus could be interceding for you: I thank You, Father, that Your house includes many dwelling places for Me to prepare for Your children (John 14:2). Give entrance to them into Our heavenly abode (John 17:24) and the joy of Our presence (Matt. 25:21, 23).

Psalm 16

The Lord the Psalmist's Portion in Life and Deliverer in Death.

A Mikhtam of David.

1   Preserve me, O God, for I take refuge in You.
2   I said to the Lord, "You are my Lord;
      I have no good besides You."
3   As for the saints who are in the earth,
      They are the majestic ones in whom is all my delight.
4   The sorrows of those who have bartered for another *god* will be
          multiplied;
      I shall not pour out their drink offerings of blood,
      Nor will I take their names upon my lips.

5   The Lord is the portion of my inheritance and my cup;
      You support my lot.
6   The lines have fallen to me in pleasant places;
      Indeed, my heritage is beautiful to me.

7   I will bless the Lord who has counseled me;
      Indeed, my mind instructs me in the night.
8   I have set the Lord continually before me;
      Because He is at my right hand, I will not be shaken.
9   Therefore my heart is glad and my glory rejoices;
      My flesh also will dwell securely.
10   For You will not abandon my soul to Sheol;
      Nor will You allow Your Holy One to undergo decay.
11   You will make known to me the path of life;
      In Your presence is fullness of joy;
      In Your right hand there are pleasures forever.

Praying Psalm 16

David's lasting, indelible (miktam) Messianic prayer.

This is my cry—preserve me, O God, for I take refuge in You (cf. Ps. 2:12). You are my Lord; I have no good besides You (vv. 1–2).

Lord, turn my heart to You and Your people—and away from the world and its idols (vv. 3–4).

Father, preserve in me a delight for my fellow believers, Your holy ones (v. 3).

I am satisfied with Your blessings—truly satisfied in You, Lord (vv. 5–6).

Your Spirit, through Your Word, directs my thoughts and keeps me steady (vv. 7–8).

I praise You, Lord, for Your counsel (v. 7).

Father, thank You for the strength You have supplied to me (v. 8).

Praise You for the promised resurrection and the glory to come! Lord Jesus, You are the first-fruits of life from the dead, and the very source of life eternal—praise be to God (Father, Son, and Spirit) (vv. 9–11).

Lord Jesus, show me the path of life and give me joy (v. 11).

How Jesus could be interceding for you: Thank You, Father, for raising Me from the dead (Matt. 17:22–23;) that I might provide redemption, eternal life, peace, and joy to all Your people (John 14:27; 17:2, 13). Pour out upon them all the hope, joy, and forgiveness they inherit through My death and resurrection (cf. Acts 2:24–28; 13:30–39; Rom. 8:34–35; 1 Pet. 1:21).

Psalm 17

Prayer for Protection against Oppressors.

A Prayer of David.

1   Hear a just cause, O LORD, give heed to my cry;
     Give ear to my prayer, which is not from deceitful lips.
2   Let my judgment come forth from Your presence;
     Let Your eyes look with equity.
3   You have tried my heart;
     You have visited *me* by night;
     You have tested me and You find nothing;
     I have purposed that my mouth will not transgress.
4   As for the deeds of men, by the word of Your lips
     I have kept from the paths of the violent.
5   My steps have held fast to Your paths.
     My feet have not slipped.

6   I have called upon You, for You will answer me, O God;
     Incline Your ear to me, hear my speech.
7   Wondrously show Your lovingkindness,
     O Savior of those who take refuge at Your right hand
     From those who rise up *against them.*
8   Keep me as the apple of the eye;
     Hide me in the shadow of Your wings
9   From the wicked who despoil me,
     My deadly enemies who surround me.
10   They have closed their unfeeling *heart,*
     With their mouth they speak proudly.
11   They have now surrounded us in our steps;
     They set their eyes to cast *us* down to the ground.
12   He is like a lion that is eager to tear,
     And as a young lion lurking in hiding places.
13   Arise, O LORD, confront him, bring him low;
     Deliver my soul from the wicked with Your sword,
14   From men with Your hand, O LORD,
     From men of the world, whose portion is in *this* life,
     And whose belly You fill with Your treasure;
     They are satisfied with children,
     And leave their abundance to their babes.
15   As for me, I shall behold Your face in righteousness;
     I will be satisfied with Your likeness when I awake.

Praying Psalm 17

David prays and presents his appeal to God for preserving his life.

Nothing is hidden from You, Lord. You know that I am not hiding some deception or sin. You know I'm seeking to walk with you in humility, truth, and justice. I am not sinless—but I feel certain that I am not living in hypocrisy (vv. 1–5).

Hear me, O Lord. My cause is just and I have been faithful (vv. 1–2).

Examine my heart, Lord (v. 3).

I trust You know and will hear my prayer. Show Your love in a mighty way. Protect me, Savior, from those who are trying to steal, kill, and destroy my faith (vv. 6–12).

Father, keep me, hide me, and preserve me from the wicked (vv. 8–9).

Lord, deal with those whose portion is in this world and in this life. As for me, I will find my portion in Your presence—seeing Your Son and being transformed into His likeness (vv. 13–15).

Lord, confront evil doers and bring them low (v. 13).

Jesus, satisfy me with Your presence and the hope of resurrection (v. 15).

How Jesus could be interceding for you: You restored to Me the glory We had shared before I took on human flesh, Father (John 17:5)—I behold You in righteousness and am completely satisfied with Your likeness (Ps. 17:15). Instill this hope in the hearts of all Your children (2 Cor. 4:14; 1 John 3: 2; Jude 24–25) and give them refuge under the shadow of Your wings (Ps. 17:8; John 17:12; 1 Pet. 1:5).

Psalm 18

The Lord Praised for Giving Deliverance.

For the choir director. A Psalm *of David the servant of the Lord, who spoke to the Lord the words of this song in the day that the Lord delivered him from the hand of all his enemies and from the hand of Saul. And he said,*

1 "I love You, O Lord, my strength."
2 The Lord is my rock and my fortress and my deliverer,
   My God, my rock, in whom I take refuge;
   My shield and the horn of my salvation, my stronghold.
3 I call upon the Lord, who is worthy to be praised,
   And I am saved from my enemies.

4 The cords of death encompassed me,
   And the torrents of ungodliness terrified me.
5 The cords of Sheol surrounded me;
   The snares of death confronted me.
6 In my distress I called upon the Lord,
   And cried to my God for help;
   He heard my voice out of His temple,
   And my cry for help before Him came into His ears.

7 Then the earth shook and quaked;
   And the foundations of the mountains were trembling
   And were shaken, because He was angry.
8 Smoke went up out of His nostrils,
   And fire from His mouth devoured;
   Coals were kindled by it.
9 He bowed the heavens also, and came down
   With thick darkness under His feet.
10 He rode upon a cherub and flew;
   And He sped upon the wings of the wind.
11 He made darkness His hiding place, His canopy around Him,
   Darkness of waters, thick clouds of the skies.
12 From the brightness before Him passed His thick clouds,
   Hailstones and coals of fire.
13 The Lord also thundered in the heavens,
   And the Most High uttered His voice,

Praying Psalm 18

*David's prayer of praise following deliverance from
Saul—recorded also in 2 Samuel 22.*

Too often I pray for help, but forget to praise You for Your deliverance. Forgive me, Lord. Thank You, Spirit of God, for moving in David to pen this praise after You delivered him from his enemies (see superscription).

I love You, O Lord, my strength—my Rock and my Fortress, my Deliverer! You are worthy to be praised (vv. 1–3).

Praise the Lord! You are my Rock and my Refuge (v. 2)!

Father, what did David experience as You came to his rescue? His description seems to transcend his deliverance from Saul. The sky was darkened, the earth quaked the day Jesus committed His spirit into Your hands. You rescued Him, making Him alive in the Spirit because He delighted in You—thank You (vv. 4–19).

Lord, help me—I'm in trouble (vv. 4–6)!

I believe You will rescue me on that day. I delight in You, Lord. Increase my delight. Let me see Your glory. Lord, I look forward to being with You when You return to rescue Israel in the day of their trouble. Hallelujah, what a Savior (vv. 4–19)!

Hailstones and coals of fire.

14 He sent out His arrows, and scattered them,
And lightning flashes in abundance, and routed them.

15 Then the channels of water appeared,
And the foundations of the world were laid bare
At Your rebuke, O Lord,
At the blast of the breath of Your nostrils.

16 He sent from on high, He took me;
He drew me out of many waters.

17 He delivered me from my strong enemy,
And from those who hated me, for they were too mighty for me.

18 They confronted me in the day of my calamity,
But the Lord was my stay.

19 He brought me forth also into a broad place;
He rescued me, because He delighted in me.

20 The Lord has rewarded me according to my righteousness;
According to the cleanness of my hands He has recompensed me.

21 For I have kept the ways of the Lord,
And have not wickedly departed from my God.

22 For all His ordinances were before me,
And I did not put away His statutes from me.

23 I was also blameless with Him,
And I kept myself from my iniquity.

24 Therefore the Lord has recompensed me according to my righteousness,
According to the cleanness of my hands in His eyes.

25 With the kind You show Yourself kind;
With the blameless You show Yourself blameless;

26 With the pure You show Yourself pure,
And with the crooked You show Yourself astute.

27 For You save an afflicted people,
But haughty eyes You abase.

28 For You light my lamp;
The Lord my God illumines my darkness.

29 For by You I can run upon a troop;
And by my God I can leap over a wall.

30 As for God, His way is blameless;
The word of the Lord is tried;
He is a shield to all who take refuge in Him.

31 For who is God, but the Lord?
And who is a rock, except our God,

Come to my aid, dear Father. Those who hate me have more power and influence than I (v. 17).

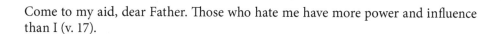

Lord, how I marvel that You actually delight in me (v. 19)!

I have sought to keep Your Word, Lord. Jesus kept it perfectly. He is His people's righteousness. Reward us, Lord, according to our righteousness (vv. 20–24).

You are perfect in all Your ways. You are kind with the kind, true to the true, and wise to the wicked. You illumine Your people. You strengthen and lead them to victory. Yet it is Your gentleness that makes us great (vv. 25–36).

O God, give me light for my darkness (v. 28).

32 The God who girds me with strength
    And makes my way blameless?
33 He makes my feet like hinds' *feet,*
    And sets me upon my high places.
34 He trains my hands for battle,
    So that my arms can bend a bow of bronze.
35 You have also given me the shield of Your salvation,
    And Your right hand upholds me;
    And Your gentleness makes me great.
36 You enlarge my steps under me,
    And my feet have not slipped.
37 I pursued my enemies and overtook them,
    And I did not turn back until they were consumed.
38 I shattered them, so that they were not able to rise;
    They fell under my feet.
39 For You have girded me with strength for battle;
    You have subdued under me those who rose up against me.
40 You have also made my enemies turn their backs to me,
    And I destroyed those who hated me.
41 They cried for help, but there was none to save,
    Even to the LORD, but He did not answer them.
42 Then I beat them fine as the dust before the wind;
    I emptied them out as the mire of the streets.
43 You have delivered me from the contentions of the people;
    You have placed me as head of the nations;
    A people whom I have not known serve me.
44 As soon as they hear, they obey me;
    Foreigners submit to me.
45 Foreigners fade away,
    And come trembling out of their fortresses.
46 The LORD lives, and blessed be my rock;
    And exalted be the God of my salvation,
47 The God who executes vengeance for me,
    And subdues peoples under me.
48 He delivers me from my enemies;
    Surely You lift me above those who rise up against me;
    You rescue me from the violent man.
49 Therefore I will give thanks to You among the nations, O LORD,
    And I will sing praises to Your name.
50 He gives great deliverance to His king,
    And shows lovingkindness to His anointed,
    To David and his descendants forever.

O, dear God, wrap me in Your strength and steady my feet so I walk wherever You lead me (vv. 32–33).

David was ultimately victorious. King Jesus will destroy His enemies at His return. Lead us to victory, Lord (vv. 37–45)!

Lord Jesus, show Yourself to all the nations! Make them know You are the only Savior (vv. 43–45, 49).

The Lord lives, and blessed be my Rock—exalted be the God of my salvation! I will praise You among the nations. Father, You have been faithful to Your King—Jesus the Messiah. Your love is better than life, Lord. Thank you (vv. 46–50).

How Jesus could be interceding for you: I am praying for Your people, Father (John 17:9). They live in a fallen world and face many troubles and dangers (John 17:11), and yet love You because You love them and keep them (John 17:23). Thank You for delivering them out of their troubles.

Psalm 19

The Works and the Word of God.

For the choir director. A Psalm of David.

1   The heavens are telling of the glory of God;
And their expanse is declaring the work of His hands.
2   Day to day pours forth speech,
And night to night reveals knowledge.
3   There is no speech, nor are there words;
Their voice is not heard.
4   Their line has gone out through all the earth,
And their utterances to the end of the world.
In them He has placed a tent for the sun,
5   Which is as a bridegroom coming out of his chamber;
It rejoices as a strong man to run his course.
6   Its rising is from one end of the heavens,
And its circuit to the other end of them;
And there is nothing hidden from its heat.

7   The law of the Lord is perfect, restoring the soul;
The testimony of the Lord is sure, making wise the simple.
8   The precepts of the Lord are right, rejoicing the heart;
The commandment of the Lord is pure, enlightening the eyes.
9   The fear of the Lord is clean, enduring forever;
The judgments of the Lord are true; they are righteous altogether.
10   They are more desirable than gold, yes, than much fine gold;
Sweeter also than honey and the drippings of the honeycomb.
11   Moreover, by them Your servant is warned;
In keeping them there is great reward.
12   Who can discern *his* errors? Acquit me of hidden *faults.*
13   Also keep back Your servant from presumptuous *sins;*
Let them not rule over me;
Then I will be blameless,
And I shall be acquitted of great transgression.
14   Let the words of my mouth and the meditation of my heart
Be acceptable in Your sight,
O Lord, my rock and my Redeemer.

Praying Psalm 19

David's prayer to his Redeemer for His acceptance of his prayer and meditation.

Father, help me to stop and appreciate Your glory in creation more often and more carefully. Guide me in seeing and listening to the testimony the heavens give regarding Your glory (vv. 1–6).

Lord, we praise You for Your handiwork (v. 1).

Your Word has become my delight (cf. Ps. 1:2). It is perfect, trustworthy, right, and the source of joy. Your Word is clear and helps me see. Thank You, Lord, for Your Word. Help me to be obedient to You (vv. 7–11).

Though I want to be obedient, I need You to reveal to me who I really am and keep me from rebelling against You. I need You (vv. 12–13).

Father, give me an understanding of my own errors (v. 12).

Cleanse me, Lord, from any hidden faults (v. 13).

Lord Jesus, don't let my sins govern me (v. 13).

Let the words of my mouth and the meditation of my heart be acceptable to You. You are the living Lord, my strength and my salvation (v. 14).

———

How Jesus could be interceding for you: Father, I praise You for creating the heavens, the earth, the seas, and all that are in them through Me and for Me (Col. 1:16). Thank You for sending Me to give Your people Your Word and to redeem them (John 17:2, 8, 14; Col. 1:14).

Psalm 20

Prayer for Victory over Enemies.

For the choir director. A Psalm of David.

1 May the LORD answer you in the day of trouble!
  May the name of the God of Jacob set you *securely* on high!
2 May He send you help from the sanctuary
  And support you from Zion!
3 May He remember all your meal offerings
  And find your burnt offering acceptable!   *Selah.*

4 May He grant you your heart's desire
  And fulfill all your counsel!
5 We will sing for joy over your victory,
  And in the name of our God we will set up our banners.
  May the LORD fulfill all your petitions.

6 Now I know that the LORD saves His anointed;
  He will answer him from His holy heaven
  With the saving strength of His right hand.
7 Some *boast* in chariots and some in horses,
  But we will boast in the name of the LORD, our God.
8 They have bowed down and fallen,
  But we have risen and stood upright.
9 Save, O LORD;
  May the King answer us in the day we call.

Praying Psalm 20

David's prayer for victory in battle against his nation's enemies.

As I pray for others, Lord, help me to seek Your blessing upon them—that You would hear their prayers and make their worship acceptable to You. Grant my family and friends the very desire of their heart so we all can rejoice together as You fulfill the desires You give to us (vv. 1–5).

Lord, send help to those seeking to protect Your people (v. 2).

Please accept my offering, Father (v. 3).

Father, fulfill not only my prayer, but Your Son's petitions on behalf of our world's leaders for the advancement of Your Kingdom purposes (v. 5).

Father, thank You for answering our prayers (vv. 5, 6).

We will boast in the name of Yahweh, our God. He is our strength. In Him we stand. Save, O Lord (vv. 6–9).

Lord Jesus, enable me to trust in You alone—increase my faith (v. 7).

How Jesus could be interceding for you: Righteous Father, advance Your Kingdom (Matt. 6:10) by giving success to those whom You have set over the world's governments who seek justice and mercy (1 Tim. 2:1–3).

Psalm 21

Praise for Deliverance.

For the choir director. A Psalm of David.

1 O LORD, in Your strength the king will be glad,
   And in Your salvation how greatly he will rejoice!
2 You have given him his heart's desire,
   And You have not withheld the request of his lips.   *Selah.*
3 For You meet him with the blessings of good things;
   You set a crown of fine gold on his head.
4 He asked life of You,
   You gave it to him,
   Length of days forever and ever.
5 His glory is great through Your salvation,
   Splendor and majesty You place upon him.
6 For You make him most blessed forever;
   You make him joyful with gladness in Your presence.

7 For the king trusts in the LORD,
   And through the lovingkindness of the Most High he will not be shaken.
8 Your hand will find out all your enemies;
   Your right hand will find out those who hate you.
9 You will make them as a fiery oven in the time of your anger;
   The LORD will swallow them up in His wrath,
   And fire will devour them.
10 Their offspring You will destroy from the earth,
   And their descendants from among the sons of men.
11 Though they intended evil against You
   And devised a plot,
   They will not succeed.
12 For You will make them turn their back;
   You will aim with Your bowstrings at their faces.
13 Be exalted, O LORD, in Your strength;
   We will sing and praise Your power.

Praying Psalm 21

David thanks the Lord for granting him victory in
battle against his nation's enemies.

Father, You blessed David the king. You blessed Jesus the King. You have given Christ the Savior length of days forever and ever. Praise be to God that in Him I too have length of days forever and ever in Your presence (vv. 1–6).

Thank You, Father, for delivering us (v. 1).

Lord Jesus, give us life everlasting (v. 4).

Father, teach me to trust You like Jesus did, and I will not be shaken (v. 7).

Deal with Your enemies (and mine) according to Your will and for Your glory (vv. 8–12).

Be exalted, O Lord. We praise you with the songs we sing (v. 13).

How Jesus could be interceding for you: Father, I delight to do Your will (Ps. 40:8) to establish Your Kingdom upon the earth by victory in battle against all the forces of evil and unrighteousness (Rev. 19:11–16).

Psalm 22

A Cry of Anguish and a Song of Praise.

For the choir director; upon Aijeleth Hashshahar. A Psalm of David.

1   My God, my God, why have You forsaken me?
     Far from my deliverance are the words of my groaning.
2   O my God, I cry by day, but You do not answer;
     And by night, but I have no rest.
3   Yet You are holy,
     O You who are enthroned upon the praises of Israel.
4   In You our fathers trusted;
     They trusted and You delivered them.
5   To You they cried out and were delivered;
     In You they trusted and were not disappointed.

6   But I am a worm and not a man,
     A reproach of men and despised by the people.
7   All who see me sneer at me;
     They separate with the lip, they wag the head, *saying,*
8   "Commit *yourself* to the LORD; let Him deliver him;
     Let Him rescue him, because He delights in him."

9   Yet You are He who brought me forth from the womb;
     You made me trust *when* upon my mother's breasts.
10   Upon You I was cast from birth;
     You have been my God from my mother's womb.
11   Be not far from me, for trouble is near;
     For there is none to help.
12   Many bulls have surrounded me;
     Strong *bulls* of Bashan have encircled me.
13   They open wide their mouth at me,
     As a ravening and a roaring lion.
14   I am poured out like water,
     And all my bones are out of joint;
     My heart is like wax;
     It is melted within me.
15   My strength is dried up like a potsherd,
     And my tongue cleaves to my jaws;

Praying Psalm 22

*David's inspired Messianic prayer revealing the execution
of Messiah and His establishing God's Kingdom.*

Lord Jesus, I cannot fully comprehend what my salvation cost You (v. 1).

Lord Jesus, this was Your cry. I'm sorry that it was for my sin—forgive me, dear God (v. 1).

As a man, Lord Jesus, You experienced the conflicting emotions and wrestlings of faith that Your people do—except to the utmost (vv. 3–18).

Father, You are holy and I trust You (vv. 3–4).

Thank You, Almighty God, that in Your sovereignty David both experienced what he did and You revealed to him what he needed to know to pen these words (vv. 6–18).

Lord, I do not deserve Your mercy—You alone are my Savior (v. 6).

The mocking, the irreverence, the pain—forgive me Lord for my own unbelief (vv. 7–8, 12–18).

O God, You are my God (v. 10)!

Father, remain near me in times of trouble—You alone are my help (v. 11).

And You lay me in the dust of death.

16   For dogs have surrounded me;
A band of evildoers has encompassed me;
They pierced my hands and my feet.

17   I can count all my bones.
They look, they stare at me;

18   They divide my garments among them,
And for my clothing they cast lots.

19   But You, O Lord, be not far off;
O You my help, hasten to my assistance.

20   Deliver my soul from the sword,
My only *life* from the power of the dog.

21   Save me from the lion's mouth;
From the horns of the wild oxen You answer me.

22   I will tell of Your name to my brethren;
In the midst of the assembly I will praise You.

23   You who fear the Lord, praise Him;
All you descendants of Jacob, glorify Him,
And stand in awe of Him, all you descendants of Israel.

24   For He has not despised nor abhorred the affliction of the afflicted;
Nor has He hidden His face from him;
But when he cried to Him for help, He heard.

25   From You *comes* my praise in the great assembly;
I shall pay my vows before those who fear Him.

26   The afflicted will eat and be satisfied;
Those who seek Him will praise the Lord.
Let your heart live forever!

27   All the ends of the earth will remember and turn to the Lord,
And all the families of the nations will worship before You.

28   For the kingdom is the Lord's
And He rules over the nations.

29   All the prosperous of the earth will eat and worship,
All those who go down to the dust will bow before Him,
Even he who cannot keep his soul alive.

30   Posterity will serve Him;
It will be told of the Lord to the *coming* generation.

31   They will come and will declare His righteousness
To a people who will be born, that He has performed *it.*

Thank You that Messiah's suffering culminated in resurrection. Thus, all the ends of the earth will turn to Him, and all the families of the nations will worship Him (vv. 22–29).

Lord Jesus, give me the desire and the courage to tell others about You and the salvation You provide (v. 22).

Praise be to You, O God, that one generation of believers has told another until this very day, that Messiah has accomplished the work of redemption. It is completed—it is finished (v. 31; cf. John 19:30).

May my children and grandchildren serve You, Lord (vv. 30–31).

How Jesus could be interceding for you: Father, You know how I endured abuse, torture, agony, and death to complete the work for which You sent Me (Matt. 26:36–39; Heb. 2:14; 5:7). Send Your people out under My authority with the gospel of salvation to all nations (Matt. 28:18–20) and give them the joy of joining Us in Your redemptive program (John 17:4, 8, 13, 18, 20–21).

Psalm 23

The Lord, the Psalmist's Shepherd.

A Psalm of David.

1 The Lord is my shepherd,
  I shall not want.
2 He makes me lie down in green pastures;
  He leads me beside quiet waters.
3 He restores my soul;
  He guides me in the paths of righteousness
  For His name's sake.

4 Even though I walk through the valley of the shadow of death,
  I fear no evil, for You are with me;
  Your rod and Your staff, they comfort me.
5 You prepare a table before me in the presence of my enemies;
  You have anointed my head with oil;
  My cup overflows.
6 Surely goodness and lovingkindness will follow me all the days of my life,
  And I will dwell in the house of the Lord forever.

Praying Psalm 23

A shepherd's prayer from a shepherd-king, David.

Show me how to live for You today, Lord (vv. 1–6).

Lord, You are the Shepherd—my Shepherd. I trust Your provision. Lead me in paths of righteousness (vv. 1–3).

I trust Your protection and direction, my Shepherd-Savior—even if it involves a valley of deepest darkness (vv. 3–4).

Father, I cling to Your promises—ultimate victory over my enemies in Christ, provision, blessing, and eternal life in Your presence (vv. 5–6).

Lord Jesus, pursue me with Your goodness and steadfast love (v. 6).

How Jesus could be interceding for you: Father, enable Your people to hear My voice and to follow only Me (John 10:3–5). I laid down My life for My sheep and am still beseeching others to follow Me (John 10:15–16). Allow Your people to rejoice with Us in finding My sheep who were lost (Luke 15:4–7).

Psalm 24

The King of Glory Entering Zion.

A Psalm of David.

1   The earth is the LORD's, and all it contains,
    The world, and those who dwell in it.
2   For He has founded it upon the seas
    And established it upon the rivers.
3   Who may ascend into the hill of the LORD?
    And who may stand in His holy place?
4   He who has clean hands and a pure heart,
    Who has not lifted up his soul to falsehood
    And has not sworn deceitfully.
5   He shall receive a blessing from the LORD
    And righteousness from the God of his salvation.
6   This is the generation of those who seek Him,
    Who seek Your face—*even* Jacob.   *Selah.*

7   Lift up your heads, O gates,
    And be lifted up, O ancient doors,
    That the King of glory may come in!
8   Who is the King of glory?
    The LORD strong and mighty,
    The LORD mighty in battle.
9   Lift up your heads, O gates,
    And lift *them* up, O ancient doors,
    That the King of glory may come in!
10 Who is this King of glory?
    The LORD of hosts,
    He is the King of glory.   *Selah.*

Praying Psalm 24

Sung during worship in the Temple after the Babylonian exile—and, on Palm Sunday in churches.

You are Sovereign, my Creator and Sustainer—the earth is Yours and so am I (vv. 1–2).

Lord, I lift up my life—thoughts, actions, words—examine them and bring me closer to You in Your holiness. Hide me in Your holiness (vv. 3–6).

Father, help me to control my tongue and to speak the truth (v. 4).

Keep my heart pure and my hands clean from sin (v. 4).

Lord Jesus, You are the God of my salvation. Thank You for saving me (v. 5).

Come in Your Kingdom glory, Lord! Let Jerusalem's gates radiate with Your splendor. Who is the King of glory? Lord Jesus, You are the King of glory (vv. 7–10)!

How Jesus could be interceding for you: May Your people rejoice in Me as their Savior-King coming to them in Your name, Father (Luke 19:37–38; John 12:27–28). May they believe that I have fulfilled all things written in Scripture about Me and will return as the King of glory (Matt. 16:27; Luke 21:27–28; 24:44–49; John 17:24).

Psalm 25

Prayer for Protection, Guidance and Pardon.

A Psalm *of David.*

1   To You, O Lord, I lift up my soul.
2   O my God, in You I trust,
Do not let me be ashamed;
Do not let my enemies exult over me.
3   Indeed, none of those who wait for You will be ashamed;
Those who deal treacherously without cause will be ashamed.

4   Make me know Your ways, O Lord;
Teach me Your paths.
5   Lead me in Your truth and teach me,
For You are the God of my salvation;
For You I wait all the day.
6   Remember, O Lord, Your compassion and Your lovingkindnesses,
For they have been from of old.
7   Do not remember the sins of my youth or my transgressions;
According to Your lovingkindness remember me,
For Your goodness' sake, O Lord.

8   Good and upright is the Lord;
Therefore He instructs sinners in the way.
9   He leads the humble in justice,
And He teaches the humble His way.
10   All the paths of the Lord are lovingkindness and truth
To those who keep His covenant and His testimonies.
11   For Your name's sake, O Lord,
Pardon my iniquity, for it is great.
12   Who is the man who fears the Lord?
He will instruct him in the way he should choose.
13   His soul will abide in prosperity,
And his descendants will inherit the land.
14   The secret of the Lord is for those who fear Him,
And He will make them know His covenant.
15   My eyes are continually toward the Lord,
For He will pluck my feet out of the net.

Praying Psalm 25

*A prayer of David asking God to walk with him on
the difficult road of righteousness.*

Lord, it seems the believing life can be a troubled life. I need You to walk with me (vv. 1–3).

Ʒ

I trust You, O God, and commit my life into Your mercy-filled hands (vv. 1–2).

Ʒ

Lord, preserve me from spiritual shame—from living a life contrary to my faith (vv. 2–3).

Ʒ

Teach me Your ways through Your Word, Father. Lead me in Your truth (vv. 4–5).

Ʒ

Remember Your infinite and eternal mercy and love, but please don't remember my past sins and rebellion (vv. 6–7).

Ʒ

Humble me before You, Lord—for your grace is great toward the humble. Please forgive me for my sins—they are many (vv. 8–11).

16 Turn to me and be gracious to me,
    For I am lonely and afflicted.
17 The troubles of my heart are enlarged;
    Bring me out of my distresses.
18 Look upon my affliction and my trouble,
    And forgive all my sins.
19 Look upon my enemies, for they are many,
    And they hate me with violent hatred.
20 Guard my soul and deliver me;
    Do not let me be ashamed, for I take refuge in You.
21 Let integrity and uprightness preserve me,
    For I wait for You.
22 Redeem Israel, O God,
    Out of all his troubles.

Lord, I am alone, and I know my sin. Be gracious to me and forgive me. Your mercy constrains me to walk in my integrity and with an upright heart (vv. 16–22).

Sinless Savior, Lord Jesus, being sinless You yet bore the wrath of God for sinners like me (v. 22).

How Jesus could be interceding for you: Father, just as I entrusted You with My spirit (Luke 23:46), instill that kind of trust in Your people—increase their faith (Luke 22:32). On the merits of My finished work of redemption (1 Pet. 2:24–25), forgive them, Father, for the sins they've committed (Luke 23:34).

Psalm 26

Protestation of Integrity and Prayer for Protection.

A Psalm *of David.*

1 Vindicate me, O Lord, for I have walked in my integrity,
   And I have trusted in the Lord without wavering.
2 Examine me, O Lord, and try me;
   Test my mind and my heart.
3 For Your lovingkindness is before my eyes,
   And I have walked in Your truth.
4 I do not sit with deceitful men,
   Nor will I go with pretenders.
5 I hate the assembly of evildoers,
   And I will not sit with the wicked.
6 I shall wash my hands in innocence,
   And I will go about Your altar, O Lord,
7 That I may proclaim with the voice of thanksgiving
   And declare all Your wonders.

8 O Lord, I love the habitation of Your house
   And the place where Your glory dwells.
9 Do not take my soul away *along* with sinners,
   Nor my life with men of bloodshed,
10 In whose hands is a wicked scheme,
   And whose right hand is full of bribes.
11 But as for me, I shall walk in my integrity;
   Redeem me, and be gracious to me.
12 My foot stands on a level place;
   In the congregations I shall bless the Lord.

Praying Psalm 26

David's prayer appealing to God for justice to His glory.

Though I know my sin, I can truly pray that I have walked in my integrity and have trusted in You without wavering. Praise be to You, O God of grace, that my sinless Savior never compromised His integrity or wavered in His faith (v. 1).

Father, help me to live for You with integrity (vv. 1, 11).

You know all things Father. You know that Your love has been my guide. I have not pursued the path of sin. I have worshiped You with sincerity and clean hands (vv. 2–7).

Examine my heart and test my faith, Lord (v. 2).

Lead me so that I walk in Your truth—in obedience to Your Word (v. 3).

O God, create in my heart a godly hatred for sin (vv. 4–5).

Don't let me get caught up with the things of this world. I need Your continuing redemption and grace. Thank You for the sure footing of Your grace—I will worship You with Your people (vv. 8–12).

Lord Jesus, give me an ever deepening love for the assembly of Your people (v. 8).

How Jesus could be interceding for you: Father, I proclaimed Your name among My brethren in My incarnation (Heb. 2:11–15). Preserve for them opportunities to meet together in assemblies praising Your name (Matt. 18:19–20; Heb. 10:23–25).

Psalm 27

A Psalm of Fearless Trust in God.

A Psalm *of David.*

1 The LORD is my light and my salvation;
   Whom shall I fear?
   The LORD is the defense of my life;
   Whom shall I dread?
2 When evildoers came upon me to devour my flesh,
   My adversaries and my enemies, they stumbled and fell.
3 Though a host encamp against me,
   My heart will not fear;
   Though war arise against me,
   In *spite of* this I shall be confident.

4 One thing I have asked from the LORD, that I shall seek:
   That I may dwell in the house of the LORD all the days of my life,
   To behold the beauty of the LORD
   And to meditate in His temple.
5 For in the day of trouble He will conceal me in His tabernacle;
   In the secret place of His tent He will hide me;
   He will lift me up on a rock.
6 And now my head will be lifted up above my enemies around me,
   And I will offer in His tent sacrifices with shouts of joy;
   I will sing, yes, I will sing praises to the LORD.

7 Hear, O LORD, when I cry with my voice,
   And be gracious to me and answer me.
8 *When You said,* "Seek My face," my heart said to You,
   "Your face, O LORD, I shall seek."
9 Do not hide Your face from me,
   Do not turn Your servant away in anger;
   You have been my help;
   Do not abandon me nor forsake me,
   O God of my salvation!
10 For my father and my mother have forsaken me,
   But the LORD will take me up.

Praying Psalm 27

A prayer traditionally recited throughout the entire month between New Year (Rosh Hashanah) and the Day of Atonement (Yom Kippur)—the "Days of Awe."

Help me to rest in Your protection, Lord—no matter the circumstances that surround me (vv. 1–3).

Lord, conquer my fears and give me courage to serve You (v. 1).

Make my heart to focus only on seeking You. Help me see Your beauty more and more every day (vv. 4–6).

Father, bring me into Your presence every day of my life (v. 4).

Lord, even when those closest to me don't understand or even betray my trust, You are my confidence. Hear my prayer and my cries (vv. 7–10).

I will sing praises to You, Lord Jesus (v. 6).

11   Teach me Your way, O LORD,
      And lead me in a level path
      Because of my foes.
12   Do not deliver me over to the desire of my adversaries,
      For false witnesses have risen against me,
      And such as breathe out violence.
13   *I would have despaired* unless I had believed that I would see the goodness
         of the LORD
      In the land of the living.
14   Wait for the LORD;
      Be strong and let your heart take courage;
      Yes, wait for the LORD.

Jesus, teach me. Deliver me. Help me to trust and wait for You—especially when I'm struggling to see Your blessings (vv. 11–14).

Father, You hear the slander of those who speak against me. Preserve me from the harm they desire to bring upon me (v. 12).

You give me hope, Lord. Help me to recognize Your goodness throughout my life and to thank You for it (v. 13).

How Jesus could be interceding for you: Remove fear and anxiety from the hearts of Your children, Father (Matt. 10:28–31; John 14:27). Enable them to know We are always present with them (Matt. 28:20; John 14:16; 17:21, 24) and to sing with joy about their salvation (Matt. 26:30; Acts 15:25; Eph. 5:19).

Psalm 28

A Prayer for Help, and Praise for Its Answer.

A Psalm *of David*.

1   To You, O LORD, I call;
    My rock, do not be deaf to me,
    For if You are silent to me,
    I will become like those who go down to the pit.
2   Hear the voice of my supplications when I cry to You for help,
    When I lift up my hands toward Your holy sanctuary.
3   Do not drag me away with the wicked
    And with those who work iniquity,
    Who speak peace with their neighbors,
    While evil is in their hearts.
4   Requite them according to their work and according to the evil of their
        practices;
    Requite them according to the deeds of their hands;
    Repay them their recompense.
5   Because they do not regard the works of the LORD
    Nor the deeds of His hands,
    He will tear them down and not build them up.

6   Blessed be the LORD,
    Because He has heard the voice of my supplication.
7   The LORD is my strength and my shield;
    My heart trusts in Him, and I am helped;
    Therefore my heart exults,
    And with my song I shall thank Him.
8   The LORD is their strength,
    And He is a saving defense to His anointed.
9   Save Your people and bless Your inheritance;
    Be their shepherd also, and carry them forever.

Praying Psalm 28

David pleads with God for help, then praises Him for answering His prayer.

Lord, please hear my prayers. Don't let me go the way of the world (vv. 1–5).

O God, hear my prayer (vv. 1–2).

Lord, don't treat me like the unbeliever and the evil doer (v. 3).

Father, bring Your justice into this world (vv. 4–5).

God, thank You, thank You that You do hear my prayers. My heart rejoices in the Lord my strength and my shield. You are my Protector, Savior, and Shepherd (vv. 5–9).

Lord Jesus, I trust You and sing my thanksgiving to You (v. 7).

Lord Jesus, You pled with Your Father to hear—and He heard. He is the saving defense of His Messiah. And You Lord, as His Messiah, are my saving defense (vv. 8–9).

Bless Your people, O Lord (v. 8).

How Jesus could be interceding for you: Father, You know what Your children need even before they ask (Matt. 6:8), so You often respond to their cries for help before they call out. I pray not only that You strengthen them (Phil. 4:13; Col. 1:9–12), but that You will enable them to strengthen one another (Luke 22:32; Acts 14:21–22).

Psalm 29

The Voice of the Lᴏʀᴅ in the Storm.

A Psalm of David.

1 Ascribe to the Lᴏʀᴅ, O sons of the mighty,
Ascribe to the Lᴏʀᴅ glory and strength.
2 Ascribe to the Lᴏʀᴅ the glory due to His name;
Worship the Lᴏʀᴅ in holy array.

3 The voice of the Lᴏʀᴅ is upon the waters;
The God of glory thunders,
The Lᴏʀᴅ is over many waters.
4 The voice of the Lᴏʀᴅ is powerful,
The voice of the Lᴏʀᴅ is majestic.
5 The voice of the Lᴏʀᴅ breaks the cedars;
Yes, the Lᴏʀᴅ breaks in pieces the cedars of Lebanon.
6 He makes Lebanon skip like a calf,
And Sirion like a young wild ox.
7 The voice of the Lᴏʀᴅ hews out flames of fire.
8 The voice of the Lᴏʀᴅ shakes the wilderness;
The Lᴏʀᴅ shakes the wilderness of Kadesh.
9 The voice of the Lᴏʀᴅ makes the deer to calve
And strips the forests bare;
And in His temple everything says, "Glory!"
10 The Lᴏʀᴅ sat *as King* at the flood;
Yes, the Lᴏʀᴅ sits as King forever.
11 The Lᴏʀᴅ will give strength to His people;
The Lᴏʀᴅ will bless His people with peace.

Praying Psalm 29

A prayer of David selected in the 17th-century church for July in a calendar of praise.

You are the true and living God Whose majesty is but only faintly—but beautifully—reflected in the wonders of creation. The waterfalls of Victoria or Niagara and their thunder only faintly reflect Your power. The forests and even the wildfires, earthquakes, and any events that shake us to the core are but the fringes of Your omnipotence (vv. 1–9; cp. Job 26:14).

You are mighty, Lord God. Let Your children say it is so (v. 1).

Lord, help to worship You in holiness (v. 2).

Father, teach me to listen to You in Your Word and in the world around me (vv. 3–10).

You rule over all—forever. You will strengthen and bless Your people, Lord. Praise be to You (vv. 10–11)!

Thank You, Jesus, for giving me strength and peace (v. 11).

How Jesus could be interceding for you: I praise You, Father, for You are indeed Lord of heaven and earth (Matt. 11:25). Just as everything in Your Temple shouted, "Glory!" (Ps. 29:9), even now prepare every knee to bow and every tongue to praise You (Isa. 45:23; Rom. 14:11). And, Father of glory (Eph. 1:17), may all Your children be to the praise of My glory, which You gave to Me (John 17:5, 22, 24; Eph. 1:13–14).

Psalm 30

Thanksgiving for Deliverance from Death.

A Psalm; a Song at the Dedication of the House. A Psalm *of David.*

1   I will extol You, O Lord, for You have lifted me up,
And have not let my enemies rejoice over me.

2   O Lord my God,
I cried to You for help, and You healed me.

3   O Lord, You have brought up my soul from Sheol;
You have kept me alive, that I would not go down to the pit.

4   Sing praise to the Lord, you His godly ones,
And give thanks to His holy name.

5   For His anger is but for a moment,
His favor is for a lifetime;
Weeping may last for the night,
But a shout of joy *comes* in the morning.

6   Now as for me, I said in my prosperity,
"I will never be moved."

7   O Lord, by Your favor You have made my mountain to stand strong;
You hid Your face, I was dismayed.

8   To You, O Lord, I called,
And to the Lord I made supplication:

9   "What profit is there in my blood, if I go down to the pit?
Will the dust praise You? Will it declare Your faithfulness?

10   "Hear, O Lord, and be gracious to me;
O Lord, be my helper."

11   You have turned for me my mourning into dancing;
You have loosed my sackcloth and girded me with gladness,

12   That *my* soul may sing praise to You and not be silent.
O Lord my God, I will give thanks to You forever.

Praying Psalm 30

A prayer the Jews recited during the festival of Hanukkah, commemorating the rededication of the Temple in 165 BC by Judas Maccabaeus after Antiochus Epiphanes had defiled it (cf. John 10:22).

Forgiving God, You are worthy to be lifted up. You have lifted me up by Your grace (vv. 1–3).

You are my song, Lord. Difficulty precedes deliverance—but Your deliverance is everlasting (vv. 4–5).

Lord Jesus, give me opportunities to sing Your praise together with other believers (v. 4).

Thank You, Lord, that my troubles are temporary while Your favor and joy last forever (v. 5).

I confess, Father, that when I am at ease I may acknowledge You, but I often take You and Your blessings for granted (vv. 6–7).

Thank You for hiding Your face when necessary, so that I will wake up and cry out to You (vv. 8–10).

I stand amazed that Almighty God is my helper (v. 10; cf. John 15:26). O Lord, keep on being my helper.

I will indeed praise You forever, O God—Father, Son, and Spirit. You turn sorrow into joy (vv. 11–12).

How Jesus could be interceding for you: You gave Your sheep to me, Father, and I delivered them out of their unbelief to give them eternal life (John 10:27–29). Let's keep them secure in Our hands. Change their mourning to rejoicing, Father, because You love to restore blessing to Your people (Isa. 61:3; Rom. 8:18–25; Rev. 21:4).

Psalm 31

A Psalm of Complaint and of Praise.

For the choir director. A Psalm of David.

1   In You, O LORD, I have taken refuge;
    Let me never be ashamed;
    In Your righteousness deliver me.
2   Incline Your ear to me, rescue me quickly;
    Be to me a rock of strength,
    A stronghold to save me.
3   For You are my rock and my fortress;
    For Your name's sake You will lead me and guide me.
4   You will pull me out of the net which they have secretly laid for me,
    For You are my strength.
5   Into Your hand I commit my spirit;
    You have ransomed me, O LORD, God of truth.

6   I hate those who regard vain idols,
    But I trust in the LORD.
7   I will rejoice and be glad in Your lovingkindness,
    Because You have seen my affliction;
    You have known the troubles of my soul,
8   And You have not given me over into the hand of the enemy;
    You have set my feet in a large place.

9   Be gracious to me, O LORD, for I am in distress;
    My eye is wasted away from grief, my soul and my body *also.*
10 For my life is spent with sorrow
    And my years with sighing;
    My strength has failed because of my iniquity,
    And my body has wasted away.
11 Because of all my adversaries, I have become a reproach,
    Especially to my neighbors,
    And an object of dread to my acquaintances;
    Those who see me in the street flee from me.
12 I am forgotten as a dead man, out of mind;
    I am like a broken vessel.

Praying Psalm 31

Many churches use verses 9–16 of this prayer of
David for worship on Passion Sunday.

Again, I come to you for refuge, Lord (v. 1).

O Lord, be my Rock during this time of great trial (v. 2).

Father, lead me and guide me for Your glory (v. 3).

Lord Jesus, I am in awe that You had this psalm in Your heart and on Your lips in Your final moments on the cross (v. 5; cf. Luke 23:46). This was Your prayer. You are the ultimate believer. Thank You.

Lord Jesus, You paid the ransom for my soul, for my life! Thank You (v. 5)!

In light of Jesus' use of this psalm, I ask, Father, that You would reorient my understanding of Your rescue. Help me to be devoted to You like Christ. Keep the resurrection glory coming to the forefront in my mind (vv. 6–16).

Lord, I rejoice in Your loyal love for me (v. 7).

Father, though others may forget me, You never will forget or forsake me (v. 12).

13   For I have heard the slander of many,
      Terror is on every side;
      While they took counsel together against me,
      They schemed to take away my life.
14   But as for me, I trust in You, O LORD,
      I say, "You are my God."
15   My times are in Your hand;
      Deliver me from the hand of my enemies and from those who persecute
         me.
16   Make Your face to shine upon Your servant;
      Save me in Your lovingkindness.
17   Let me not be put to shame, O LORD, for I call upon You;
      Let the wicked be put to shame, let them be silent in Sheol.
18   Let the lying lips be mute,
      Which speak arrogantly against the righteous
      With pride and contempt.
19   How great is Your goodness,
      Which You have stored up for those who fear You,
      Which You have wrought for those who take refuge in You,
      Before the sons of men!
20   You hide them in the secret place of Your presence from the conspiracies
         of man;
      You keep them secretly in a shelter from the strife of tongues.
21   Blessed be the LORD,
      For He has made marvelous His lovingkindness to me in a besieged city.
22   As for me, I said in my alarm,
      "I am cut off from before Your eyes";
      Nevertheless You heard the voice of my supplications
      When I cried to You.
23   O love the LORD, all you His godly ones!
      The LORD preserves the faithful
      And fully recompenses the proud doer.
24   Be strong and let your heart take courage,
      All you who hope in the LORD.

I place my life and the times of my life in Your loving hands, dear God. Deliver me from persecution in Your loyal love and kindness (vv. 15–16).

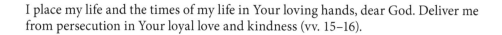

I love You, Lord! By Your grace, I will be strong and take courage because of the hope I have in You (vv. 17–24).

Thank You, Father, for providing me with Your protection and care (vv. 19–21, 23).

How Jesus could be interceding for you: Enable Your children, Father, to trust You fully with their lives the way I committed My life to You on the cross (Luke 23:46; Ps. 31:5a). By My sacrificial death I provided the ransom (Ps. 31:5b) for them—I completed it as You intended (John 17:4). Help them understand that You have given them to Me as a result of that ransom and they are also Yours (John 17:7–10).

Psalm 32

Blessedness of Forgiveness and of Trust in God.

A Psalm of David. A Maskil.

1 How blessed is he whose transgression is forgiven,
Whose sin is covered!
2 How blessed is the man to whom the Lord does not impute iniquity,
And in whose spirit there is no deceit!

3 When I kept silent *about my sin,* my body wasted away
Through my groaning all day long.
4 For day and night Your hand was heavy upon me;
My vitality was drained away *as* with the fever heat of summer.   *Selah.*
5 I acknowledged my sin to You,
And my iniquity I did not hide;
I said, "I will confess my transgressions to the Lord";
And You forgave the guilt of my sin.   *Selah.*
6 Therefore, let everyone who is godly pray to You in a time when You may
be found;
Surely in a flood of great waters they will not reach him.
7 You are my hiding place; You preserve me from trouble;
You surround me with songs of deliverance.   *Selah.*

8 I will instruct you and teach you in the way which you should go;
I will counsel you with My eye upon you.
9 Do not be as the horse or as the mule which have no understanding,
Whose trappings include bit and bridle to hold them in check,
Otherwise they will not come near to you.
10 Many are the sorrows of the wicked,
But he who trusts in the Lord, lovingkindness shall surround him.
11 Be glad in the Lord and rejoice, you righteous ones;
And shout for joy, all you who are upright in heart.

Praying Psalm 32

After his sin, David prayed this confession before the
Lord and praised Him for forgiving him.

I am blessed beyond measure. Praise be to Jesus Christ! Thank You, my sin is covered and my transgression is forgiven (vv. 1–2)

Thank You for conviction of sin and the burden of a guilty conscience, because it compels me to confess my transgressions to You. Thank You, Lord, for the grace of forgiveness and lifting of my guilt (vv. 3–6).

Father, teach me to always confess my sin rather than to remain silent (v. 3).

Thank You for teaching me over the years to pray more consistently, more fervently. You are my hiding place, my shelter (vv. 6–7).

Lord Jesus, I pray that other believers around me might come to You in prayer for forgiveness (v. 6).

Lord, remove my stubbornness, my reluctance to run to You for help (v. 9).

Your love surrounds me, Lord. Hallelujah! (vv. 10–11).

How Jesus could be interceding for you: Merciful and gracious Father, thank You for forgiving Your children by means of the saving work You accomplished through Me (Matt. 26:28; Eph. 4:32). Forgive them for Your name's sake, O God of their salvation (Ps. 79:9). Cleanse them from all unrighteousness (1 John 1:9).

Psalm 33

Praise to the Creator and Preserver.

1 Sing for joy in the LORD, O you righteous ones;
   Praise is becoming to the upright.
2 Give thanks to the LORD with the lyre;
   Sing praises to Him with a harp of ten strings.
3 Sing to Him a new song;
   Play skillfully with a shout of joy.
4 For the word of the LORD is upright,
   And all His work is *done* in faithfulness.
5 He loves righteousness and justice;
   The earth is full of the lovingkindness of the LORD.

6 By the word of the LORD the heavens were made,
   And by the breath of His mouth all their host.
7 He gathers the waters of the sea together as a heap;
   He lays up the deeps in storehouses.
8 Let all the earth fear the LORD;
   Let all the inhabitants of the world stand in awe of Him.
9 For He spoke, and it was done;
   He commanded, and it stood fast.
10 The LORD nullifies the counsel of the nations;
    He frustrates the plans of the peoples.
11 The counsel of the LORD stands forever,
    The plans of His heart from generation to generation.
12 Blessed is the nation whose God is the LORD,
    The people whom He has chosen for His own inheritance.
13 The LORD looks from heaven;
    He sees all the sons of men;
14 From His dwelling place He looks out
    On all the inhabitants of the earth,
15 He who fashions the hearts of them all,
    He who understands all their works.
16 The king is not saved by a mighty army;
    A warrior is not delivered by great strength.
17 A horse is a false hope for victory;
    Nor does it deliver anyone by its great strength.

Praying Psalm 33

The prayer of an anonymous believer in song-filled worship.

The earth is full of Your love, O Lord. Let the world and all that is in it praise You (vv. 1–5).

Father, I praise You for who You are and for what You have done (v. 1).

Thank You for Your Word, O God (v. 4).

Your living Word is Jesus Christ (John 1:1). By Your Word the heavens and their hosts came into being. I stand in awe of You, Lord (vv. 6–11).

Turn my nation to You, God. Teach us not to depend on human wisdom, power, or wealth. Teach us to seek You for all things (vv. 12–17).

Lord Jesus, You know my heart and thoughts as well as those of my neighbors. Enable me to speak Your word to them with boldness and compassion (vv. 13–15).

Father, help me to stop depending on my own strength (vv. 16–17).

18 Behold, the eye of the LORD is on those who fear Him,
    On those who hope for His lovingkindness,
19 To deliver their soul from death
    And to keep them alive in famine.
20 Our soul waits for the LORD;
    He is our help and our shield.
21 For our heart rejoices in Him,
    Because we trust in His holy name.
22 Let Your lovingkindness, O LORD, be upon us,
    According as we have hoped in You.

Look, and see my heart. I trust in You, Lord—I fear Your Holy name. I hope in Your love. You are the joy of Your people (vv. 18–22).

Father, teach me that there are times when I should give to those who are hungry even while I am praying for them (v. 19).

Holy Spirit, thank You for uniting believers together as one and teach me to pray with the pronoun "our" as much as I do with "my" (v. 20).

How Jesus could be interceding for you: Father, in Your presence is fullness of joy (Ps. 16:11; John 15:11; 17:13) and in You are all the springs of joy (Ps. 87:7). Put a song of praise in Your people's hearts and on their lips because You have provided refuge for them even in the midst of life's trials (Pss. 5:11; 59:16; Luke 6:22–23).

Psalm 34

The Lord, a Provider and Deliverer.

*A Psalm of David when he feigned madness before Abimelech,
who drove him away and he departed.*

1   I will bless the Lord at all times;
His praise shall continually be in my mouth.

2   My soul will make its boast in the Lord;
The humble will hear it and rejoice.

3   O magnify the Lord with me,
And let us exalt His name together.

4   I sought the Lord, and He answered me,
And delivered me from all my fears.

5   They looked to Him and were radiant,
And their faces will never be ashamed.

6   This poor man cried, and the Lord heard him
And saved him out of all his troubles.

7   The angel of the Lord encamps around those who fear Him,
And rescues them.

8   O taste and see that the Lord is good;
How blessed is the man who takes refuge in Him!

9   O fear the Lord, you His saints;
For to those who fear Him there is no want.

10   The young lions do lack and suffer hunger;
But they who seek the Lord shall not be in want of any good thing.

11   Come, you children, listen to me;
I will teach you the fear of the Lord.

12   Who is the man who desires life
And loves *length of* days that he may see good?

13   Keep your tongue from evil
And your lips from speaking deceit.

14   Depart from evil and do good;
Seek peace and pursue it.

15   The eyes of the Lord are toward the righteous
And His ears are *open* to their cry.

Praying Psalm 34

*In the early church, believers often associated this prayer
with the observance of the Lord's Supper.*

Lord, Your grace is amazing. David feigned madness before Abimelech—then David praised You for deliverance (superscription; cf. 1 Sam. 21:11–22:1).

Captivate me with Your grace in such a way that I call others to magnify You and exalt Your name together with me (vv. 1–3).

You alone can deliver us from our fears, Lord. May Your people seek You (vv. 4–7).

Father, thank You for saving me out of all my troubles this week (v. 6).

There it is again. How blessed is the one who takes refuge in You (v. 8).

Lord, teach me how to fear You in the way You have commanded (v. 11).

Father, give me a clean mouth with pure and honest speech (v. 13).

16   The face of the LORD is against evildoers,
      To cut off the memory of them from the earth.
17   *The righteous* cry, and the LORD hears
      And delivers them out of all their troubles.
18   The LORD is near to the brokenhearted
      And saves those who are crushed in spirit.
19   Many are the afflictions of the righteous,
      But the LORD delivers him out of them all.
20   He keeps all his bones,
      Not one of them is broken.
21   Evil shall slay the wicked,
      And those who hate the righteous will be condemned.
22   The LORD redeems the soul of His servants,
      And none of those who take refuge in Him will be condemned.

Blessed are those who mourn—because You draw near to those who are crushed in spirit (v. 18; Matt. 5:3–4).

Thank You for revealing the truth. Many are the afflictions of the righteous, but You will ultimately rescue Your people (vv. 19–22).

Lord Jesus, enable me to endure my afflictions and to trust You to do what is best for me and to Your glory (v. 19; see v. 8).

How Jesus could be interceding for you: I fulfilled Your Word, Father, in my suffering as the perfect, sinless sacrifice for sin (Ps. 34:12–16, 20; John 19:36; 1 Pet. 3:8–12). Give Your children the desire to pursue unity, kindness, humility, righteousness, and peace—to follow My example (Luke 9:23; John 17:25–26; 1 Pet. 2:21; 3:15).

Psalm 35

Prayer for Rescue from Enemies.

A Psalm *of David.*

1   Contend, O Lord, with those who contend with me;
Fight against those who fight against me.

2   Take hold of buckler and shield
And rise up for my help.

3   Draw also the spear and the battle-axe to meet those who pursue me;
Say to my soul, "I am your salvation."

4   Let those be ashamed and dishonored who seek my life;
Let those be turned back and humiliated who devise evil against me.

5   Let them be like chaff before the wind,
With the angel of the Lord driving *them* on.

6   Let their way be dark and slippery,
With the angel of the Lord pursuing them.

7   For without cause they hid their net for me;
Without cause they dug a pit for my soul.

8   Let destruction come upon him unawares,
And let the net which he hid catch himself;
Into that very destruction let him fall.

9   And my soul shall rejoice in the Lord;
It shall exult in His salvation.

10 All my bones will say, "Lord, who is like You,
Who delivers the afflicted from him who is too strong for him,
And the afflicted and the needy from him who robs him?"

11 Malicious witnesses rise up;
They ask me of things that I do not know.

12 They repay me evil for good,
To the bereavement of my soul.

13 But as for me, when they were sick, my clothing was sackcloth;
I humbled my soul with fasting,
And my prayer kept returning to my bosom.

14 I went about as though it were my friend or brother;
I bowed down mourning, as one who sorrows for a mother.

Praying Psalm 35

*King David's prayer for justice on behalf of those
who suffer oppression and injustice.*

O Lord, come to our nation's aid (vv. 1–3)!

Praise be to You—the Spirit of God has said to my soul, "I am your salvation" (v. 3).

Let all the enemies of Jesus Your Messiah stand before You in judgment, Father (vv. 4–8).

Judge those who are my enemies because they are Your enemies. I will leave their judgment in Your hands, O righteous Judge. Help me to love my enemies as You would have me love them (vv. 8–16).

Your are truly incomparable, Lord—there is no one like You (v. 10)!

O God, enable me to mourn over sinners as much as I grieve over evil and injustice (vv. 11–14).

15   But at my stumbling they rejoiced and gathered themselves together;
     The smiters whom I did not know gathered together against me,
     They slandered me without ceasing.
16   Like godless jesters at a feast,
     They gnashed at me with their teeth.
17   Lord, how long will You look on?
     Rescue my soul from their ravages,
     My only *life* from the lions.
18   I will give You thanks in the great congregation;
     I will praise You among a mighty throng.
19   Do not let those who are wrongfully my enemies rejoice over me;
     Nor let those who hate me without cause wink maliciously.
20   For they do not speak peace,
     But they devise deceitful words against those who are quiet in the land.
21   They opened their mouth wide against me;
     They said, "Aha, aha, our eyes have seen it!"
22   You have seen it, O Lord, do not keep silent;
     O Lord, do not be far from me.
23   Stir up Yourself, and awake to my right
     And to my cause, my God and my Lord.
24   Judge me, O Lord my God, according to Your righteousness,
     And do not let them rejoice over me.
25   Do not let them say in their heart, "Aha, our desire!"
     Do not let them say, "We have swallowed him up!"
26   Let those be ashamed and humiliated altogether who rejoice at my
          distress;
     Let those be clothed with shame and dishonor who magnify themselves
          over me.
27   Let them shout for joy and rejoice, who favor my vindication;
     And let them say continually, "The Lord be magnified,
     Who delights in the prosperity of His servant."
28   And my tongue shall declare Your righteousness
     And Your praise all day long.

Lord Jesus, thank You for entrusting Yourself to Your Father in the midst of those who were seeking to destroy You (vv. 17–26).

Father, replace injustice with justice and unrighteousness with righteousness (vv. 22–24).

You know where and how Your people are being persecuted today, Lord. Bring them relief with Your justice and mercy (v. 22).

Savior, judge me according to Your Word and Your righteousness (v. 24).

Hallelujah for the resurrection and vindication of my Lord and Savior (vv. 27–28)!

How Jesus could be interceding for you: Holy Father, You anointed Me as Your King to bring unbelievers to judgment with a rod of iron (Ps. 2:9; Rev. 19:15). You gave Me full authority to judge (John 5:22). I ask that You will bring justice for Your people and destruction of the wicked through Me in Your appointed time (Matt. 6:9–10; John 8:16).

Psalm 36

Wickedness of Men and Lovingkindness of God.

For the choir director. A Psalm *of David the servant of the* Lord.

1 Transgression speaks to the ungodly within his heart;
There is no fear of God before his eyes.
2 For it flatters him in his *own* eyes
Concerning the discovery of his iniquity *and* the hatred *of it.*
3 The words of his mouth are wickedness and deceit;
He has ceased to be wise *and* to do good.
4 He plans wickedness upon his bed;
He sets himself on a path that is not good;
He does not despise evil.

5 Your lovingkindness, O Lord, extends to the heavens,
Your faithfulness *reaches* to the skies.
6 Your righteousness is like the mountains of God;
Your judgments are *like* a great deep.
O Lord, You preserve man and beast.
7 How precious is Your lovingkindness, O God!
And the children of men take refuge in the shadow of Your wings.
8 They drink their fill of the abundance of Your house;
And You give them to drink of the river of Your delights.
9 For with You is the fountain of life;
In Your light we see light.
10 O continue Your lovingkindness to those who know You,
And Your righteousness to the upright in heart.
11 Let not the foot of pride come upon me,
And let not the hand of the wicked drive me away.
12 There the doers of iniquity have fallen;
They have been thrust down and cannot rise.

Praying Psalm 36

*A prayer of a servant of the Lord, exalting God's loyal
love while living in a fallen, corrupt world.*

God, create in me a holy hatred for evil. Let me not be flattered by the deceitfulness
of my sin (vv. 1–4).

⋘⋙

Use me, Lord, to speak the truth of the good news of Jesus Christ to the wicked and
deceitful so they might come to fear You (v. 1).

⋘⋙

Thank you for Your love, Your faithfulness, Your protection, and Your abundant
provision (vv. 5–9).

⋘⋙

Father, preserve me in the shadow of Your wings (vv. 6–7)!

⋘⋙

Thank You for the abundance of blessings I have in You (vv. 8–9).

⋘⋙

Keep me in Your love, O Lord (vv. 10–12).

⋘⋙

Continue Your lovingkindness, Your loyal love, to me, Lord Jesus (v. 10).

How Jesus could be interceding for you: I am Your Servant, Father (Isa. 49:5–7;
53:11; Matt. 12:18). Bring Your people to Me for refuge (Pss. 2:12; 36:7; Matt. 11:28).
Satisfy Your children's thirst through Me, the water of life (Ps. 36:8; John 4:10–14;
7:37–38). Grant them an abundant spiritual life through Me, for I am the Life (Ps.
36:9a; John 11:25; 14:6). Give them My light in their darkness, for I am the Light of
the world (Ps. 36:9b; John 8:12).

Psalm 37

Security of Those Who Trust in the Lord, and Insecurity of the Wicked.

A Psalm *of David.*

1 Do not fret because of evildoers,
  Be not envious toward wrongdoers.
2 For they will wither quickly like the grass
  And fade like the green herb.
3 Trust in the Lord and do good;
  Dwell in the land and cultivate faithfulness.
4 Delight yourself in the Lord;
  And He will give you the desires of your heart.
5 Commit your way to the Lord,
  Trust also in Him, and He will do it.
6 He will bring forth your righteousness as the light
  And your judgment as the noonday.

7 Rest in the Lord and wait patiently for Him;
  Do not fret because of him who prospers in his way,
  Because of the man who carries out wicked schemes.
8 Cease from anger and forsake wrath;
  Do not fret; *it leads* only to evildoing.
9 For evildoers will be cut off,
  But those who wait for the Lord, they will inherit the land.
10 Yet a little while and the wicked man will be no more;
  And you will look carefully for his place and he will not be *there.*
11 But the humble will inherit the land
  And will delight themselves in abundant prosperity.
12 The wicked plots against the righteous
  And gnashes at him with his teeth.
13 The Lord laughs at him,
  For He sees his day is coming.
14 The wicked have drawn the sword and bent their bow
  To cast down the afflicted and the needy,
  To slay those who are upright in conduct.
15 Their sword will enter their own heart,
  And their bows will be broken.

Praying Psalm 37

A prayer of David in his old age.

Lord, keep me from fretting over the success of wicked people (v. 1).

Give me Your desires, Lord. I commit my way to You and trust You to guide me in Your ways (vv. 4–5).

Blessed are the humble, Father. Help me to wait patiently for You and Your vindication (vv. 7–11).

I will trust that You will vindicate Your own and those who plot against Your Messiah and His people will bear their punishment (vv. 12–15).

16   Better is the little of the righteous
     Than the abundance of many wicked.
17   For the arms of the wicked will be broken,
     But the LORD sustains the righteous.
18   The LORD knows the days of the blameless,
     And their inheritance will be forever.
19   They will not be ashamed in the time of evil,
     And in the days of famine they will have abundance.
20   But the wicked will perish;
     And the enemies of the LORD will be like the glory of the pastures,
     They vanish—like smoke they vanish away.
21   The wicked borrows and does not pay back,
     But the righteous is gracious and gives.
22   For those blessed by Him will inherit the land,
     But those cursed by Him will be cut off.
23   The steps of a man are established by the LORD,
     And He delights in his way.
24   When he falls, he will not be hurled headlong,
     Because the LORD is the One who holds his hand.
25   I have been young and now I am old,
     Yet I have not seen the righteous forsaken
     Or his descendants begging bread.
26   All day long he is gracious and lends,
     And his descendants are a blessing.
27   Depart from evil and do good,
     So you will abide forever.
28   For the LORD loves justice
     And does not forsake His godly ones;
     They are preserved forever,
     But the descendants of the wicked will be cut off.
29   The righteous will inherit the land
     And dwell in it forever.
30   The mouth of the righteous utters wisdom,
     And his tongue speaks justice.
31   The law of his God is in his heart;
     His steps do not slip.
32   The wicked spies upon the righteous
     And seeks to kill him.
33   The LORD will not leave him in his hand
     Or let him be condemned when he is judged.

Father, enable me to be satisfied with what I have, even if it is only a little (v. 16).

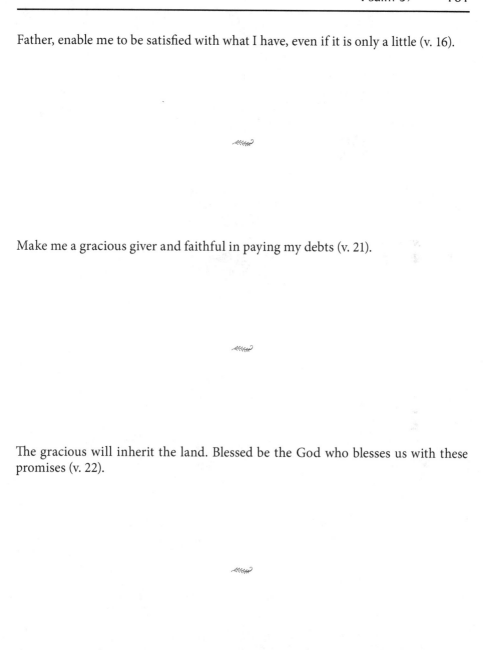

Make me a gracious giver and faithful in paying my debts (v. 21).

The gracious will inherit the land. Blessed be the God who blesses us with these promises (v. 22).

Thank You for this Word. When I stumble I will get up, because You hold my hand, Lord. Thank You (vv. 23–26).

34 Wait for the Lord and keep His way,
    And He will exalt you to inherit the land;
    When the wicked are cut off, you will see it.

35 I have seen a wicked, violent man
    Spreading himself like a luxuriant tree in its native soil.

36 Then he passed away, and lo, he was no more;
    I sought for him, but he could not be found.

37 Mark the blameless man, and behold the upright;
    For the man of peace will have a posterity.

38 But transgressors will be altogether destroyed;
    The posterity of the wicked will be cut off.

39 But the salvation of the righteous is from the Lord;
    He is their strength in time of trouble.

40 The Lord helps them and delivers them;
    He delivers them from the wicked and saves them,
    Because they take refuge in Him.

Blessed is the man of peace, for he will have an eternal inheritance. Thank You, Father (v. 37).

☙

Thank You, Jesus, for being there for me in my times of trouble (vv. 39–40).

☙

Again Lord, I take refuge in You (v. 40).

How Jesus could be interceding for you: Exalted and Mighty Father, humble Your servants so they will inherit the blessings You have prepared for them (Ps. 37:11; Matt. 5:5; 1 Pet. 5:6–7). Thank You for appointing Me as Your Shepherd to gently lead and care for the aged among Your children (Ps. 37:25; Isa. 46:4). I will never leave them nor forsake them (Ps. 37:25; Heb. 13:5).

Psalm 38

Prayer of a Suffering Penitent.

A Psalm of David, for a memorial.

1 O Lord, rebuke me not in Your wrath,
And chasten me not in Your burning anger.
2 For Your arrows have sunk deep into me,
And Your hand has pressed down on me.
3 There is no soundness in my flesh because of Your indignation;
There is no health in my bones because of my sin.
4 For my iniquities are gone over my head;
As a heavy burden they weigh too much for me.
5 My wounds grow foul *and* fester
Because of my folly.
6 I am bent over and greatly bowed down;
I go mourning all day long.
7 For my loins are filled with burning,
And there is no soundness in my flesh.
8 I am benumbed and badly crushed;
I groan because of the agitation of my heart.

9 Lord, all my desire is before You;
And my sighing is not hidden from You.
10 My heart throbs, my strength fails me;
And the light of my eyes, even that has gone from me.
11 My loved ones and my friends stand aloof from my plague;
And my kinsmen stand afar off.
12 Those who seek my life lay snares *for me;*
And those who seek to injure me have threatened destruction,
And they devise treachery all day long.
13 But I, like a deaf man, do not hear;
And *I am* like a mute man who does not open his mouth.
14 Yes, I am like a man who does not hear,
And in whose mouth are no arguments.
15 For I hope in You, O Lord;
You will answer, O Lord my God.
16 For I said, "May they not rejoice over me,
Who, when my foot slips, would magnify themselves against me."

Praying Psalm 38

A "memorial" prayer of David as he confesses his sin and seeks to remember the consequences of sin.

Father, thank You for the overwhelming sense of sickness and sorrow that comes when I sin and I don't deal with it immediately (vv. 1–8).

Lord Jesus, though You are sinless You felt this burden as You were broken and smitten for my iniquity. I'm sorry for my sin, Lord. Forgive me. Thank You (vv. 1–4).

How foolish I have been to sin against You, Lord (v. 5)!

Jesus, when you were reviled by sinful men, You did not open Your mouth. Your hope was in Your Father and Your God. Help me to place my hope in God as well (vv. 9–17).

Behold my illness with which You discipline me, Lord, and grant me relief (v. 9).

God of Abraham, Isaac, and Jacob—enable the remnant of Israel to pray this corporately before Your Son comes to establish His Kingdom (vv. 15–18).

17 For I am ready to fall,
    And my sorrow is continually before me.
18 For I confess my iniquity;
    I am full of anxiety because of my sin.
19 But my enemies are vigorous *and* strong,
    And many are those who hate me wrongfully.
20 And those who repay evil for good,
    They oppose me, because I follow what is good.
21 Do not forsake me, O Lord;
    O my God, do not be far from me!
22 Make haste to help me,
    O Lord, my salvation!

Living God, You alone are my salvation. Come quickly to my aid. Though I have sinned, You know my heart's desire and my aim are to follow You (vv. 18–22).

Father, forgive me, because I have sinned against You (v. 18).

Lord Jesus, lift the consequences of my sin from upon me and cause me never to forget how my foolish disobedience brought them upon me (v. 22).

How Jesus could be interceding for you: Father, cause sinners to tremble before You and Your Word (Isa. 66:2; 1 John 1:9). Bring them to truly confess that You have chastised them justly and yet lovingly (Heb. 12:5–11).

Psalm 39

The Vanity of Life.

For the choir director, for Jeduthun. A Psalm of David.

1   I said, "I will guard my ways
     That I may not sin with my tongue;
     I will guard my mouth as with a muzzle
     While the wicked are in my presence."
2   I was mute and silent,
     I refrained *even* from good,
     And my sorrow grew worse.
3   My heart was hot within me,
     While I was musing the fire burned;
     Then I spoke with my tongue:
4   "Lord, make me to know my end
     And what is the extent of my days;
     Let me know how transient I am.
5   "Behold, You have made my days *as* handbreadths,
     And my lifetime as nothing in Your sight;
     Surely every man at his best is a mere breath.   *Selah.*
6   "Surely every man walks about as a phantom;
     Surely they make an uproar for nothing;
     He amasses *riches* and does not know who will gather them.

7   "And now, Lord, for what do I wait?
     My hope is in You.
8   "Deliver me from all my transgressions;
     Make me not the reproach of the foolish.
9   "I have become mute, I do not open my mouth,
     Because it is You who have done *it*.
10   "Remove Your plague from me;
     Because of the opposition of Your hand I am perishing.
11   "With reproofs You chasten a man for iniquity;
     You consume as a moth what is precious to him;
     Surely every man is a mere breath.   *Selah.*

12   "Hear my prayer, O Lord, and give ear to my cry;
     Do not be silent at my tears;
     For I am a stranger with You,
     A sojourner like all my fathers.
13   "Turn Your gaze away from me, that I may smile *again*
     Before I depart and am no more."

Praying Psalm 39

*David prays for God to make him fully aware of
his immortality and his immoralities.*

David did not open his mouth to Shimei—neither did Jesus when His accusers
sought His life. Teach me the path of trust, Lord. Teach me to control my tongue
(vv. 1–3).

Lord, help me to understand the brevity of life (vv. 4–6).

All my hope is in You, Lord (v. 7).

Lord, enable me to be humbled under Your chastening and to realize the depth of
my disobedience (vv. 8–11).

Jesus, deliver me from my sins and their effects upon my life and the lives of those
around me (v. 8).

My hope is indeed in You, Father. Lift the burden that is weighing down my soul,
dear God (vv. 12–13).

How Jesus could be interceding for you: Eternal Father, the earthly lives of Your
children are but a breath in time (Luke 12:19–20). Teach them to consider the brevity of life (Ps. 90:12) and to trust You for all their needs (Matt. 6:25–31).

Psalm 40

God Sustains His Servant.

For the choir director. A Psalm of David.

1 I waited patiently for the Lord;
 And He inclined to me and heard my cry.
2 He brought me up out of the pit of destruction, out of the miry clay,
 And He set my feet upon a rock making my footsteps firm.
3 He put a new song in my mouth, a song of praise to our God;
 Many will see and fear
 And will trust in the Lord.

4 How blessed is the man who has made the Lord his trust,
 And has not turned to the proud, nor to those who lapse into falsehood.
5 Many, O Lord my God, are the wonders which You have done,
 And Your thoughts toward us;
 There is none to compare with You.
 If I would declare and speak of them,
 They would be too numerous to count.

6 Sacrifice and meal offering You have not desired;
 My ears You have opened;
 Burnt offering and sin offering You have not required.
7 Then I said, "Behold, I come;
 In the scroll of the book it is written of me.
8 "I delight to do Your will, O my God;
 Your Law is within my heart."

9 I have proclaimed glad tidings of righteousness in the great congregation;
 Behold, I will not restrain my lips,
 O Lord, You know.
10 I have not hidden Your righteousness within my heart;
 I have spoken of Your faithfulness and Your salvation;
 I have not concealed Your lovingkindness and Your truth from the great
  congregation.
11 You, O Lord, will not withhold Your compassion from me;
 Your lovingkindness and Your truth will continually preserve me.

Praying Psalm 40

A prayer expressing David's thanks for God's gracious deliverance.

Those who wait on You, Lord, never wait in vain. Praise God (vv. 1–3)!

O Father, teach me how to patiently wait for You in the midst of the problems my own sin has brought upon me (v. 1).

Thank You, Lord Jesus, that You were the perfect disciple. You always delighted to do God's will (vv. 6–8).

Father, teach me to delight in doing Your will (v. 8).

Jesus, open my mouth to speak the good news concerning Your salvation (v. 9).

I know that sense of overwhelming dread over the multitude of my sins—what must have You felt, Lord—when my iniquities and those of the world were laid to Your account? (vv. 10–12).

12 For evils beyond number have surrounded me;
    My iniquities have overtaken me, so that I am not able to see;
    They are more numerous than the hairs of my head,
    And my heart has failed me.
13 Be pleased, O Lord, to deliver me;
    Make haste, O Lord, to help me.
14 Let those be ashamed and humiliated together
    Who seek my life to destroy it;
    Let those be turned back and dishonored
    Who delight in my hurt.
15 Let those be appalled because of their shame
    Who say to me, "Aha, aha!"
16 Let all who seek You rejoice and be glad in You;
    Let those who love Your salvation say continually,
    "The Lord be magnified!"
17 Since I am afflicted and needy,
    Let the Lord be mindful of me.
    You are my help and my deliverer;
    Do not delay, O my God.

Father, may I always seek what pleases You, rather than what pleases me (v. 13)

When I see how others delight in hurting me, keep me from delighting in causing hurt to others (v. 14).

The Lord be magnified and glorified (v. 16).

Remember me, Lord. I need You (v. 17).

How Jesus could be interceding for you: Father, I came to do Your will—Your written revelation spoke of Me and Your Word was in My heart (Ps. 40:7–10; Matt. 26:42; Heb. 10:4–10). I obeyed You unto death and gave Your Word to Your children (John 17:8, 14). Save Your people, Father, and preserve them (Ps. 40:11). Bless those who trust in You (Ps. 40:4; John 20:29).

Psalm 41

The Psalmist in Sickness Complains of Enemies and False Friends.

For the choir director. A Psalm of David.

1   How blessed is he who considers the helpless;
The Lord will deliver him in a day of trouble.
2   The Lord will protect him and keep him alive,
And he shall be called blessed upon the earth;
And do not give him over to the desire of his enemies.
3   The Lord will sustain him upon his sickbed;
In his illness, You restore him to health.

4   As for me, I said, "O Lord, be gracious to me;
Heal my soul, for I have sinned against You."
5   My enemies speak evil against me,
"When will he die, and his name perish?"
6   And when he comes to see *me,* he speaks falsehood;
His heart gathers wickedness to itself;
When he goes outside, he tells it.
7   All who hate me whisper together against me;
Against me they devise my hurt, *saying,*
8   "A wicked thing is poured out upon him,
That when he lies down, he will not rise up again."
9   Even my close friend in whom I trusted,
Who ate my bread,
Has lifted up his heel against me.
10   But You, O Lord, be gracious to me and raise me up,
That I may repay them.
11   By this I know that You are pleased with me,
Because my enemy does not shout in triumph over me.
12   As for me, You uphold me in my integrity,
And You set me in Your presence forever.
13   Blessed be the Lord, the God of Israel,
From everlasting to everlasting.
Amen and Amen.

Praying Psalm 41

Book One (Pss. 1–41) of the Psalter closes with this prayer for relief from life's afflictions and for the assurance of salvation from God.

How blessed are the merciful, for they will receive mercy (vv. 1–3; cf. Matt. 5:7).

Lord, make me biblically "considerate" of the helpless (v. 1).

Be gracious to me, Father, in the face of man's betrayal of me (vv. 4–9). Your Son knows what it's like to be betrayed by a trusted friend. Thank You for a merciful and faithful High Priest in Him.

Father, protect me from my enemies (vv. 2, 4–9).

Heal me from my illness and forgive my sin (v. 4).

Lord Jesus, keep me faithful to You as I seek after You (v. 12).

Set me in Your presence forever, O God (v. 12).

You are the most blessed God—the Giver of every blessing—forever and ever. Amen and amen (v. 13).

How Jesus could be interceding for you: Loving Father, give blessing (Matt. 5:3–11; 25:34), healing (Luke 5:17), and comfort (2 Cor. 1:3–5) to Your child.

Psalm 42

Thirsting for God in Trouble and Exile.

For the choir director. A Maskil of the sons of Korah.

1   As the deer pants for the water brooks,
    So my soul pants for You, O God.
2   My soul thirsts for God, for the living God;
    When shall I come and appear before God?
3   My tears have been my food day and night,
    While *they* say to me all day long, "Where is your God?"
4   These things I remember and I pour out my soul within me.
    For I used to go along with the throng *and* lead them in procession to the
        house of God,
    With the voice of joy and thanksgiving, a multitude keeping festival.

5   Why are you in despair, O my soul?
    And *why* have you become disturbed within me?
    Hope in God, for I shall again praise Him
    For the help of His presence.
6   O my God, my soul is in despair within me;
    Therefore I remember You from the land of the Jordan
    And the peaks of Hermon, from Mount Mizar.
7   Deep calls to deep at the sound of Your waterfalls;
    All Your breakers and Your waves have rolled over me.
8   The LORD will command His lovingkindness in the daytime;
    And His song will be with me in the night,
    A prayer to the God of my life.

9   I will say to God my rock, "Why have You forgotten me?
    Why do I go mourning because of the oppression of the enemy?"
10 As a shattering of my bones, my adversaries revile me,
    While they say to me all day long, "Where is your God?"
11 Why are you in despair, O my soul?
    And why have you become disturbed within me?
    Hope in God, for I shall yet praise Him,
    The help of my countenance and my God.

Praying Psalm 42

*Book Two (Pss. 42–72) of the Psalter opens with a psalm by the
sons of Korah, descendants of the Korah of Numbers 16 (see Num.
26:10–11)—living testimonies to God's amazing grace.*

Father, my soul does thirst for You, the living God. But there are times when my
spiritual senses seem dulled and my longing is not what it should be. Please create
in me a greater and greater longing for Your presence (vv. 1–2).

When I am struggling in faith or in the midst of a spiritual battle, the world—and
even sometimes those who profess faith in You—question why I'm going through
these things if I trust in You. I'm bringing all of it to You (vv. 3–4).

Lord, no matter what my tears are about, my hope remains in You and You alone
(v. 5).

Bring to my mind and memory all the many things You have done for me, Lord
Jesus (v. 6).

I need You, Lord. Life feels like waves crashing over me and I can't keep my footing.
Remember me, O God (v. 7).

Lord Jesus, I'm humbled and sorry that while here on earth, facing the prospect of
bearing the sins of Your people, You too felt overwhelming despair. Thank You for
determining not to escape the trial that burdened Your soul to the point of death
(cf. Matt. 26:38; John 12:27).

I believe Your love will be with me by day and Your comfort by night (v. 8).

Father, even though I might not feel like singing in the midst of difficult nights and
unable to sleep, put Your song in my heart and my mouth (v. 8).

I feel like You've forgotten me, O God of my life. Everything and everyone seem
to be against me. I will take counsel from Your Word—"Why are you despairing,
O my soul?" I will hope in God. I will praise You, because You are my help, my
hope, my Savior (vv. 9–11).

How Jesus could be interceding for you: Father, on the cross I experienced thirst,
both physical and spiritual (John 19:28; Ps. 22:14–15). Because I am the Water of
Life, satisfy Your children's longings, the panting of their souls, with Me (John
4:13–14).

Psalm 43

Prayer for Deliverance.

1   Vindicate me, O God, and plead my case against an ungodly nation;
    O deliver me from the deceitful and unjust man!
2   For You are the God of my strength; why have You rejected me?
    Why do I go mourning because of the oppression of the enemy?

3   O send out Your light and Your truth, let them lead me;
    Let them bring me to Your holy hill
    And to Your dwelling places.
4   Then I will go to the altar of God,
    To God my exceeding joy;
    And upon the lyre I shall praise You, O God, my God.

5   Why are you in despair, O my soul?
    And why are you disturbed within me?
    Hope in God, for I shall again praise Him,
    The help of my countenance and my God.

Praying Psalm 43

*Absence of a psalm heading indicates the continuation
of the previous prayer by the sons of Korah.*

Lord, I can imagine You wrestling in prayer, guided by this psalm, as the leaders of Israel turned against You and You sought to do Your Father's will.

I'm under attack by my enemies, Lord. Defend me, vindicate my faith, and deliver me from their clutches (v. 1).

Father, I flee to You for refuge. Don't turn me away (v. 2).

Lead me, Father, by Your Word. Draw me near to You. Enable and ennoble my worship with joy, singing, and praise (vv. 3–4).

What my soul pants for, Lord Jesus, is to be with You, in Your presence with everlasting joy (v.4).

God, help me to hope in You and turn away from the thoughts that disturb me and tempt me to despair (v. 5).

How Jesus could be interceding for you: Father, I endured Your rejection as one who became sin, so Your people might possess Your righteousness (2 Cor. 5:21). I am their truth (John 14:6) and their light (John 8:12), grant them entrance to Your holiest hill, Your heavenly throne room (John 17:24).

Psalm 44

Former Deliverances and Present Troubles.

For the choir director. A Maskil of the sons of Korah.

1   O God, we have heard with our ears,
    Our fathers have told us
    The work that You did in their days,
    In the days of old.
2   You with Your own hand drove out the nations;
    Then You planted them;
    You afflicted the peoples,
    Then You spread them abroad.
3   For by their own sword they did not possess the land,
    And their own arm did not save them,
    But Your right hand and Your arm and the light of Your presence,
    For You favored them.

4   You are my King, O God;
    Command victories for Jacob.
5   Through You we will push back our adversaries;
    Through Your name we will trample down those who rise up against us.
6   For I will not trust in my bow,
    Nor will my sword save me.
7   But You have saved us from our adversaries,
    And You have put to shame those who hate us.
8   In God we have boasted all day long,
    And we will give thanks to Your name forever.   *Selah.*

9   Yet You have rejected *us* and brought us to dishonor,
    And do not go out with our armies.
10 You cause us to turn back from the adversary;
    And those who hate us have taken spoil for themselves.
11 You give us as sheep to be eaten
    And have scattered us among the nations.
12 You sell Your people cheaply,
    And have not profited by their sale.
13 You make us a reproach to our neighbors,
    A scoffing and a derision to those around us.

Praying Psalm 44

*An artistically written psalm of wisdom by the sons
of Korah at a time of national disaster.*

Countless times I've read of Your mighty deeds in regard to Israel. By Your power and truth You saved that blessed the nation through which my Redeemer has come (vv. 1–3).

Father, how I long for You to delight in me. Thank You for saving me, for I could never have saved myself (v. 3).

You are my King, O God—*the* King of all—and the King of Israel. Grant your nation repentance and faith to see their Messiah, so that they may boast in You once more (vv. 4–19).

Lord Jesus, You are the King of my life. I will obey You and serve You (v. 4).

Though sometimes I'm tempted to think I can trust my own wisdom and strength, Lord, enable me to trust You completely and to give You thanks forever (vv. 6–8).

Father, in this fallen world I feel like I'm a lamb being led to slaughter. If it's not the opposition of those who hate You, then it's one natural disaster after another testing my faith in You and Your goodness. I'm ashamed of my unbelief. Increase my faith (vv. 9–12).

Precious Jesus, You endured mocking from sinful people. Help me to endure such treatment and not to be ashamed of my failure to have Your calmness in the midst of persecution (vv. 13–16).

14 You make us a byword among the nations,
    A laughingstock among the peoples.
15 All day long my dishonor is before me
    And my humiliation has overwhelmed me,
16 Because of the voice of him who reproaches and reviles,
    Because of the presence of the enemy and the avenger.
17 All this has come upon us, but we have not forgotten You,
    And we have not dealt falsely with Your covenant.
18 Our heart has not turned back,
    And our steps have not deviated from Your way,
19 Yet You have crushed us in a place of jackals
    And covered us with the shadow of death.
20 If we had forgotten the name of our God
    Or extended our hands to a strange god,
21 Would not God find this out?
    For He knows the secrets of the heart.
22 But for Your sake we are killed all day long;
    We are considered as sheep to be slaughtered.
23 Arouse Yourself, why do You sleep, O Lord?
    Awake, do not reject us forever.
24 Why do You hide Your face
    And forget our affliction and our oppression?
25 For our soul has sunk down into the dust;
    Our body cleaves to the earth.
26 Rise up, be our help,
    And redeem us for the sake of Your lovingkindness.

O God, keep my heart focused on You and keep me from turning away from You (v. 18).

⋘

I, like the remnant of believers in Israel, pledge my fidelity to You, the all-knowing, Almighty God. Many of Your sheep are being persecuted and even slaughtered for Your Son's sake. Father, rise up and be our help because of Your great love (vv. 20–26).

⋘

Examine my heart and purify it, Lord, because You know its secrets (v. 21).

⋘

Because You Yourself suffered and died for me, O Lamb of God, make me willing to die for You (v. 22).

———

How Jesus could be interceding for you: I am the Author of Your people's salvation through My suffering, O God (Heb. 2:10). And, I am the Perfecter of their faith (Heb. 12:2). By Your Spirit, enable them to follow My example in suffering (1 Pet. 2:21) and to grow in their faith (Luke 22:32).

Psalm 45

A Song Celebrating the King's Marriage.

For the choir director; according to the Shoshannim.
A Maskil of the sons of Korah. A Song of Love.

1   My heart overflows with a good theme;
    I address my verses to the King;
    My tongue is the pen of a ready writer.
2   You are fairer than the sons of men;
    Grace is poured upon Your lips;
    Therefore God has blessed You forever.

3   Gird Your sword on *Your* thigh, O Mighty One,
    In Your splendor and Your majesty!
4   And in Your majesty ride on victoriously,
    For the cause of truth and meekness *and* righteousness;
    Let Your right hand teach You awesome things.
5   Your arrows are sharp;
    The peoples fall under You;
    Your arrows are in the heart of the King's enemies.

6   Your throne, O God, is forever and ever;
    A scepter of uprightness is the scepter of Your kingdom.
7   You have loved righteousness and hated wickedness;
    Therefore God, Your God, has anointed You
    With the oil of joy above Your fellows.
8   All Your garments are *fragrant with* myrrh and aloes *and* cassia;
    Out of ivory palaces stringed instruments have made You glad.
9   Kings' daughters are among Your noble ladies;
    At Your right hand stands the queen in gold from Ophir.
10 Listen, O daughter, give attention and incline your ear:
    Forget your people and your father's house;
11 Then the King will desire your beauty.
    Because He is your Lord, bow down to Him.
12 The daughter of Tyre *will come* with a gift;
    The rich among the people will seek your favor.
13 The King's daughter is all glorious within;
    Her clothing is interwoven with gold.

Praying Psalm 45

A prayer of praise as a wedding song fit for a king.

My Lord Jesus Christ—You are the most beautiful of all men, God blessed forever—my God, my Lord, my King (vv. 1–2).

Lord of heaven and earth, enable my mind, my heart, and my lips to speak words befitting of praise to You as my King (v. 1).

Come, Lord. In glory come to judge Your enemies and reign over all the nations of the earth (vv. 3–5).

Messiah, Your throne is forever and ever. You are God and You rule with integrity. I offer You my praise, Lord (vv. 6–7).

How majestic You are in all Your royal glory, Lord! The scepter, indeed, has not departed from You, O Lion of the tribe of Judah (v. 6; Gen. 49:10).

Lord, the Church which You redeemed will be made a glorious bride for You. We will give thanks to You forever and ever (vv. 10–17).

Father, help me place my marriage ahead of my birth family (v. 10).

Enable Your people, O God, to celebrate the marriage of believing men and women and to hold the institution of marriage in high regard (v. 15).

14   She will be led to the King in embroidered work;
    The virgins, her companions who follow her,
    Will be brought to You.

15   They will be led forth with gladness and rejoicing;
    They will enter into the King's palace.

16   In place of your fathers will be your sons;
    You shall make them princes in all the earth.

17   I will cause Your name to be remembered in all generations;
    Therefore the peoples will give You thanks forever and ever.

Teach me, Lord, how I might cause Your name to be remembered among my descendants (v. 17).

———

How Jesus could be interceding for you: Father, You anointed me as Your appointed ruler over all the earth. I pray that Your people might behold My glory as King of kings and Lord of lords (John 17:24; 1 Tim. 6:14–15).

Psalm 46

God the Refuge of His People.

For the choir director. A Psalm *of the sons of Korah, set to Alamoth. A Song.*

1 God is our refuge and strength,
A very present help in trouble.
2 Therefore we will not fear, though the earth should change
And though the mountains slip into the heart of the sea;
3 Though its waters roar *and* foam,
Though the mountains quake at its swelling pride.   *Selah.*

4 There is a river whose streams make glad the city of God,
The holy dwelling places of the Most High.
5 God is in the midst of her, she will not be moved;
God will help her when morning dawns.
6 The nations made an uproar, the kingdoms tottered;
He raised His voice, the earth melted.
7 The Lord of hosts is with us;
The God of Jacob is our stronghold.   *Selah.*

8 Come, behold the works of the Lord,
Who has wrought desolations in the earth.
9 He makes wars to cease to the end of the earth;
He breaks the bow and cuts the spear in two;
He burns the chariots with fire.
10 "Cease *striving* and know that I am God;
I will be exalted among the nations, I will be exalted in the earth."
11 The Lord of hosts is with us;
The God of Jacob is our stronghold.   *Selah.*

Praying Psalm 46

A prayer to praise the Lord for delivering His people from destruction.

Even if everything in all of creation were to convulse and disintegrate, by Your grace I will not fear. You are my refuge and strength, O God (vv. 1–3).

Thank You, Lord, for being my help just when I need Your comforting presence and assurance (v. 1).

Where You dwell as the Lord of Hosts, there is peace—no matter the uproar of nations and kingdoms. You are the fortress of Your people (vv. 4–8).

We praise You, Jesus, for being with us and for us (vv. 7, 11).

I will be still and trust in You, my God. Be exalted as Lord among the nations and in the whole earth (vv. 9–11).

Lord, when I face what seem to be insurmountable problems, help me to know You are God (v. 10).

Be exalted, O God (v. 10)!

How Jesus could be interceding for you: You appointed from ages past, Father, that I would serve as Immanuel to Your people (Isa. 7:14; Matt. 1:23). In the midst of their many challenges in a fallen world, may they realize that I will never leave them nor forsake them (Matt. 28:20; Heb. 13:5).

Psalm 47

God the King of the Earth.

For the choir director. A Psalm of the sons of Korah.

1   O clap your hands, all peoples;
    Shout to God with the voice of joy.
2   For the LORD Most High is to be feared,
    A great King over all the earth.
3   He subdues peoples under us
    And nations under our feet.
4   He chooses our inheritance for us,
    The glory of Jacob whom He loves.   *Selah.*

5   God has ascended with a shout,
    The LORD, with the sound of a trumpet.
6   Sing praises to God, sing praises;
    Sing praises to our King, sing praises.
7   For God is the King of all the earth;
    Sing praises with a skillful psalm.
8   God reigns over the nations,
    God sits on His holy throne.
9   The princes of the people have assembled themselves *as* the people of the
       God of Abraham,
    For the shields of the earth belong to God;
    He is highly exalted.

Praying Psalm 47

Communal praise to the Lord Most High with choral responses.

Lord Most High, hallowed be Your name. Let all people rejoice and tremble before You (vv. 1–2).

⫷⫸

Your Kingdom come, Lord Jesus, for Yours is the Kingdom and the power and the glory forever and ever (vv. 3–9).

⫷⫸

O God, we praise You for Your deeds on behalf of Your people Israel (vv. 3, 4).

⫷⫸

Lord, we praise You for Your sovereign reign over all the earth and all its peoples (vv. 2, 7, 8).

⫷⫸

Be most highly exalted, O God (v. 9)!

How Jesus could be interceding for you: Sovereign Father, You have given Me the Kingdom (Luke 19:11–12). Send me back to earth to establish My Kingdom (Rev. 11:15), in answer to the prayer of Your people whom I taught to pray, "Your Kingdom come" (Matt. 6:10).

Psalm 48

The Beauty and Glory of Zion.

A Song; a Psalm of the sons of Korah.

1   Great is the LORD, and greatly to be praised,
   In the city of our God, His holy mountain.
2   Beautiful in elevation, the joy of the whole earth,
   Is Mount Zion *in* the far north,
   The city of the great King.
3   God, in her palaces,
   Has made Himself known as a stronghold.

4   For, lo, the kings assembled themselves,
   They passed by together.
5   They saw *it,* then they were amazed;
   They were terrified, they fled in alarm.
6   Panic seized them there,
   Anguish, as of a woman in childbirth.
7   With the east wind
   You break the ships of Tarshish.
8   As we have heard, so have we seen
   In the city of the LORD of hosts, in the city of our God;
   God will establish her forever.   *Selah.*

9   We have thought on Your lovingkindness, O God,
   In the midst of Your temple.
10 As is Your name, O God,
   So is Your praise to the ends of the earth;
   Your right hand is full of righteousness.
11 Let Mount Zion be glad,
   Let the daughters of Judah rejoice
   Because of Your judgments.
12 Walk about Zion and go around her;
   Count her towers;
13 Consider her ramparts;
   Go through her palaces,
   That you may tell *it* to the next generation.
14 For such is God,
   Our God forever and ever;
   He will guide us until death.

Praying Psalm 48

A "song of Zion" offering praise-filled prayer to God, the great King.

One day, God the Lord—Jesus Christ Himself—will rule the world from Jerusalem. Lord, I am looking forward to that day when all will confess that You are great and greatly to be praised. Jerusalem will be exalted, but You will be Your people's fortress (vv. 1–3).

Be exalted and be great in all You do, O Lord God, our Great High King (v. 1)!

Come to rule the nations, Lord Jesus (vv. 4–8).

May the kings of the earth be amazed at Your works, O Father (vv. 4, 5).

When I think of Your love and Your name, eternity will not be able to exhaust the praise due to You for Your glorious character (vv. 9–10).

Father, focus my thought on Your lovingkindness and steadfast loyalty (v. 9).

Your presence, O King, will make Jerusalem and the New Jerusalem glad, glorious, and beautiful. Guide us home, dear Lord (vv. 11–14).

Lord Jesus, guide me all of every day until the day I go to be with You (v. 14).

How Jesus could be interceding for you: As the Holy One of Israel, Father, I went to Zion, Your city (Isa. 12:6; Zech. 9:9). Encourage Zion and allow them to sing and rejoice when I return to reign as their King (Zech. 2:10–12). Save Israel (Rom. 9:32–10:1), Father, and teach Your Church true wisdom and obedience (Rom. 11:25–33).

Psalm 49

The Folly of Trusting in Riches.

For the choir director. A Psalm of the sons of Korah.

1   Hear this, all peoples;
      Give ear, all inhabitants of the world,
2   Both low and high,
      Rich and poor together.
3   My mouth will speak wisdom,
      And the meditation of my heart *will be* understanding.
4   I will incline my ear to a proverb;
      I will express my riddle on the harp.

5   Why should I fear in days of adversity,
      When the iniquity of my foes surrounds me,
6   Even those who trust in their wealth
      And boast in the abundance of their riches?
7   No man can by any means redeem *his* brother
      Or give to God a ransom for him—
8   For the redemption of his soul is costly,
      And he should cease *trying* forever—
9   That he should live on eternally,
      That he should not undergo decay.
10   For he sees *that even* wise men die;
      The stupid and the senseless alike perish
      And leave their wealth to others.
11   Their inner thought is *that* their houses are forever
      And their dwelling places to all generations;
      They have called their lands after their own names.
12   But man in *his* pomp will not endure;
      He is like the beasts that perish.
13   This is the way of those who are foolish,
      And of those after them who approve their words.   *Selah.*
14   As sheep they are appointed for Sheol;
      Death shall be their shepherd;
      And the upright shall rule over them in the morning,
      And their form shall be for Sheol to consume
      So that they have no habitation.

Praying Psalm 49

A prayerful meditation on the meaning and means of redemption from sin.

God, whether rich or poor, all men everywhere need to know that only You can ransom sinners and save us from our sins (vv. 1–9).

Lord, help me to meditate on Your Word so that I understand what You would have me know (v. 3).

Teach me not to fear the "days of adversity," Father (v. 5).

Thank You, Jesus, for the priceless ransom You paid for my soul (vv. 8, 9).

Experience tells us, O Lord, that the wise and the foolish both die—after death our bodies decay just like animals. Father, those who do not trust in You try to build a name for themselves yet are heading for destruction. (vv. 10–14).

Do not allow me to focus more on my house and possessions than on You, O God (v. 11).

Praise be to You, O God, for You sent Jesus to be the Shepherd of my soul by delivering me from the power of the shepherd of death (v. 14).

15   But God will redeem my soul from the power of Sheol,
     For He will receive me.   *Selah.*
16   Do not be afraid when a man becomes rich,
     When the glory of his house is increased;
17   For when he dies he will carry nothing away;
     His glory will not descend after him.
18   Though while he lives he congratulates himself—
     And though *men* praise you when you do well for yourself—
19   He shall go to the generation of his fathers;
     They will never see the light.
20   Man in *his* pomp, yet without understanding,
     Is like the beasts that perish.

Father, I trust that, because of Your Son, the grave has no ultimate hold on me. I will rise and abide in Your presence (v. 15).

Lord, help me not to envy the godless who prosper here on earth. They will perish and not rise to life, but live in death and everlasting darkness (vv. 16–20).

How Jesus could be interceding for you: Continue to glorify Your name, Father, by delivering individuals from the power of Satan on the basis of the redemption price I gave through My sacrificial death (Matt. 20:28; Heb. 2:14–15). By the power of My ransom, give to each true believer abundant life now and eternal life forever and ever (Matt. 25:46; John 10:10–11; 17:2–3).

Psalm 50

God the Judge of the Righteous and the Wicked.

A Psalm of Asaph.

1   The Mighty One, God, the Lord, has spoken,
    And summoned the earth from the rising of the sun to its setting.
2   Out of Zion, the perfection of beauty,
    God has shone forth.
3   May our God come and not keep silence;
    Fire devours before Him,
    And it is very tempestuous around Him.
4   He summons the heavens above,
    And the earth, to judge His people:
5   "Gather My godly ones to Me,
    Those who have made a covenant with Me by sacrifice."
6   And the heavens declare His righteousness,
    For God Himself is judge.   *Selah.*

7   "Hear, O My people, and I will speak;
    O Israel, I will testify against you;
    I am God, your God.
8   "I do not reprove you for your sacrifices,
    And your burnt offerings are continually before Me.
9   "I shall take no young bull out of your house
    Nor male goats out of your folds.
10 "For every beast of the forest is Mine,
    The cattle on a thousand hills.
11 "I know every bird of the mountains,
    And everything that moves in the field is Mine.
12 "If I were hungry I would not tell you,
    For the world is Mine, and all it contains.
13 "Shall I eat the flesh of bulls
    Or drink the blood of male goats?
14 "Offer to God a sacrifice of thanksgiving
    And pay your vows to the Most High;
15 Call upon Me in the day of trouble;
    I shall rescue you, and you will honor Me."

Praying Psalm 50

Asaph's prayer about God as Judge and the proper offering from His people.

I'm watching and waiting—come, Lord. Come in glory to judge and to reign (vv. 1–6).

Amen! Come quickly, Lord Jesus (vv. 1–6; cp. Rev. 22:20).

Father, keep me from a mere rule-keeping religion. I want to obey You from a heart of faith. I want to worship You as You deserve (vv. 7–15).

Teach me how to offer sacrifices of thanksgiving that meet with Your approval, Father (v. 14).

16   But to the wicked God says,
     "What right have you to tell of My statutes
     And to take My covenant in your mouth?
17   "For you hate discipline,
     And you cast My words behind you.
18   "When you see a thief, you are pleased with him,
     And you associate with adulterers.
19   "You let your mouth loose in evil
     And your tongue frames deceit.
20   "You sit and speak against your brother;
     You slander your own mother's son.
21   "These things you have done and I kept silence;
     You thought that I was just like you;
     I will reprove you and state *the case* in order before your eyes.

22   "Now consider this, you who forget God,
     Or I will tear *you* in pieces, and there will be none to deliver.
23   "He who offers a sacrifice of thanksgiving honors Me;
     And to him who orders *his* way *aright*
     I shall show the salvation of God."

God, thank You that You're not like men. Keep me from hypocrisy and from loving the world and the things of the world (vv. 16–21).

Merciful Father, teach me to love Your Word and Your discipline (v. 17).

Thank You, dear God, for Your mercy and revealing Your salvation in Christ (vv. 22–23).

Lord Jesus, cause me to focus on spiritual things—heavenly things, rather than earthly (v. 23).

How Jesus could be interceding for you: You are a consuming fire, Father (Heb. 12:29). You keep Your covenants with Your people Israel (Dan. 9:4; Rom. 9:4). Pour out on Your Church the benefits of the New Covenant, which You established by My blood (Luke 22:20). By Your Spirit, cause Your people to offer to You their sacrifices of praise (Heb. 13:15).

Psalm 51

A Contrite Sinner's Prayer for Pardon.

For the choir director. A Psalm of David, when Nathan the prophet came to him, after he had gone in to Bathsheba.

1 Be gracious to me, O God, according to Your lovingkindness;
According to the greatness of Your compassion blot out my
transgressions.
2 Wash me thoroughly from my iniquity
And cleanse me from my sin.
3 For I know my transgressions,
And my sin is ever before me.
4 Against You, You only, I have sinned
And done what is evil in Your sight,
So that You are justified when You speak
And blameless when You judge.

5 Behold, I was brought forth in iniquity,
And in sin my mother conceived me.
6 Behold, You desire truth in the innermost being,
And in the hidden part You will make me know wisdom.
7 Purify me with hyssop, and I shall be clean;
Wash me, and I shall be whiter than snow.
8 Make me to hear joy and gladness,
Let the bones which You have broken rejoice.
9 Hide Your face from my sins
And blot out all my iniquities.
10 Create in me a clean heart, O God,
And renew a steadfast spirit within me.
11 Do not cast me away from Your presence
And do not take Your Holy Spirit from me.
12 Restore to me the joy of Your salvation
And sustain me with a willing spirit.
13 *Then* I will teach transgressors Your ways,
And sinners will be converted to You.
14 Deliver me from bloodguiltiness, O God, the God of my salvation;
Then my tongue will joyfully sing of Your righteousness.

Praying Psalm 51

*David's prayer confessing his sin of adultery with
Bathsheba and murder of her husband Uriah.*

Even when I'm not feeling the weight of my sin, as David did when confronted with
his adultery and his murderous scheme concerning Bathsheba's husband—help me
to know my need for Your compassion and grace (superscription and v. 1).

What kind of love blots out transgression and washes us thoroughly from our iniquity? Only infinite and eternal love, infinite and eternal grace. Praise be to God my
Savior (vv. 1–2).

Father, be gracious and merciful to me, though I don't deserve any of it (v. 1).

I have sinned against You, Lord! Forgive me (v.4)!

Forgive my sin, dear Lord. I am a sinner by birth and by choice. But You can make
me whiter than snow. Cleanse me, Lord, and blot out every stain (vv. 5–9).

Father, help me to rejoice in Your loving discipline (v. 8).

Create in me a clean heart that is faithful to You. Please, somehow preserve my
usefulness for Your glory and restore to me the joy of Your salvation. Enable me to
call others to repent and look to You for mercy (vv. 10–13).

Grant me a broken and contrite heart and draw near, O God. I will worship You in
spirit and in truth (vv. 14–19).

You alone are righteous, Lord (v. 14).

15 O Lord, open my lips,
    That my mouth may declare Your praise.
16 For You do not delight in sacrifice, otherwise I would give it;
    You are not pleased with burnt offering.
17 The sacrifices of God are a broken spirit;
    A broken and a contrite heart, O God, You will not despise.
18 By Your favor do good to Zion;
    Build the walls of Jerusalem.
19 Then You will delight in righteous sacrifices,
    In burnt offering and whole burnt offering;
    Then young bulls will be offered on Your altar.

Father, give me the courage to praise You in front of others (v. 15).

May the sacrifices of my lips be accepted as righteous sacrifices before You, Lord (vv. 16–19; cf. Heb. 13:15–16).

O God, I pray for the restoration of Your people and for peace for Jerusalem (v. 18).

How Jesus could be interceding for you: Gracious and merciful Father, accept Your child's confession of sin, forgive the sin, cleanse from every unrighteousness, and restore the joy of salvation (1 John 1:4, 9).

Psalm 52

Futility of Boastful Wickedness.

For the choir director. A Maskil of David, when Doeg the Edomite came and told Saul and said to him, "David has come to the house of Ahimelech."

1   Why do you boast in evil, O mighty man?
      The lovingkindness of God *endures* all day long.
2   Your tongue devises destruction,
      Like a sharp razor, O worker of deceit.
3   You love evil more than good,
      Falsehood more than speaking what is right.   *Selah.*
4   You love all words that devour,
      O deceitful tongue.

5   But God will break you down forever;
      He will snatch you up and tear you away from *your* tent,
      And uproot you from the land of the living.   *Selah.*
6   The righteous will see and fear,
      And will laugh at him, *saying,*
7   "Behold, the man who would not make God his refuge,
      But trusted in the abundance of his riches
      And was strong in his *evil* desire."

8   But as for me, I am like a green olive tree in the house of God;
      I trust in the lovingkindness of God forever and ever.
9   I will give You thanks forever, because You have done *it,*
      And I will wait on Your name, for *it is* good, in the presence of Your godly
      ones.

Praying Psalm 52

David's skillfully composed prayer while being pursued by wicked men.

Lord, Doeg was a murderer and a liar, consumed with personal gain. Deal justly and swiftly with all those who trust in the power of men rather than the true and living God (superscription, 1 Sam. 22:9; and vv. 1–7).

Thank You, Father, for always being faithful (v. 1).

Teach me to love good more than evil (v. 3).

O God, keep me from using my words as a malicious weapon against others (v. 4).

Help me not to trust money more than You, Savior (v. 7).

Turn my heart away from wanting anything that keeps me from trusting in Your love (v. 8).

Father, I will give You thanks forever and wait for You with all those who trust in You (v. 9).

Dear Jesus, may everyone around me witness my hope in You (v. 9).

How Jesus could be interceding for you: Evil men conspired to kill Me, Father, while I pursued Your will during My incarnation (Matt. 26:3–4, 59). Wicked people persecute My sheep, because the world hates Me (John 15:18–19; 17:14). Give My sheep faithful hearts and lives committed to serving You (Matt. 24:45–46; Luke 22:31–32), and protect them (John 17:15).

Psalm 53

Folly and Wickedness of Men.

For the choir director; according to Mahalath. A Maskil of David.

1 The fool has said in his heart, "There is no God,"
They are corrupt, and have committed abominable injustice;
There is no one who does good.

2 God has looked down from heaven upon the sons of men
To see if there is anyone who understands,
Who seeks after God.

3 Every one of them has turned aside; together they have become corrupt;
There is no one who does good, not even one.

4 Have the workers of wickedness no knowledge,
Who eat up My people *as though* they ate bread
And have not called upon God?

5 There they were in great fear *where* no fear had been;
For God scattered the bones of him who encamped against you;
You put *them* to shame, because God had rejected them.

6 Oh, that the salvation of Israel would come out of Zion!
When God restores His captive people,
Let Jacob rejoice, let Israel be glad.

Praying Psalm 53

David's prayer for the salvation of Israel in the light of the depravity of mankind.

Lord, don't let me be a fool by sinning against You (v. 1).

All of us, God, are corrupt and rebellious apart from Your grace in Christ (vv. 1–3).

O God, I am a sinner—there is nothing good in me that I should deserve salvation from my sin (vv. 1, 3).

Messiah, Savior, how our unbelief and wicked hearts must have grieved You—and still grieve You (vv. 4–5).

Protect Your people from wicked people, Father (v. 5).

Redeem Your covenant nation, Lord, so that from You and through You and to You be the glory forever and ever (v. 6; cf. Rom. 11).

O precious Savior, fulfill Your name "Jesus" by saving Your people Israel. Deliver Zion (v. 6)!

How Jesus could be interceding for you: Father, I gave My life as a sacrifice for those who are ungodly, sinners, and Your enemies (Rom. 5:6, 8, 10). Teach Your people to love their enemies and to pray for their persecutors (Matt. 5:43–48). Lead them to obey My words, so they do not act like fools (Matt. 7:26).

Psalm 54

Prayer for Defense against Enemies.

For the choir director; on stringed instruments. A Maskil of David, when the Ziphites came and said to Saul, "Is not David hiding himself among us?"

1 Save me, O God, by Your name,
And vindicate me by Your power.
2 Hear my prayer, O God;
Give ear to the words of my mouth.
3 For strangers have risen against me
And violent men have sought my life;
They have not set God before them.   *Selah.*

4 Behold, God is my helper;
The Lord is the sustainer of my soul.
5 He will recompense the evil to my foes;
Destroy them in Your faithfulness.

6 Willingly I will sacrifice to You;
I will give thanks to Your name, O LORD, for it is good.
7 For He has delivered me from all trouble,
And my eye has looked *with satisfaction* upon my enemies.

Praying Psalm 54

David's prayer of thanks when he had been betrayed.

Lord Jesus, Son of David, thank you that You know what it's like to be betrayed—yet Your faith prevailed. Strengthen my faith, Lord (superscription).

When I am faced with those who seek my life, teach my heart to seek You—to say, "Save me, Lord" (vv. 1–3).

Save me from my enemies, God, but by Your power, not mine (v. 1).

O Father, hear the prayer of Your child who feels betrayed and rejected (v. 2).

Be my helper and my support, Lord (v. 3).

That the Almighty would be my Helper I find hard to comprehend. I praise You, Father, for Your Son, and the gift of the Helper, the Holy Spirit (v. 4).

Judge Your enemies, Lord—they are mine as well. I will wait for You to vindicate me (vv. 5–7).

Thank You, Jesus, for saving me and caring for me (v. 6).

How Jesus could be interceding for you: Father, You heard my prayers while I made My life an offering for sin (Eph. 5:2; Heb. 5:7–9; 10:12). You gave me victory over death and the grave (Rom. 6:9). Vindicate Your people's faith; make them more than victors (1 Cor. 15:54–57; 1 John 5:4–5).

Psalm 55

Prayer for the Destruction of the Treacherous.

For the choir director; on stringed instruments. A Maskil of David.

1   Give ear to my prayer, O God;
    And do not hide Yourself from my supplication.
2   Give heed to me and answer me;
    I am restless in my complaint and am surely distracted,
3   Because of the voice of the enemy,
    Because of the pressure of the wicked;
    For they bring down trouble upon me
    And in anger they bear a grudge against me.

4   My heart is in anguish within me,
    And the terrors of death have fallen upon me.
5   Fear and trembling come upon me,
    And horror has overwhelmed me.
6   I said, "Oh, that I had wings like a dove!
    I would fly away and be at rest.
7   "Behold, I would wander far away,
    I would lodge in the wilderness.   *Selah.*
8   "I would hasten to my place of refuge
    From the stormy wind *and* tempest."

9   Confuse, O Lord, divide their tongues,
    For I have seen violence and strife in the city.
10 Day and night they go around her upon her walls,
    And iniquity and mischief are in her midst.
11 Destruction is in her midst;
    Oppression and deceit do not depart from her streets.
12 For it is not an enemy who reproaches me,
    Then I could bear *it;*
    Nor is it one who hates me who has exalted himself against me,
    Then I could hide myself from him.
13 But it is you, a man my equal,
    My companion and my familiar friend;
14 We who had sweet fellowship together
    Walked in the house of God in the throng.

Praying Psalm 55

*In Jerusalem David prays over the sin-filled city and
about a friend's deceit and betrayal.*

Hear me as I cry to You, Lord. I am restless and in distress. I feel overwhelmed and drowning in sorrow (vv. 1–5).

O God, I'm frustrated by this city's wickedness, and I'm restless—I want to escape. Give me rest for my mind and heart (v. 2).

I know our warfare is not against flesh and blood, but against spiritual forces in the heavenlies (cf. Eph. 6:12). But at times people seem to be their instruments. Help me, Father, to withstand the onslaught of those who have a grudge to bear (v. 3).

Father, give me relief from the pressures of wicked people (v. 3).

I want to run away from this, Lord. Help me; deliver me, Father (vv. 6–11).

What a mess this fallen world is! Be my refuge from this world, Lord (v. 8).

Lord Jesus, I read these verses and I think of Your betrayal by a friend and companion. It reminds me of my sinfulness and Your sinlessness. If I am betrayed, it is far less injustice than when You were betrayed. I'm sorry, my Savior, that You were betrayed for my sake. Thank You for the deceit and betrayal You endured for me (vv. 12–14).

Give me patience, humility, and compassion to develop sweet fellowship with fellow believers. Teach me to forgive those by whom I might be offended (v. 14).

15 Let death come deceitfully upon them;
    Let them go down alive to Sheol,
    For evil is in their dwelling, in their midst.
16 As for me, I shall call upon God,
    And the LORD will save me.
17 Evening and morning and at noon, I will complain and murmur,
    And He will hear my voice.
18 He will redeem my soul in peace from the battle *which is* against me,
    For they are many *who strive* with me.
19 God will hear and answer them—
    Even the one who sits enthroned from of old—   *Selah.*
    With whom there is no change,
    And who do not fear God.
20 He has put forth his hands against those who were at peace with him;
    He has violated his covenant.
21 His speech was smoother than butter,
    But his heart was war;
    His words were softer than oil,
    Yet they were drawn swords.
22 Cast your burden upon the LORD and He will sustain you;
    He will never allow the righteous to be shaken.
23 But You, O God, will bring them down to the pit of destruction;
    Men of bloodshed and deceit will not live out half their days.
    But I will trust in You.

You could pray this concerning the son of perdition, Lord Jesus (cf. John 17:12). May all who refuse Your love and salvation be damned (v. 15).

Father in heaven, I will call and keep calling until You save. You will deal justly with the wicked and deliver those who trust in You (vv. 16–22).

Dear Jesus, give me peace from the daily battle—Your precious peace (v. 18).

Take my burdens, Father. Enable me to cast all my anxieties on my Savior (v. 22; cp. 1 Pet. 5:7).

How Jesus could be interceding for you: In Your mercy and Your love, dear Father, answer Your child's prayer for relief from anxiety (Matt. 6:27; Phil. 4:6). Give each believer peace in every circumstance (John 14:27; Phil. 4:7). I care for each one of My sheep and desire to lead each one to their rest in Me (Matt. 11:28; Heb. 4:9–10).

Psalm 56

Supplication for Deliverance and Grateful Trust in God.

For the choir director; according to Jonath elem rehokim. A Mikhtam of David, when the Philistines seized him in Gath.

1   Be gracious to me, O God, for man has trampled upon me;
    Fighting all day long he oppresses me.
2   My foes have trampled upon me all day long,
    For they are many who fight proudly against me.
3   When I am afraid,
    I will put my trust in You.
4   In God, whose word I praise,
    In God I have put my trust;
    I shall not be afraid.
    What can *mere* man do to me?
5   All day long they distort my words;
    All their thoughts are against me for evil.
6   They attack, they lurk,
    They watch my steps,
    As they have waited *to take* my life.
7   Because of wickedness, cast them forth,
    In anger put down the peoples, O God!

8   You have taken account of my wanderings;
    Put my tears in Your bottle.
    Are *they* not in Your book?
9   Then my enemies will turn back in the day when I call;
    This I know, that God is for me.
10 In God, *whose* word I praise,
    In the LORD, *whose* word I praise,
11 In God I have put my trust, I shall not be afraid.
    What can man do to me?
12 Your vows are *binding* upon me, O God;
    I will render thank offerings to You.
13 For You have delivered my soul from death,
    Indeed my feet from stumbling,
    So that I may walk before God
    In the light of the living.

Praying Psalm 56

A prayer of David who trusts God with his life when the captive of one enemy and pursued by another.

Father, I am not a king on the run from his enemies, but I am one who through faith in Your Son will rule with Him one day. I am afraid more often than I'd like to admit. When I am afraid, I will purposely put my trust in You—then I am not afraid. You will save me from my enemies (vv. 1–4).

O God, I praise You for Your Word (vv. 4, 10)!

Teach me to trust You when I am afraid, Lord (v. 3).

O God, I praise You for Your Word (vv. 4, 10)!

Thank You, Lord Jesus, that You know what it's like to be misrepresented, misunderstood, and slandered. Deal with those who perpetrate hate upon Your people (vv. 5–7).

Praise be to the Compassionate One—the Savior, my Lord! You know the reasons for every tear I've shed and every tear each of Your beloved ones have shed. And You care (v. 8)!

Thank You, Father, for caring about my troubles and my tears (v. 8).

I will not be afraid, because You're listening when I pray. I trust You, Lord. I will not be afraid. You will bring me safely to Your Kingdom (vv. 9–13).

Lord Jesus, my Shepherd, lead me in Your ways while I have life (v. 13).

How Jesus could be interceding for you: Mighty Father, calm the fears of Your people (Matt. 8:26–27; 2 Tim. 1:7). Immerse their minds and hearts in Your Word (Matt. 4:4; John 14:23–24). Teach them by Your Spirit (John 14:26) and heal each heartache (Matt. 5:4; Luke 4:18).

Psalm 57

Prayer for Rescue from Persecutors.

For the choir director; set to Al-tashheth. A Mikhtam of David,
when he fled from Saul in the cave.

1 Be gracious to me, O God, be gracious to me,
For my soul takes refuge in You;
And in the shadow of Your wings I will take refuge
Until destruction passes by.
2 I will cry to God Most High,
To God who accomplishes *all things* for me.
3 He will send from heaven and save me;
He reproaches him who tramples upon me.   *Selah.*
God will send forth His lovingkindness and His truth.

4 My soul is among lions;
I must lie among those who breathe forth fire,
Even the sons of men, whose teeth are spears and arrows
And their tongue a sharp sword.
5 Be exalted above the heavens, O God;
Let Your glory *be* above all the earth.
6 They have prepared a net for my steps;
My soul is bowed down;
They dug a pit before me;
They *themselves* have fallen into the midst of it.   *Selah.*

7 My heart is steadfast, O God, my heart is steadfast;
I will sing, yes, I will sing praises!
8 Awake, my glory!
Awake, harp and lyre!
I will awaken the dawn.
9 I will give thanks to You, O Lord, among the peoples;
I will sing praises to You among the nations.
10 For Your lovingkindness is great to the heavens
And Your truth to the clouds.
11 Be exalted above the heavens, O God;
Let Your glory *be* above all the earth.

Praying Psalm 57

*David prays to God Most High in a dangerous situation
for which he needs God's protection.*

God, Savior, You are my place of rest, protection, safety, and solace from the onslaught of the world and those who want to destroy my faith and destroy my life (superscription and v. 1).

Please, let me experience Your grace, my God (v. 1).

Accusations and slander surrounded You, Lord Jesus, as they surrounded David. Did You take comfort in this psalm? Thank You for it. I feel I'm under attack. Hear my prayer and hide me. Save me, Lord (vv. 2–6).

Thank You, Lord, for accomplishing Your will in me even in such dangerous circumstances (v. 2).

Be exalted, O God! Be exalted (vv. 5, 11)!

You have strengthened my faith and called me to praise. I love You because You first loved me—and Your love fills the heavens. You are faithful and true. Be exalted, O Lord, above all (vv. 7–11).

Lord Jesus, make my heart steadfast and loyal to You no matter what (v. 7).

Even in the night, fill my heart and my mouth with songs of praises to You (v. 8).

How Jesus could be interceding for you: Faithful, loving Father, Your glory covers the earth. I share that glory with You again after completing My work of redemption (John 17:5). Though I am now with You, fill the mouths of Your people with praise for what they know of Me from Your Word (John 1:14; 2:11). Preserve in them the hope of Your glory that I gave to them (John 17:22; Rom. 5:2).

Psalm 58

Prayer for the Punishment of the Wicked.

For the choir director; set to Al-tashheth. A Mikhtam of David.

1 Do you indeed speak righteousness, O gods?
Do you judge uprightly, O sons of men?
2 No, in heart you work unrighteousness;
On earth you weigh out the violence of your hands.
3 The wicked are estranged from the womb;
These who speak lies go astray from birth.
4 They have venom like the venom of a serpent;
Like a deaf cobra that stops up its ear,
5 So that it does not hear the voice of charmers,
Or a skillful caster of spells.

6 O God, shatter their teeth in their mouth;
Break out the fangs of the young lions, O LORD.
7 Let them flow away like water that runs off;
When he aims his arrows, let them be as headless shafts.
8 *Let them be* as a snail which melts away as it goes along,
Like the miscarriages of a woman which never see the sun.
9 Before your pots can feel *the fire of* thorns
He will sweep them away with a whirlwind, the green and the burning
alike.
10 The righteous will rejoice when he sees the vengeance;
He will wash his feet in the blood of the wicked.
11 And men will say, "Surely there is a reward for the righteous;
Surely there is a God who judges on earth!"

Praying Psalm 58

Sadly, some churches have removed this prayer from their hymnbooks and from their services, because of its petition to bring judgment on the wicked.

Lord Jesus, as I read these words I think of how You must have felt and how You prayed facing such injustice from wicked rulers (John 10:34–39; Acts 2:23). As Your representatives they should have shepherded the people, but they perverted justice against You, the very Son of God. It was for me, Lord, You endured this. Forgive me. Thank you for enduring faithfully in love (vv. 1–5).

Preserve our nation from corrupt leaders, Father (v. 1).

O God, stop those who would terrorize with violent deeds (v. 2).

Father, help me to understand that I, too, am infected with sin (v. 3).

By Your grace and in Your Son, Father, I pray for Your righteous judgment to come upon all who hate Your righteous Son and those He has redeemed with His own blood. Judge the wicked judges. I will rejoice with all Your people in the righteous judgment of the wicked (vv. 6–11; cf. 2 Thess. 1:5–12).

How I praise You for the ultimate demise of the wicked (v. 10)!

Lord, thank You for being a God concerned about justice (v. 11).

How Jesus could be interceding for you: I taught Your children to pray for Your Kingdom to come and Your will to be done on earth as it is in heaven (Matt. 6:9–10). Your answer to their prayer means You must send Me to rid the earth of all the wicked and to bring about justice with sword and rod (Rev. 19:11–16). Bring righteousness and justice to Your people, Almighty Father.

Psalm 59

Prayer for Deliverance from Enemies.

*For the choir director; set to Al-tashheth. A Mikhtam of David, when Saul
sent men and they watched the house in order to kill him.*

1   Deliver me from my enemies, O my God;
    Set me *securely* on high away from those who rise up against me.
2   Deliver me from those who do iniquity
    And save me from men of bloodshed.
3   For behold, they have set an ambush for my life;
    Fierce men launch an attack against me,
    Not for my transgression nor for my sin, O LORD,
4   For no guilt of *mine,* they run and set themselves against me.
    Arouse Yourself to help me, and see!
5   You, O LORD God of hosts, the God of Israel,
    Awake to punish all the nations;
    Do not be gracious to any *who are* treacherous in iniquity.   *Selah.*
6   They return at evening, they howl like a dog,
    And go around the city.
7   Behold, they belch forth with their mouth;
    Swords are in their lips,
    For, *they say,* "Who hears?"
8   But You, O LORD, laugh at them;
    You scoff at all the nations.

9   *Because of* his strength I will watch for You,
    For God is my stronghold.
10   My God in His lovingkindness will meet me;
    God will let me look *triumphantly* upon my foes.
11   Do not slay them, or my people will forget;
    Scatter them by Your power, and bring them down,
    O Lord, our shield.
12   *On account of* the sin of their mouth *and* the words of their lips,
    Let them even be caught in their pride,
    And on account of curses and lies which they utter.
13   Destroy *them* in wrath, destroy *them* that they may be no more;
    That *men* may know that God rules in Jacob
    To the ends of the earth.   *Selah.*

Praying Psalm 59

This prayer of David expresses his dependence upon God's protection when his enemies seek his life even in Jerusalem.

Father, as David penned these words guided by Your Spirit, did he know they would minister to countless believers throughout the ages? David prayed as Saul sought his life. The future covenant nation, once made alive to the gospel, will pray for Your deliverance as the nations surround Jerusalem (cf. Zech. 13–14). Your Messiah may well have prayed in similar fashion as He was surrounded by enemies seeking to thwart Your plan of redemption through Him. Now I pray, deliver me from my enemies, Lord (vv. 1–8).

Keep me safe, Lord, from criminals and those who would harm me or my family (vv. 1–2).

Come quickly, Lord Jesus, to bring final judgment upon all nations (v. 5).

Vicious dogs seek to devour Your people. Deliver us, Lord, and deliver Your covenant nation. May Your Kingdom come. We will sing of Your strength and Your love (vv. 9–17).

Thank You, Lord, for being steadfastly and lovingly loyal to me (v. 10).

O Lord Jesus, may all the earth know that You are King (v. 13).

14   They return at evening, they howl like a dog,
      And go around the city.
15   They wander about for food
      And growl if they are not satisfied.
16   But as for me, I shall sing of Your strength;
      Yes, I shall joyfully sing of Your lovingkindness in the morning,
      For You have been my stronghold
      And a refuge in the day of my distress.
17   O my strength, I will sing praises to You;
      For God is my stronghold, the God who shows me lovingkindness.

Father, I live among people who behave more like dogs than people—they're always growling about something. When I'm tempted to act in the same way, strengthen me and fill my heart and mouth with songs of praise for You (v. 16).

How I praise you, O God, for being my strength and my refuge (v. 17).

How Jesus could be interceding for you: Father, protect Your children from those who would hound them and persecute them. My enemies attacked me like wild dogs (Ps. 22:16). Because the wicked hate Me, they hate My sheep (John 15:18–19) and evildoers seek like dogs to frighten them and drive them to doctrinal error (Phil. 3:2). Protect them, Father.

Psalm 60

Lament over Defeat in Battle, and Prayer for Help.

*For the choir director; according to Shushan Eduth. A Mikhtam of David, to
teach; when he struggled with Aram-naharaim and with Aram-zobah, and Joab
returned, and smote twelve thousand of Edom in the Valley of Salt.*

1   O God, You have rejected us. You have broken us;
   You have been angry; O, restore us.
2   You have made the land quake, You have split it open;
   Heal its breaches, for it totters.
3   You have made Your people experience hardship;
   You have given us wine to drink that makes us stagger.
4   You have given a banner to those who fear You,
   That it may be displayed because of the truth.   *Selah.*
5   That Your beloved may be delivered,
   Save with Your right hand, and answer us!

6   God has spoken in His holiness:
   "I will exult, I will portion out Shechem and measure out the valley of
     Succoth.
7   "Gilead is Mine, and Manasseh is Mine;
   Ephraim also is the helmet of My head;
   Judah is My scepter.
8   "Moab is My washbowl;
   Over Edom I shall throw My shoe;
   Shout loud, O Philistia, because of Me!"

9   Who will bring me into the besieged city?
   Who will lead me to Edom?
10 Have not You Yourself, O God, rejected us?
   And will You not go forth with our armies, O God?
11 O give us help against the adversary,
   For deliverance by man is in vain.
12 Through God we shall do valiantly,
   And it is He who will tread down our adversaries.

Praying Psalm 60

*King David prays this psalm as a wartime king and
commander in chief of Israel's armies.*

God, thank You for the gift of prayer in the midst of severe discipline and training.
We can cry to You and ask You why, and seek Your mercy. I feel like I'm facing
defeat in circumstances that only You know fully, Lord. Why? How long? Please
heal. Don't allow me to hold the flag of truth in Your name, then flee in defeat
before the enemy of my soul (superscription and vv. 1–5).

Restore me to fellowship with You, merciful Father (v. 1).

Thank You, Lord, for providing for Your people (vv. 4–5).

You answered David with victory. You will give Your covenant nation victory in
their future day of trouble (cf. Zech. 14). Through God I, too, will do valiantly in the
faith, and He will bring me safely into His Kingdom (vv. 6–12).

Teach me to trust You, rather than people (v. 11).

Lord, thank You for enabling Your people to be victorious (v. 12).

How Jesus could be interceding for you: Holy Father, teach Your children to trust
in You and Your power (Luke 22:31–32; 1 Pet. 4:19), rather than in their own arm
of flesh, which will fail them (2 Cor. 10:3–6). Give them victory over the world's
temptations and in their spiritual battles—answer their prayers (John 14:12–14;
Eph. 6:10–18).

Psalm 61

Confidence in God's Protection.

For the choir director; on a stringed instrument. A Psalm *of David.*

1   Hear my cry, O God;
    Give heed to my prayer.
2   From the end of the earth I call to You when my heart is faint;
    Lead me to the rock that is higher than I.
3   For You have been a refuge for me,
    A tower of strength against the enemy.
4   Let me dwell in Your tent forever;
    Let me take refuge in the shelter of Your wings.   *Selah.*

5   For You have heard my vows, O God;
    You have given *me* the inheritance of those who fear Your name.
6   You will prolong the king's life;
    His years will be as many generations.
7   He will abide before God forever;
    Appoint lovingkindness and truth that they may preserve him.
8   So I will sing praise to Your name forever,
    That I may pay my vows day by day.

Praying Psalm 61

*David's circumstances lead him to pray for personal protection
as well as for the preservation of his throne.*

Teach me how to be patient while learning that faith's greatest victories come mainly through the most difficult of trials (vv. 1–4).

⋘

O God, You are our strong tower and shelter. Let everyone who is weary come to You for rest and safety, Lord (vv. 1–4).

⋘

Hear my humble prayer while I grow faint-hearted in my daily trials and troubles, Father (vv. 1–2).

⋘

Lord, lead me and protect me, for I am weak, stressed, and exhausted (v. 2).

⋘

Jesus, let me find refuge and rest in You—casting all my cares on You (v. 4).

⋘

I will worship You, Father, forever and ever, in the inheritance that will never fade away—because You have raised the King—Your Son, my Savior, from the grave. In Him I have and will fulfill every vow. I will worship You in obedience and sing Your praises forever (vv. 5–8).

⋘

Father, send Your Son to reign as King over His Kingdom (v. 6)!

———

How Jesus could be interceding for you: My dwelling place has been with You from before the creation of the universe (John 17:5). According to Your promise (Deut. 6:2; Ps. 91:16), prolong the lives of Your children until You bring them into Your house where I prepare a place for them to be with Us forever and ever (John 14:1–3; 17:24).

Psalm 62

God Alone a Refuge from Treachery and Oppression.

For the choir director; according to Jeduthun. A Psalm of David.

1   My soul *waits* in silence for God only;
    From Him is my salvation.
2   He only is my rock and my salvation,
    My stronghold; I shall not be greatly shaken.

3   How long will you assail a man,
    That you may murder *him,* all of you,
    Like a leaning wall, like a tottering fence?
4   They have counseled only to thrust him down from his high position;
    They delight in falsehood;
    They bless with their mouth,
    But inwardly they curse.   *Selah.*

5   My soul, wait in silence for God only,
    For my hope is from Him.
6   He only is my rock and my salvation,
    My stronghold; I shall not be shaken.
7   On God my salvation and my glory *rest;*
    The rock of my strength, my refuge is in God.
8   Trust in Him at all times, O people;
    Pour out your heart before Him;
    God is a refuge for us.   *Selah.*

9   Men of low degree are only vanity and men of rank are a lie;
    In the balances they go up;
    They are together lighter than breath.
10 Do not trust in oppression
    And do not vainly hope in robbery;
    If riches increase, do not set *your* heart *upon them.*
11 Once God has spoken;
    Twice I have heard this:
    That power belongs to God;
12 And lovingkindness is Yours, O Lord,
    For You recompense a man according to his work.

Praying Psalm 62

In this prayer expressing his trust in God, David understands that only God can provide the security he needs.

People are fickle and weak—often filled with hypocrisy. You are not. You are my rock and my fortress, dear Lord (vv. 1–4).

Dear God, men fail, You do not. In You only will I put my trust and hope (vv. 1–2).

Lord, help me to wait patiently for You no matter what my circumstances might be (v. 1).

Prop me up, when I am like a leaning wall or a tottering fence, dear Father (v. 3).

Teach me to be discerning in regard to people's words—give me wisdom (v. 4).

Thank You for being our refuge, our shelter, and immovable rock of defense. Let all who trust in You pour out their hearts to You (vv. 5–8).

Thank You for giving me unshakable calm in the midst of difficult trials (vv. 5–6).

Father, social status, rank, wealth—or lack thereof—are of no account to You. I will not trust in men. Power, love, and justice belong to You. I will hope in the Lord (vv. 9–12).

Lord Jesus, train me to listen to Your Word and to draw on Your power through Your Word (v. 11).

———

How Jesus could be interceding for you: Your words, Father, sustained Me in the wilderness when Satan tempted Me (Matt. 4:4). Give Your people wisdom (Matt. 7:24), understanding (Matt. 13:23), blessing (Luke 11:28), answered prayer (John 15:7), sanctification (John 17:17), and power (Acts 19:20; 1 Cor. 1:18) through Our Word (John 17:8, 14).

Psalm 63

The Thirsting Soul Satisfied in God.

A Psalm of David, when he was in the wilderness of Judah.

1   O God, You are my God; I shall seek You earnestly;
      My soul thirsts for You, my flesh yearns for You,
      In a dry and weary land where there is no water.
2   Thus I have seen You in the sanctuary,
      To see Your power and Your glory.
3   Because Your lovingkindness is better than life,
      My lips will praise You.
4   So I will bless You as long as I live;
      I will lift up my hands in Your name.
5   My soul is satisfied as with marrow and fatness,
      And my mouth offers praises with joyful lips.

6   When I remember You on my bed,
      I meditate on You in the night watches,
7   For You have been my help,
      And in the shadow of Your wings I sing for joy.
8   My soul clings to You;
      Your right hand upholds me.

9   But those who seek my life to destroy it,
      Will go into the depths of the earth.
10   They will be delivered over to the power of the sword;
      They will be a prey for foxes.
11   But the king will rejoice in God;
      Everyone who swears by Him will glory,
      For the mouths of those who speak lies will be stopped.

Praying Psalm 63

*David spent much time in the wilderness praying, even though
he also spent time with God at the Tabernacle.*

Lord God, please increase my thirst for You, so that I may see Your power and Your glory (vv. 1–2).

I desire You. I want to know You better, O God (v. 1).

Lord, teach me to sing in the desert, to worship You in the wilderness (v. 1).

Your love, Father, is better than life. I want to know You more and love You more—and praise You as You deserve (vv. 3–5).

Thank You, Lord, for Your unchanging loyal love (v. 3).

In the middle of the night, when I awake, I will seek You. You are my strength (vv. 6–8).

Father, I rejoice in Your protection and care (v. 7).

Help me to cling to You all the days of my life (v. 8).

King Jesus, You persevered in faith in the midst of liars and murderers seeking to take Your life. I will trust in You and Your ultimate victory (vv. 9–11).

In the midst of national and international troubles and uncertainties, teach our leaders to rejoice in You, my God and my King (v. 11).

How Jesus could be interceding for you: Like my human ancestral father David, I spent much time praying in the wilderness (Mark 1:35; 6:46). Draw Your people to Yourself in prayer whether they are in church, in the wilderness, or on their beds at home. Cause them to cling to You and to Me, loving Father (John 15:1–11; 1 John 2:24).

Psalm 64

Prayer for Deliverance from Secret Enemies.

For the choir director. A Psalm of David.

1 Hear my voice, O God, in my complaint;
Preserve my life from dread of the enemy.
2 Hide me from the secret counsel of evildoers,
From the tumult of those who do iniquity,
3 Who have sharpened their tongue like a sword.
They aimed bitter speech *as* their arrow,
4 To shoot from concealment at the blameless;
Suddenly they shoot at him, and do not fear.
5 They hold fast to themselves an evil purpose;
They talk of laying snares secretly;
They say, "Who can see them?"
6 They devise injustices, *saying,*
"We are ready with a well-conceived plot";
For the inward thought and the heart of a man are deep.

7 But God will shoot at them with an arrow;
Suddenly they will be wounded.
8 So they will make him stumble;
Their own tongue is against them;
All who see them will shake the head.
9 Then all men will fear,
And they will declare the work of God,
And will consider what He has done.
10 The righteous man will be glad in the Lord and will take refuge in Him;
And all the upright in heart will glory.

Praying Psalm 64

The target of a plot (perhaps started by his own son),
David lays his complaint before God in prayer.

I need Your protection, Lord—physically, spiritually, emotionally—in every way (vv. 1-6).

Father, free me from the fear I have of opposition and danger (v. 1).

Protect me, Lord, from hidden harm—dangers of which I am unaware (v. 2).

O dear God, teach me to use my words for good, rather than for evil (v. 3).

Lord Jesus, remind me again and again that You see everything (v. 5).

I know You will bring justice to this world. Then everyone will fear You as You deserve, Lord (vv. 7-9).

Righteous and Almighty God, turn the words of the wicked back upon their own heads (v. 8).

I will rejoice in You, Father, take refuge in You, Lord Jesus, and rely on You, Holy Spirit, to teach me to walk uprightly (v. 10).

Father, give me a heart of rejoicing and of praising You always (v. 10).

How Jesus could be interceding for you: Living Father, Protector of Your people, hear My prayer on behalf of your endangered child. Turn the wicked from terrorizing Your people to confessing that You are the One to Whom they must give an account for every word they speak (Matt. 12:36-37). Teach Your child that You turn their pain into praise (Matt. 5:3-12; John 14:27-31) and their desperation into hope (1 Pet. 3:13-17).

Psalm 65

God's Abundant Favor to Earth and Man.

For the choir director. A Psalm of David. A Song.

1   There will be silence before You, *and* praise in Zion, O God,
     And to You the vow will be performed.
2   O You who hear prayer,
     To You all men come.
3   Iniquities prevail against me;
     As for our transgressions, You forgive them.
4   How blessed is the one whom You choose and bring near *to You*
     To dwell in Your courts.
     We will be satisfied with the goodness of Your house,
     Your holy temple.

5   By awesome *deeds* You answer us in righteousness, O God of our
          salvation,
     You who are the trust of all the ends of the earth and of the farthest sea;
6   Who establishes the mountains by His strength,
     Being girded with might;
7   Who stills the roaring of the seas,
     The roaring of their waves,
     And the tumult of the peoples.
8   They who dwell in the ends *of the earth* stand in awe of Your signs;
     You make the dawn and the sunset shout for joy.

9   You visit the earth and cause it to overflow;
     You greatly enrich it;
     The stream of God is full of water;
     You prepare their grain, for thus You prepare the earth.
10   You water its furrows abundantly,
     You settle its ridges,
     You soften it with showers,
     You bless its growth.
11   You have crowned the year with Your bounty,
     And Your paths drip *with* fatness.
12   The pastures of the wilderness drip,
     And the hills gird themselves with rejoicing.
13   The meadows are clothed with flocks
     And the valleys are covered with grain;
     They shout for joy, yes, they sing.

Praying Psalm 65

This prayer of David could have been sung or recited at the Feast of Tabernacles (Lev. 23:33–43), which came shortly after the Day of Atonement (Lev. 16).

Fill my mouth with praise to You, Lord, and enable me to keep any promises I have made to You (v. 1).

O Hearer of prayer—sweet grace to know this is one of Your great names (v. 2).

Oh, praise God! Thank You, Lord Jesus—my sins are forgiven (v. 3)!

You are the blessed One Who forgives all of our transgressions and sins! I know that Your justice demands a satisfactory penalty for those sins against an infinitely holy God. Praise be to Jesus Christ, Who has procured our forgiveness (v. 3)!

It will be a glorious day when all the ends of the earth trust in You, Lord (v. 5).

Gracious Father, thank You for the beautiful sunrise and sunset with which You bless me (v. 8).

The blessings of Your Kingdom will overflow in all of creation. Creation's groaning will cease (cf. Rom. 8:22). May Your Kingdom come, Lord Jesus (vv. 9–13).

Merciful Father, thank You for the rain You cause to fall upon the just and the unjust (vv. 9–10).

Lord Jesus, keep me singing Your praise all my life (v. 13)!

How Jesus could be interceding for you: Father, in Your wisdom and omniscience You made Me Savior (Luke 19:10; Col. 1:14), Sovereign Lord (Luke 2:11; 1 Tim. 6:13–16), and Sustainer of creation (Col. 1:17). Give Your people joy in singing praise to You, to Me, and to Your Holy Spirit for salvation, answered prayer, and the bounty of creation's blessings (Eph. 5:18–20; 1 Pet. 1:8; Rev. 15:3–4).

Psalm 66

Praise for God's Mighty Deeds and for His Answer to Prayer.

For the choir director. A Song. A Psalm.

1   Shout joyfully to God, all the earth;
2   Sing the glory of His name;
    Make His praise glorious.
3   Say to God, "How awesome are Your works!
    Because of the greatness of Your power Your enemies will give feigned
        obedience to You.
4   "All the earth will worship You,
    And will sing praises to You;
    They will sing praises to Your name."   *Selah.*

5   Come and see the works of God,
    Who is awesome in *His* deeds toward the sons of men.
6   He turned the sea into dry land;
    They passed through the river on foot;
    There let us rejoice in Him!
7   He rules by His might forever;
    His eyes keep watch on the nations;
    Let not the rebellious exalt themselves.   *Selah.*

8   Bless our God, O peoples,
    And sound His praise abroad,
9   Who keeps us in life
    And does not allow our feet to slip.
10 For You have tried us, O God;
    You have refined us as silver is refined.
11 You brought us into the net;
    You laid an oppressive burden upon our loins.
12 You made men ride over our heads;
    We went through fire and through water,
    Yet You brought us out into *a place of* abundance.
13 I shall come into Your house with burnt offerings;
    I shall pay You my vows,
14 Which my lips uttered
    And my mouth spoke when I was in distress.

Praying Psalm 66

An anonymous psalmist composed this prayer expressing universal praise.

Oh, Lord, teach me how to praise You (vv. 1–3).

Deliver Your people, Father, that Your people may call all the earth to shout joyfully to You (v. 1).

May all the earth worship You, O Lord God (v. 4).

One day all will know that You rule in power, Lord, and that You keep watch over the nations (v. 7).

Thank You, God, for being in control of the world as well as of my life (v. 7).

Jacob's distress will result in Israel's deliverance. Then all will hear of Your faithfulness and mercy (vv. 8–17).

We come to You, O Refiner's Fire, to refine us through the trials You deem necessary for us to experience (v. 10–12).

Lord Jesus, thank You for saving us and for providing us with abundant blessing (v. 12).

15   I shall offer to You burnt offerings of fat beasts,
      With the smoke of rams;
      I shall make *an offering of* bulls with male goats.   *Selah.*
16   Come *and* hear, all who fear God,
      And I will tell of what He has done for my soul.
17   I cried to Him with my mouth,
      And He was extolled with my tongue.
18   If I regard wickedness in my heart,
      The Lord will not hear;
19   But certainly God has heard;
      He has given heed to the voice of my prayer.
20   Blessed be God,
      Who has not turned away my prayer
      Nor His lovingkindness from me.

You know the hearts of all men, dear God. If I hold onto sin in my heart You will not listen to my prayers. But You have listened and acted for me. Blessed be the living God Who has given His love to me (vv. 18–20)!

⸨⸨⸨⸝

Father, remove wickedness from my thoughts and my actions (v. 18).

How Jesus could be interceding for you: Glorious Father, You are worthy of Your people's worship. May this psalm guide them in their praise; may My word abound in their hearts as they sing this psalm (Col. 3:16). Yours, Father, is the greatness, the power, the victory, the majesty, the Kingdom, and the glory (1 Chron. 29:11; Dan. 2:37; Phil. 2:11).

Psalm 67

The Nations Exhorted to Praise God.

For the choir director; with stringed instruments. A Psalm. A Song.

1   God be gracious to us and bless us,
    And cause His face to shine upon us—   *Selah.*
2   That Your way may be known on the earth,
    Your salvation among all nations.
3   Let the peoples praise You, O God;
    Let all the peoples praise You.
4   Let the nations be glad and sing for joy;
    For You will judge the peoples with uprightness
    And guide the nations on the earth.   *Selah.*
5   Let the peoples praise You, O God;
    Let all the peoples praise You.
6   The earth has yielded its produce;
    God, our God, blesses us.
7   God blesses us,
    That all the ends of the earth may fear Him.

Praying Psalm 67

Synagogues sometimes display this prayer on the front of the reader's stand with its words arranged in the form of a seven-branched menorah. Some Jews recite the 49 Hebrew words of this prayer on each of the 49 nights between Passover (Pesach) and Pentecost (Shavuot). The congregation sings it at the Feast of Pentecost.

Bless Your people, Lord, that Christ Who is Your Way and Your salvation may be known to all nations (vv. 1–3).

Father, bless Your people and show them Your favor (v. 1).

Lord Jesus, lead me to take the proclamation of salvation to those around me wherever I go (v. 2).

Cause all people to give You praise, Lord God, and to rejoice in Your salvation (vv. 3, 5).

The nations will be glad when You—the Righteous One, the Lord Jesus Christ—rule the nations and judge the people with uprightness (vv. 4–7).

Thank You, Father, for the abundance of Your blessings to us (vv. 6, 7).

How Jesus could be interceding for you: By Your decree, Father, I purchased the Church with My blood (Acts 20:28) and the Holy Spirit established it on Pentecost (Acts 2; 1 Cor. 12:13). Empower Your people to enter Your harvest fields throughout the world to teach the gospel of salvation to all peoples (Matt. 28:18–20).

Psalm 68

The God of Sinai and of the Sanctuary.

For the choir director. A Psalm of David. A Song.

1 Let God arise, let His enemies be scattered,
   And let those who hate Him flee before Him.
2 As smoke is driven away, *so* drive *them* away;
   As wax melts before the fire,
   So let the wicked perish before God.
3 But let the righteous be glad; let them exult before God;
   Yes, let them rejoice with gladness.
4 Sing to God, sing praises to His name;
   Lift up *a song* for Him who rides through the deserts,
   Whose name is the LORD, and exult before Him.

5 A father of the fatherless and a judge for the widows,
   Is God in His holy habitation.
6 God makes a home for the lonely;
   He leads out the prisoners into prosperity,
   Only the rebellious dwell in a parched land.

7 O God, when You went forth before Your people,
   When You marched through the wilderness,   *Selah.*
8 The earth quaked;
   The heavens also dropped *rain* at the presence of God;
   Sinai itself *quaked* at the presence of God, the God of Israel.
9 You shed abroad a plentiful rain, O God;
   You confirmed Your inheritance when it was parched.
10 Your creatures settled in it;
   You provided in Your goodness for the poor, O God.
11 The Lord gives the command;
   The women who proclaim the *good* tidings are a great host:
12 "Kings of armies flee, they flee,
   And she who remains at home will divide the spoil!"
13 When you lie down among the sheepfolds,
   You are like the wings of a dove covered with silver,
   And its pinions with glistening gold.

Praying Psalm 68

*This prayer of King David expresses a great celebration of God's greatness,
perhaps following a significant military victory for which he gives God the glory.*

Arise, O God, and scatter Your enemies. The wicked will run away, but the righteous will rejoice (vv. 1–4).

Please take action on behalf of Your people, Almighty God (v. 1).

Father, You are so compassionate and gracious. You are high and lifted up, but dwell with the lowly and broken (vv. 5–6).

Thank You, Lord, for Your loving care for widows and orphans. Cause Your people to do the same (v. 5; Jas. 1:27).

Your mercies in Your care for Your people Israel in the wilderness and Your law's provision for the poor cause us to praise You, O God (vv. 7–10).

Your final victory will never be overturned. Our resurrected and ascended Lord will reign in power (vv. 11–18).

Father, help me to be a bearer of the good news of Your salvation (v. 11).

14   When the Almighty scattered the kings there,
     It was snowing in Zalmon.
15   A mountain of God is the mountain of Bashan;
     A mountain *of many* peaks is the mountain of Bashan.
16   Why do you look with envy, O mountains with *many* peaks,
     At the mountain which God has desired for His abode?
     Surely the Lord will dwell *there* forever.
17   The chariots of God are myriads, thousands upon thousands;
     The Lord is among them *as at* Sinai, in holiness.
18   You have ascended on high, You have led captive *Your* captives;
     You have received gifts among men,
     Even *among* the rebellious also, that the Lord God may dwell *there*.
19   Blessed be the Lord, who daily bears our burden,
     The God *who* is our salvation.   *Selah.*
20   God is to us a God of deliverances;
     And to God the Lord belong escapes from death.
21   Surely God will shatter the head of His enemies,
     The hairy crown of him who goes on in his guilty deeds.
22   The Lord said, "I will bring *them* back from Bashan.
     I will bring *them* back from the depths of the sea;
23   That your foot may shatter *them* in blood,
     The tongue of your dogs *may have* its portion from *your* enemies."
24   They have seen Your procession, O God,
     The procession of my God, my King, into the sanctuary.
25   The singers went on, the musicians after *them,*
     In the midst of the maidens beating tambourines.
26   Bless God in the congregations,
     Even the Lord, *you who are* of the fountain of Israel.
27   There is Benjamin, the youngest, ruling them,
     The princes of Judah *in* their throng,
     The princes of Zebulun, the princes of Naphtali.
28   Your God has commanded your strength;
     Show Yourself strong, O God, who have acted on our behalf.
29   Because of Your temple at Jerusalem
     Kings will bring gifts to You.
30   Rebuke the beasts in the reeds,
     The herd of bulls with the calves of the peoples,
     Trampling under foot the pieces of silver;
     He has scattered the peoples who delight in war.
31   Envoys will come out of Egypt;
     Ethiopia will quickly stretch out her hands to God.

My Creator and Savior, when I am in the mountains, give me an overwhelming sense of Your presence and Your greatness. Enable me to understand how insignificant I am before You and how amazing it is that You love me (vv. 15–17).

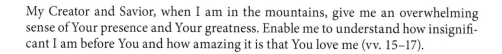

I praise You, Lord Jesus, for bearing my burdens (v. 19; 1 Pet. 5:7).

Shatter the head of Your enemies, Lord of the armies (vv. 21–23).

Father, as Your people gather for worship, hear our songs of praise (vv. 24–26).

King of all nations, bring the leaders of Your people and the kings of the earth to their knees before You (vv. 27–31).

32 Sing to God, O kingdoms of the earth,
    Sing praises to the Lord,   *Selah.*
33 To Him who rides upon the highest heavens, which are from ancient
        times;
    Behold, He speaks forth with His voice, a mighty voice.
34 Ascribe strength to God;
    His majesty is over Israel
    And His strength is in the skies.
35 O God, *You are* awesome from Your sanctuary.
    The God of Israel Himself gives strength and power to the people.
    Blessed be God!

Oh, God, what an awesome and powerful God You are (vv. 32–35)!

As I gaze upon the stars at night or at the sun and clouds in the daylight, I praise You for Your majesty and strength, Lord (vv. 33–34).

You are awesome indeed! Blessed be the Lord God Almighty (v. 35)!

How Jesus could be interceding for you: Omnipotent Father, bring Your Kingdom program to completion at the time of Your choosing (Matt. 24:36). Send Me as Your anointed King to Whom all peoples will bow their knees and praise with their mouths (Ps. 2; Phil. 2:9–11). Allow Your People to see all My glory, for My glory is also Your glory (Matt. 24:30–31; Luke 9:26).

Psalm 69

A Cry of Distress and Imprecation on Adversaries.

For the choir director; according to Shoshannim. A Psalm *of David.*

1   Save me, O God,
    For the waters have threatened my life.
2   I have sunk in deep mire, and there is no foothold;
    I have come into deep waters, and a flood overflows me.
3   I am weary with my crying; my throat is parched;
    My eyes fail while I wait for my God.
4   Those who hate me without a cause are more than the hairs of my head;
    Those who would destroy me are powerful, being wrongfully my enemies;
    What I did not steal, I then have to restore.

5   O God, it is You who knows my folly,
    And my wrongs are not hidden from You.
6   May those who wait for You not be ashamed through me, O Lord God of
        hosts;
    May those who seek You not be dishonored through me, O God of Israel,
7   Because for Your sake I have borne reproach;
    Dishonor has covered my face.
8   I have become estranged from my brothers
    And an alien to my mother's sons.
9   For zeal for Your house has consumed me,
    And the reproaches of those who reproach You have fallen on me.
10 When I wept in my soul with fasting,
    It became my reproach.
11 When I made sackcloth my clothing,
    I became a byword to them.
12 Those who sit in the gate talk about me,
    And I *am* the song of the drunkards.
13 But as for me, my prayer is to You, O Lord, at an acceptable time;
    O God, in the greatness of Your lovingkindness,
    Answer me with Your saving truth.
14 Deliver me from the mire and do not let me sink;
    May I be delivered from my foes and from the deep waters.
15 May the flood of water not overflow me
    Nor the deep swallow me up,
    Nor the pit shut its mouth on me.

Praying Psalm 69

King David prays for God to deliver him from the depths of his distressing circumstances and the deceit and hatred of his enemies seeking to dethrone him.

I know Your Kingdom is coming—but Lord, save me. I'm overwhelmed and feel like my life is faltering (vv. 1–4).

O please, vindicate me, O my Lord (vv. 3–4).

Save me, O God, from my troubles that overwhelm me like a flood (vv. 1–2).

Lord Jesus, again I'm struck by this psalm and how it must have ministered to You. You were dishonored, estranged from Your brothers—yet zealous for Your Father's house. You were a man of sorrows and a song of the drunkards—for me! Lord, forgive me. Thank You for taking my place. Thank You for bearing my shame—sinless Son of God (vv. 5–12)!

You know what I am and what I have done, Lord. My own sins have contributed to my current circumstances. Forgive me (v. 5).

Father, do not allow Your people to be slandered because of me (v. 6).

May I be zealous for You, Lord, and willingly bear the suffering it brings (v. 9).

You prayed, and Your Father ultimately answered with Your resurrection. But Lord, the shame, the pain, the reproach was for me (vv. 13–21).

Merciful Father, please answer my prayer (vv. 13, 16, 17).

16 Answer me, O Lᴏʀᴅ, for Your lovingkindness is good;
    According to the greatness of Your compassion, turn to me,
17 And do not hide Your face from Your servant,
    For I am in distress; answer me quickly.
18 Oh draw near to my soul *and* redeem it;
    Ransom me because of my enemies!
19 You know my reproach and my shame and my dishonor;
    All my adversaries are before You.
20 Reproach has broken my heart and I am so sick.
    And I looked for sympathy, but there was none,
    And for comforters, but I found none.
21 They also gave me gall for my food
    And for my thirst they gave me vinegar to drink.
22 May their table before them become a snare;
    And when they are in peace, *may it become* a trap.
23 May their eyes grow dim so that they cannot see,
    And make their loins shake continually.
24 Pour out Your indignation on them,
    And may Your burning anger overtake them.
25 May their camp be desolate;
    May none dwell in their tents.
26 For they have persecuted him whom You Yourself have smitten,
    And they tell of the pain of those whom You have wounded.
27 Add iniquity to their iniquity,
    And may they not come into Your righteousness.
28 May they be blotted out of the book of life
    And may they not be recorded with the righteous.
29 But I am afflicted and in pain;
    May Your salvation, O God, set me *securely* on high.
30 I will praise the name of God with song
    And magnify Him with thanksgiving.
31 And it will please the Lᴏʀᴅ better than an ox
    Or a young bull with horns and hoofs.
32 The humble have seen *it and* are glad;
    You who seek God, let your heart revive.
33 For the Lᴏʀᴅ hears the needy
    And does not despise His *who are* prisoners.
34 Let heaven and earth praise Him,
    The seas and everything that moves in them.
35 For God will save Zion and build the cities of Judah,
    That they may dwell there and possess it.
36 The descendants of His servants will inherit it,
    And those who love His name will dwell in it.

Jesus, Savior, You prayed, "Forgive them." But as for those who refuse to look to You in faith, may they be blotted out of the book of life (vv. 22–28).

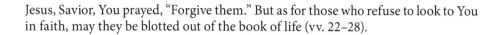

Righteous Father, bring justice upon the wicked—vengeance belongs to You, not to me (vv. 22–28).

Lord Jesus, accept my praise as an offering better than any sacrifice (vv. 30–31).

Revive the hearts of those who seek You (v. 32).

I love Your name, Lord (v. 36).

How Jesus could be interceding for you: Zeal for Your temple consumed Me (John 2:17), so I cleansed it. For the salvation of Your people, Father, I endured undeserved rejection, conspiracy, lies, insults, shame, hatred, cursing, scourging, and death at the hands of wicked people (John 1:11; 15:25; Rom. 15:3; Heb. 12:2). As I hung on the cross, they gave Me bitter wine for My thirst (Matt. 27:34, 48). For My sake, Father, relieve this beleaguered believer from his/her distressing circumstances.

Psalm 70

Prayer for Help against Persecutors.

For the choir director. A Psalm *of David; for a memorial.*

1   O God, *hasten* to deliver me;
     O LORD, hasten to my help!
2   Let those be ashamed and humiliated
     Who seek my life;
     Let those be turned back and dishonored
     Who delight in my hurt.
3   Let those be turned back because of their shame
     Who say, "Aha, aha!"

4   Let all who seek You rejoice and be glad in You;
     And let those who love Your salvation say continually,
     "Let God be magnified."
5   But I am afflicted and needy;
     Hasten to me, O God!
     You are my help and my deliverer;
     O LORD, do not delay.

Praying Psalm 70

David's prayer (perhaps a Spirit-led excerpt from Ps. 40) may have been accompanied by a sacrifice to "remind" ("memorial") God of his request.

Help, Lord! I need You now (v. 1).

I love Your salvation. Be magnified, dear God—You are indeed great (v. 4).

Let those who want to see my faith falter be ashamed and humiliated (vv. 2–3).

Thank You, Lord, for being my help and my deliverer (v. 5).

How Jesus could be interceding for you: O Help of the helpless (Matt. 9:36; Heb. 4:16), deliver them. Enable them to magnify Your name through their vindication and the shame You bring upon their persecutors (Mark 8:38; 1 Pet. 3:14–16).

Psalm 71

Prayer of an Old Man for Deliverance.

1 In You, O Lord, I have taken refuge;
Let me never be ashamed.

2 In Your righteousness deliver me and rescue me;
Incline Your ear to me and save me.

3 Be to me a rock of habitation to which I may continually come;
You have given commandment to save me,
For You are my rock and my fortress.

4 Rescue me, O my God, out of the hand of the wicked,
Out of the grasp of the wrongdoer and ruthless man,

5 For You are my hope;
O Lord God, *You are* my confidence from my youth.

6 By You I have been sustained from *my* birth;
You are He who took me from my mother's womb;
My praise is continually of You.

7 I have become a marvel to many,
For You are my strong refuge.

8 My mouth is filled with Your praise
And with Your glory all day long.

9 Do not cast me off in the time of old age;
Do not forsake me when my strength fails.

10 For my enemies have spoken against me;
And those who watch for my life have consulted together,

11 Saying, "God has forsaken him;
Pursue and seize him, for there is no one to deliver."

12 O God, do not be far from me;
O my God, hasten to my help!

13 Let those who are adversaries of my soul be ashamed *and* consumed;
Let them be covered with reproach and dishonor, who seek to injure me.

14 But as for me, I will hope continually,
And will praise You yet more and more.

15 My mouth shall tell of Your righteousness
And of Your salvation all day long;
For I do not know the sum *of them.*

16 I will come with the mighty deeds of the Lord God;
I will make mention of Your righteousness, Yours alone.

Praying Psalm 71

*This anonymous prayer of an aged believer lifts up
the righteousness of God in praise.*

Here I am again, Lord, seeking refuge and crying for help, even as an old person. Don't let me be ashamed (vv. 1–6).

Father, be my rock and my fortress (v. 3).

Lord, help me to trust You from my youth onward into old age (v. 5).

The world wants to find a reason to say that You have forsaken Your people. Jesus, You experienced this. Let all of Your chosen ones pray, "I will keep waiting for You, and praise You yet more and more" (vv. 7–16).

O God, fill my mouth with Your praise and Your glory (v. 8).

Continue to be with me and carry me along even in my old age, gracious Lord (v. 9).

Lord Jesus, give me continual hope all my days (v. 14).

17 O God, You have taught me from my youth,
    And I still declare Your wondrous deeds.
18 And even when *I am* old and gray, O God, do not forsake me,
    Until I declare Your strength to *this* generation,
    Your power to all who are to come.
19 For Your righteousness, O God, *reaches* to the heavens,
    You who have done great things;
    O God, who is like You?
20 You who have shown me many troubles and distresses
    Will revive me again,
    And will bring me up again from the depths of the earth.
21 May You increase my greatness
    And turn *to* comfort me.
22 I will also praise You with a harp,
    Even Your truth, O my God;
    To You I will sing praises with the lyre,
    O Holy One of Israel.
23 My lips will shout for joy when I sing praises to You;
    And my soul, which You have redeemed.
24 My tongue also will utter Your righteousness all day long;
    For they are ashamed, for they are humiliated who seek my hurt.

Like the psalmist, I too can testify that You have done great things in my life—as well as exposed me to many problems and troubles. I look to You, Father, as the One who will deliver me safely to Your Kingdom (vv. 17–21).

Father, give me strength to declare Your goodness, power, and righteousness to my children and grandchildren (v. 18).

O Holy One of Israel, I will sing praise to You as the God of my righteousness (vv. 22–24).

How Jesus could be interceding for you: Holy and righteous Father, older saints served You with joy in preparation for My incarnation (Luke 1:7, 18, 36; 2:36–38). Preserve, bless, and empower older saints to carry on such praise to their descendants until I come again (Luke 1:50; 1 Tim. 5:4).

Psalm 72

The Reign of the Righteous King.

A Psalm of Solomon.

1   Give the king Your judgments, O God,
     And Your righteousness to the king's son.
2   May he judge Your people with righteousness
     And Your afflicted with justice.
3   Let the mountains bring peace to the people,
     And the hills, in righteousness.
4   May he vindicate the afflicted of the people,
     Save the children of the needy
     And crush the oppressor.

5   Let them fear You while the sun *endures,*
     And as long as the moon, throughout all generations.
6   May he come down like rain upon the mown grass,
     Like showers that water the earth.
7   In his days may the righteous flourish,
     And abundance of peace till the moon is no more.

8   May he also rule from sea to sea
     And from the River to the ends of the earth.
9   Let the nomads of the desert bow before him,
     And his enemies lick the dust.
10   Let the kings of Tarshish and of the islands bring presents;
     The kings of Sheba and Seba offer gifts.
11   And let all kings bow down before him,
     All nations serve him.
12   For he will deliver the needy when he cries for help,
     The afflicted also, and him who has no helper.
13   He will have compassion on the poor and needy,
     And the lives of the needy he will save.
14   He will rescue their life from oppression and violence,
     And their blood will be precious in his sight;
15   So may he live, and may the gold of Sheba be given to him;
     And let them pray for him continually;
     Let them bless him all day long.

Praying Psalm 72

*A prayer of King Solomon closes Book Two asking the
Lord to establish His Kingdom with His King.*

Jesus is the King! Your Kingdom come, Your will be done on earth as it is in heaven (Matt. 6:10).

Lord God Almighty, establish Your chosen King to exercise justice, righteousness, and compassion over Your Kingdom (vv. 1–4)

While we await the return of our Savior as King, Father, give us leaders who rule with justice (v. 1).

Rule forever, dear God (vv. 5–7).

Rule to the ends of the earth, Lord (v. 8).

Father, may all nations and people worship the Messiah (v. 11).

Rule with compassion and mercy, Lord Jesus (vv. 12–15).

Thank You for valuing our lives, dear God (v. 14).

While I pray for my Lord to return quickly, teach me to pray for those who are in authority over me, Lord (v. 15).

16   May there be abundance of grain in the earth on top of the mountains;
     Its fruit will wave like *the cedars of* Lebanon;
     And may those from the city flourish like vegetation of the earth.
17   May his name endure forever;
     May his name increase as long as the sun *shines;*
     And let *men* bless themselves by him;
     Let all nations call him blessed.
18   Blessed be the LORD God, the God of Israel,
     Who alone works wonders.
19   And blessed be His glorious name forever;
     And may the whole earth be filled with His glory.
     Amen, and Amen.
20   The prayers of David the son of Jesse are ended.

Blessed be the name of the Lord (v. 17).

May the whole earth be filled with the King's glory. Amen and amen (v. 19).

Father, teach me to pray like David (v. 20).

How Jesus could be interceding for you: You anointed Me, Father, to reign as King, just as You promised David (2 Sam. 7:8–16; Ps. 2:8). As David's greater Son, send Me as the answer to his own son's prayer (Isa. 9:7; Jer. 23:5; Luke 1:32). Allow me to fulfill the prayer I taught My disciples—to bring in the Kingdom (Matt. 6:10; Rev. 5:5).

Psalm 73

The End of the Wicked Contrasted with That of the Righteous.

A Psalm of Asaph.

1   Surely God is good to Israel,
      To those who are pure in heart!
2   But as for me, my feet came close to stumbling,
      My steps had almost slipped.
3   For I was envious of the arrogant
      As I saw the prosperity of the wicked.
4   For there are no pains in their death,
      And their body is fat.
5   They are not in trouble *as other* men,
      Nor are they plagued like mankind.
6   Therefore pride is their necklace;
      The garment of violence covers them.
7   Their eye bulges from fatness;
      The imaginations of *their* heart run riot.
8   They mock and wickedly speak of oppression;
      They speak from on high.
9   They have set their mouth against the heavens,
      And their tongue parades through the earth.
10   Therefore his people return to this place,
      And waters of abundance are drunk by them.
11   They say, "How does God know?
      And is there knowledge with the Most High?"
12   Behold, these are the wicked;
      And always at ease, they have increased *in* wealth.
13   Surely in vain I have kept my heart pure
      And washed my hands in innocence;
14   For I have been stricken all day long
      And chastened every morning.
15   If I had said, "I will speak thus,"
      Behold, I would have betrayed the generation of Your children.
16   When I pondered to understand this,
      It was troublesome in my sight
17   Until I came into the sanctuary of God;

Praying Psalm 73

*In this prayer opening Book Three, Asaph confesses his struggle
with how the wicked prosper and praises God for giving him a good
far greater than what the wicked enjoy in their lifetime.*

No matter what happens, Father, You are good (v. 1).

I confess that I too have been envious of sinners at times, Lord (v. 3).

Deliver me from envy and its damaging effects (v. 3).

O Sovereign Lord, You know all things. None of the doubts of my heart remain hidden from You (v. 11).

I also have questioned whether following You has been worth it (v. 13).

Father, help me to remain faithful despite all my doubts (v. 13).

Then I perceived their end.

18 Surely You set them in slippery places;
    You cast them down to destruction.

19 How they are destroyed in a moment!
    They are utterly swept away by sudden terrors!

20 Like a dream when one awakes,
    O Lord, when aroused, You will despise their form.

21 When my heart was embittered
    And I was pierced within,

22 Then I was senseless and ignorant;
    I was *like* a beast before You.

23 Nevertheless I am continually with You;
    You have taken hold of my right hand.

24 With Your counsel You will guide me,
    And afterward receive me to glory.

25 Whom have I in heaven *but You?*
    And besides You, I desire nothing on earth.

26 My flesh and my heart may fail,
    But God is the strength of my heart and my portion forever.

27 For, behold, those who are far from You will perish;
    You have destroyed all those who are unfaithful to You.

28 But as for me, the nearness of God is my good;
    I have made the Lord God my refuge,
    That I may tell of all Your works.

Thank You, my God, for teaching me Your truth when I hear Your Word spoken within the assembly of believers (v. 17).

Forgive me, Father, for my faithlessness and self-focus. Animals live by sight and their natural senses, but I will live by faith and trust in Your faithfulness (vv. 21–22).

O God, remove my ignorance (v. 22).

Dear Lord, thank You for taking my hand and guiding me through life (vv. 23–24).

You are my true and eternal satisfaction, Lord. You will destroy the faithless and deliver those who take refuge in Your Son. I believe, Lord. Strengthen my faith and use me to tell others of You (vv. 25–28).

Lord Jesus, You are all that I desire (v. 25).

May my prayer always be, "Nearer, my God, to You" (v. 28).

How Jesus could be interceding for you: Yes, Father, You alone are good (Mark 10:18). Bless Your people when they gather together for worship, for when they meet, I am in their midst (Matt. 18:20). Remove their doubts, their bitterness, and their fears (John 14:27). Give them a desire to be in Our presence (John 14:2–3, 23; 17:24).

Psalm 74

An Appeal against the Devastation of the Land by the Enemy.

A Maskil of Asaph.

1   O God, why have You rejected *us* forever?
Why does Your anger smoke against the sheep of Your pasture?

2   Remember Your congregation, which You have purchased of old,
Which You have redeemed to be the tribe of Your inheritance;
And this Mount Zion, where You have dwelt.

3   Turn Your footsteps toward the perpetual ruins;
The enemy has damaged everything within the sanctuary.

4   Your adversaries have roared in the midst of Your meeting place;
They have set up their own standards for signs.

5   It seems as if one had lifted up
His axe in a forest of trees.

6   And now all its carved work
They smash with hatchet and hammers.

7   They have burned Your sanctuary to the ground;
They have defiled the dwelling place of Your name.

8   They said in their heart, "Let us completely subdue them."
They have burned all the meeting places of God in the land.

9   We do not see our signs;
There is no longer any prophet,
Nor is there any among us who knows how long.

10   How long, O God, will the adversary revile,
And the enemy spurn Your name forever?

11   Why do You withdraw Your hand, even Your right hand?
From within Your bosom, destroy *them!*

12   Yet God is my king from of old,
Who works deeds of deliverance in the midst of the earth.

13   You divided the sea by Your strength;
You broke the heads of the sea monsters in the waters.

14   You crushed the heads of Leviathan;
You gave him as food for the creatures of the wilderness.

15   You broke open springs and torrents;
You dried up ever-flowing streams.

16   Yours is the day, Yours also is the night;
You have prepared the light and the sun.

Praying Psalm 74

Asaph prays for his people who, despite being the sheep of God's pasture, have experienced destruction from an invading army.

Father, as I read the prayer of the remnant suffering in the face of exile, I am reminded of suffering believers today. Strengthen and encourage them in their faith. Grant my brothers and sisters relief. Don't let the enemy oppress them forever (vv. 1–11).

Thank You, Lord, for redeeming me, for paying the redemption price for Your people (v. 2).

Fill my mind and my heart with Your Word, Father (v. 9).

You are King forever, Lord. You won everything. You rule over everything. I will trust in You (vv. 12–17).

We praise You, O God, for day and night, summer and winter (vv. 16–17).

17   You have established all the boundaries of the earth;
       You have made summer and winter.
18   Remember this, O Lord, that the enemy has reviled,
       And a foolish people has spurned Your name.
19   Do not deliver the soul of Your turtledove to the wild beast;
       Do not forget the life of Your afflicted forever.
20   Consider the covenant;
       For the dark places of the land are full of the habitations of violence.
21   Let not the oppressed return dishonored;
       Let the afflicted and needy praise Your name.
22   Arise, O God, *and* plead Your own cause;
       Remember how the foolish man reproaches You all day long.
23   Do not forget the voice of Your adversaries,
       The uproar of those who rise against You which ascends continually.

Hold the oppressors of Your people guilty, O Sovereign Lord. Arise and remember Israel. Arise and remember Your afflicted church as well (vv. 18–23).

When I feel like a dove attacked by a wild beast, protect me, Father (v. 19).

Lord, fulfill Your covenant with Your people (v. 20).

How Jesus could be interceding for you: I taught Your words to My disciples regarding Jerusalem's destruction in their day (Matt. 24; John 17:8, 14). I redeemed Your congregation, the sheep of Your pasture, by My own blood (Acts 20:28). In all their affliction I was afflicted (Isa. 63:9). Comfort them, loving Father (2 Cor. 1:3–5), and prepare them for eternal glory (2 Cor. 4:17).

Psalm 75

God Abases the Proud, but Exalts the Righteous.

For the choir director; set to Al-tashheth. A Psalm of Asaph, a Song.

1   We give thanks to You, O God, we give thanks,
     For Your name is near;
     Men declare Your wondrous works.
2   "When I select an appointed time,
     It is I who judge with equity.
3   "The earth and all who dwell in it melt;
     It is I who have firmly set its pillars.   *Selah.*
4   "I said to the boastful, 'Do not boast,'
     And to the wicked, 'Do not lift up the horn;
5   Do not lift up your horn on high,
     Do not speak with insolent pride.' "

6   For not from the east, nor from the west,
     Nor from the desert *comes* exaltation;
7   But God is the Judge;
     He puts down one and exalts another.
8   For a cup is in the hand of the LORD, and the wine foams;
     It is well mixed, and He pours out of this;
     Surely all the wicked of the earth must drain *and* drink down its dregs.

9   But as for me, I will declare *it* forever;
     I will sing praises to the God of Jacob.
10   And all the horns of the wicked He will cut off,
     But the horns of the righteous will be lifted up.

Praying Psalm 75

Asaph prays for the Judge of all the earth to act and then thanks Him for doing so.

Thank You, God. Your character is our comfort and You are always near (v. 1).

Praise be to the Judge of all mankind. You will exalt those who trust in You. You will debase the treacherous who trust in and exalt themselves. I will sing Your praises forever (vv. 2–10).

Give me patience to wait for You to judge the wicked, Lord (v. 2).

Father, remove any pride or arrogance in my life (vv. 4–5).

O God, help me to be faithful in praising You (v. 9).

How Jesus could be interceding for you: As the Judge of all the earth (John 5:22–23), I intercede with You, Father, on behalf of Your servants (Rom. 8:34; Heb. 7:25). Grant relief to Your people in place of the afflictions they bear (2 Thess. 1:5–8).

Psalm 76

The Victorious Power of the God of Jacob.

For the choir director; on stringed instruments. A Psalm of Asaph, a Song.

1 God is known in Judah;
   His name is great in Israel.
2 His tabernacle is in Salem;
   His dwelling place also is in Zion.
3 There He broke the flaming arrows,
   The shield and the sword and the weapons of war.   *Selah.*

4 You are resplendent,
   More majestic than the mountains of prey.
5 The stouthearted were plundered,
   They sank into sleep;
   And none of the warriors could use his hands.
6 At Your rebuke, O God of Jacob,
   Both rider and horse were cast into a dead sleep.
7 You, even You, are to be feared;
   And who may stand in Your presence when once You are angry?

8 You caused judgment to be heard from heaven;
   The earth feared and was still
9 When God arose to judgment,
   To save all the humble of the earth.   *Selah.*
10 For the wrath of man shall praise You;
   With a remnant of wrath You will gird Yourself.
11 Make vows to the LORD your God and fulfill *them;*
   Let all who are around Him bring gifts to Him who is to be feared.
12 He will cut off the spirit of princes;
   He is feared by the kings of the earth.

Praying Psalm 76

As Asaph prays, he praises the Lord for delivering His people from powerful enemies.

Lord Jesus, when You come back to reign in Zion, the armies will flee and fall at Your feet. You indeed are to be feared, for Your holy anger will consume Your enemies (vv. 1–7).

You are great in this world, in our church, and in my life, Lord (v. 1).

Lord God, put an end to wars against Your people (vv. 3–6).

Create in my heart a godly fear of You, dear Father (v. 7).

O God, humble my soul before You. For You will save all the humble of the earth. Blessed are the humble for they will inherit the earth (v. 9).

Every tongue will confess—even kings and princes—that You alone are sovereign Master, even the Lord Jesus Christ (vv. 11–12).

My Savior, help me to fulfill my commitment to honor and serve You (v. 11).

How Jesus could be interceding for you: At Your rebuke, righteous Father, You cause the enemies of Your people to flee. I await the time when You will make the enemies My footstool (Ps. 110:1; Heb. 10:12–13). Bless those who fear You (Luke 1:50; 1 Pet. 2:17) and are humble (1 Pet. 5:6–7).

Psalm 77

Comfort in Trouble from Recalling God's Mighty Deeds.

For the choir director; according to Jeduthun. A Psalm of Asaph.

1   My voice *rises* to God, and I will cry aloud;
    My voice *rises* to God, and He will hear me.
2   In the day of my trouble I sought the Lord;
    In the night my hand was stretched out without weariness;
    My soul refused to be comforted.
3   *When* I remember God, then I am disturbed;
    When I sigh, then my spirit grows faint.   *Selah.*
4   You have held my eyelids *open;*
    I am so troubled that I cannot speak.
5   I have considered the days of old,
    The years of long ago.
6   I will remember my song in the night;
    I will meditate with my heart,
    And my spirit ponders:

7   Will the Lord reject forever?
    And will He never be favorable again?
8   Has His lovingkindness ceased forever?
    Has *His* promise come to an end forever?
9   Has God forgotten to be gracious,
    Or has He in anger withdrawn His compassion?   *Selah.*
10 Then I said, "It is my grief,
    That the right hand of the Most High has changed."
11 I shall remember the deeds of the LORD;
    Surely I will remember Your wonders of old.
12 I will meditate on all Your work
    And muse on Your deeds.
13 Your way, O God, is holy;
    What god is great like our God?
14 You are the God who works wonders;
    You have made known Your strength among the peoples.
15 You have by Your power redeemed Your people,
    The sons of Jacob and Joseph.   *Selah.*

Praying Psalm 77

In a time of severe trouble, Asaph appeals to God for strength, comfort, and relief.

Lord, sometimes I pray and find no comfort. I can't sleep, and I can't really articulate what's disturbing my troubled soul (vv. 1–3).

Comfort me, Lord, for I am deeply troubled and distressed (vv. 1–2).

Father, give me songs of praise during those nights when I am sleepless (v. 6).

I don't seem to feel Your love and grace. Is it some sin, or is it just a season for building my faith (vv. 7–10)?

Help me to express my doubts to You, rather than to hide them (vv. 7–9).

I will purposely recount Your works and Your wondrous acts as revealed in Your Word. You are indeed holy—there is none like You (vv. 11–15).

O Lord Jesus, cause me to focus on You rather than on myself and my troubles (vv. 11–14).

16   The waters saw You, O God;
      The waters saw You, they were in anguish;
      The deeps also trembled.
17   The clouds poured out water;
      The skies gave forth a sound;
      Your arrows flashed here and there.
18   The sound of Your thunder was in the whirlwind;
      The lightnings lit up the world;
      The earth trembled and shook.
19   Your way was in the sea
      And Your paths in the mighty waters,
      And Your footprints may not be known.
20   You led Your people like a flock
      By the hand of Moses and Aaron.

The God who redeemed Israel and parted the sea is my God. I believe, Lord. Help my unbelief (vv. 16–20).

⸙

Whenever I experience a tremendous and awesome thunderstorm, remind me that You send the rain and display Your power in the thunder and lightning. O Lord God, teach me to trust You in all of life's "storms" (vv. 16–18).

———

How Jesus could be interceding for you: Gracious Father, I have walked where Your servant walks (John 1:14; Phil. 2:6–8) and have experienced the troubling circumstances that cause anguish and distress (Mark 14:33–36; Heb. 2:14–18). Enable Your child to follow My example in doing Your will and enduring the long, difficult nights (1 Pet. 2:21; 1 John 2:6).

Psalm 78

God's Guidance of His People in Spite of Their Unfaithfulness.

A Maskil of Asaph.

1   Listen, O my people, to my instruction;
      Incline your ears to the words of my mouth.
2   I will open my mouth in a parable;
      I will utter dark sayings of old,
3   Which we have heard and known,
      And our fathers have told us.
4   We will not conceal them from their children,
      But tell to the generation to come the praises of the Lord,
      And His strength and His wondrous works that He has done.

5   For He established a testimony in Jacob
      And appointed a law in Israel,
      Which He commanded our fathers
      That they should teach them to their children,
6   That the generation to come might know, *even* the children *yet* to be born,
      That they may arise and tell *them* to their children,
7   That they should put their confidence in God
      And not forget the works of God,
      But keep His commandments,
8   And not be like their fathers,
      A stubborn and rebellious generation,
      A generation that did not prepare its heart
      And whose spirit was not faithful to God.

9   The sons of Ephraim were archers equipped with bows,
      Yet they turned back in the day of battle.
10   They did not keep the covenant of God
      And refused to walk in His law;
11   They forgot His deeds
      And His miracles that He had shown them.
12   He wrought wonders before their fathers
      In the land of Egypt, in the field of Zoan.
13   He divided the sea and caused them to pass through,
      And He made the waters stand up like a heap.

Praying Psalm 78

The second longest psalm in the Psalter, Asaph's prayer focuses on*
God's covenant with David and presents him as the second Moses.

Father, help me to tell others about what You've revealed in the Bible about Yourself (vv. 1–4).

Cause me to listen to and obey Your instruction, Lord (v. 1).

Teach me how to pass on Your instruction to my children and my grandchildren (vv. 4–8).

Thank You for the inspired record of Israel's history. Turn Your people's hearts to You (vv. 5–8).

Father, forgive me for my stubbornness, rebellion, and unfaithfulness (v. 8).

Forgive me, Lord, for forgetting the great things You have done. Forgive me for my faithless thoughts and actions (vv. 9–20).

Lord Jesus, thank You for sending the Holy Spirit to remind me of Your deeds and Your miracles. Help me never to forget (v. 11)!

---

*   In what ways can we consider a historical psalm like Psalm 78 a prayer? (1) The psalm focuses primarily on God—specifically the faithfulness and perseverance of God. (2) The psalm is reflective—a meditation comparing Israel's faithlessness with God's faithfulness. (3) The psalm concludes with the tribe of Judah (Gen. 49:10) and David (2 Sam. 7)—pointing to Messiah for Israel's ultimate redemption. Therefore, Psalm 78 praises God by contemplating how and why He brought Israel out of Egypt.

14   Then He led them with the cloud by day
      And all the night with a light of fire.

15   He split the rocks in the wilderness
      And gave *them* abundant drink like the ocean depths.

16   He brought forth streams also from the rock
      And caused waters to run down like rivers.

17   Yet they still continued to sin against Him,
      To rebel against the Most High in the desert.

18   And in their heart they put God to the test
      By asking food according to their desire.

19   Then they spoke against God;
      They said, "Can God prepare a table in the wilderness?

20   "Behold, He struck the rock so that waters gushed out,
      And streams were overflowing;
      Can He give bread also?
      Will He provide meat for His people?"

21   Therefore the LORD heard and was full of wrath;
      And a fire was kindled against Jacob
      And anger also mounted against Israel,

22   Because they did not believe in God
      And did not trust in His salvation.

23   Yet He commanded the clouds above
      And opened the doors of heaven;

24   He rained down manna upon them to eat
      And gave them food from heaven.

25   Man did eat the bread of angels;
      He sent them food in abundance.

26   He caused the east wind to blow in the heavens
      And by His power He directed the south wind.

27   When He rained meat upon them like the dust,
      Even winged fowl like the sand of the seas,

28   Then He let *them* fall in the midst of their camp,
      Round about their dwellings.

29   So they ate and were well filled,
      And their desire He gave to them.

30   Before they had satisfied their desire,
      While their food was in their mouths,

31   The anger of God rose against them
      And killed some of their stoutest ones,
      And subdued the choice men of Israel.

32   In spite of all this they still sinned

As I read of Your care for Israel in the wilderness, teach me to recognize Your gracious provision when I and my family need Your leading or we lack adequate food and drink. Increase my trust in You, Lord (vv. 14–16).

Keep my heart set upon You and not upon my fleshly desires (v. 18).

Father, by Your Spirit teach me that Your Son is the Bread of Life. Satisfy my heart with Him so that I will not rebel against You and seek after things in this world that cannot satisfy (vv. 21–33).

O God, keep me from failing to trust Your saving work in my life (v. 22).

Merciful Creator and Lord, You know my needs, You provide my food, You control the birds of the sky, and You know the desires of my heart. Fulfill those desires that honor You and remove from me those desires that dishonor You (vv. 23–31).

Thank You for teaching me that I too often repeat Israel's sins despite having far greater revelation and evidence of Your grace and mercy (v. 32).

And did not believe in His wonderful works.
33   So He brought their days to an end in futility
And their years in sudden terror.
34   When He killed them, then they sought Him,
And returned and searched diligently for God;
35   And they remembered that God was their rock,
And the Most High God their Redeemer.
36   But they deceived Him with their mouth
And lied to Him with their tongue.
37   For their heart was not steadfast toward Him,
Nor were they faithful in His covenant.
38   But He, being compassionate, forgave *their* iniquity and did not destroy *them;*
And often He restrained His anger
And did not arouse all His wrath.
39   Thus He remembered that they were but flesh,
A wind that passes and does not return.
40   How often they rebelled against Him in the wilderness
And grieved Him in the desert!
41   Again and again they tempted God,
And pained the Holy One of Israel.
42   They did not remember His power,
The day when He redeemed them from the adversary,
43   When He performed His signs in Egypt
And His marvels in the field of Zoan,
44   And turned their rivers to blood,
And their streams, they could not drink.
45   He sent among them swarms of flies which devoured them,
And frogs which destroyed them.
46   He gave also their crops to the grasshopper
And the product of their labor to the locust.
47   He destroyed their vines with hailstones
And their sycamore trees with frost.
48   He gave over their cattle also to the hailstones
And their herds to bolts of lightning.
49   He sent upon them His burning anger,
Fury and indignation and trouble,
A band of destroying angels.
50   He leveled a path for His anger;
He did not spare their soul from death,
But gave over their life to the plague,
51   And smote all the firstborn in Egypt,

Thank You for Your compassion and patience in preserving Israel and thus the nation through which the Redeemer would come (vv. 34–39).

Lord, thank You for restraining Your anger against me and for forgiving my sins (v. 38).

How often I forget, Lord—You are the same God who sovereignly directed the plagues on Egypt to deliver Your people and judge those who refuse to believe (vv. 40–53).

Father, like Your people of old, I have too often wandered from You while ignoring all Your mighty deeds (vv. 42–52).

Forgive my failure to remember and to tell others about how You have displayed Your power in my life and delivered me from my rebellion and from harmful circumstances (v. 42).

The first *issue* of their virility in the tents of Ham.
52 But He led forth His own people like sheep
    And guided them in the wilderness like a flock;
53 He led them safely, so that they did not fear;
    But the sea engulfed their enemies.
54 So He brought them to His holy land,
    To this hill country which His right hand had gained.
55 He also drove out the nations before them
    And apportioned them for an inheritance by measurement,
    And made the tribes of Israel dwell in their tents.
56 Yet they tempted and rebelled against the Most High God
    And did not keep His testimonies,
57 But turned back and acted treacherously like their fathers;
    They turned aside like a treacherous bow.
58 For they provoked Him with their high places
    And aroused His jealousy with their graven images.
59 When God heard, He was filled with wrath
    And greatly abhorred Israel;
60 So that He abandoned the dwelling place at Shiloh,
    The tent which He had pitched among men,
61 And gave up His strength to captivity
    And His glory into the hand of the adversary.
62 He also delivered His people to the sword,
    And was filled with wrath at His inheritance.
63 Fire devoured His young men,
    And His virgins had no wedding songs.
64 His priests fell by the sword,
    And His widows could not weep.
65 Then the Lord awoke as *if from* sleep,
    Like a warrior overcome by wine.
66 He drove His adversaries backward;
    He put on them an everlasting reproach.
67 He also rejected the tent of Joseph,
    And did not choose the tribe of Ephraim,
68 But chose the tribe of Judah,
    Mount Zion which He loved.
69 And He built His sanctuary like the heights,
    Like the earth which He has founded forever.
70 He also chose David His servant
    And took him from the sheepfolds;
71 From the care of the ewes with suckling lambs He brought him
    To shepherd Jacob His people,
    And Israel His inheritance.
72 So he shepherded them according to the integrity of his heart,
    And guided them with his skillful hands.

Teach me to trust You (vv. 54–64).

Deliver me, O God, from the idols of my own heart (v. 58).

Lord Jesus, how I thank You that when I deserved wrath, abhorrence, and abandonment, You showed me mercy, love, and Your continuing presence in my life, because You purchased my salvation by Your sacrificial death (vv. 59–64).

Thank You, Father, for the promises You made to David. I worship You now through Your Son Jesus, because of Your faithfulness to that covenant You made with David (vv. 65–72).

I have a greater Shepherd than King David, so I offer You praise, dear Lord, for His caring for me (vv. 70–72).

How Jesus could be interceding for you: As the greater Son of David (Matt. 1:1), the One greater than Moses (Heb. 3:1–6), and the Shepherd of all Your sheep (Matt. 2:5–6; John 10:11–18), I praise You, merciful Father, for Your love and forgiveness for the sins of the sheep of Your pasture (Luke 12:32; Acts 20:28; Heb. 13:20).

Psalm 79

A Lament over the Destruction of Jerusalem, and Prayer for Help.

A Psalm of Asaph.

1   O God, the nations have invaded Your inheritance;
     They have defiled Your holy temple;
     They have laid Jerusalem in ruins.
2   They have given the dead bodies of Your servants for food to the birds of
          the heavens,
     The flesh of Your godly ones to the beasts of the earth.
3   They have poured out their blood like water round about Jerusalem;
     And there was no one to bury them.
4   We have become a reproach to our neighbors,
     A scoffing and derision to those around us.
5   How long, O Lord? Will You be angry forever?
     Will Your jealousy burn like fire?
6   Pour out Your wrath upon the nations which do not know You,
     And upon the kingdoms which do not call upon Your name.
7   For they have devoured Jacob
     And laid waste his habitation.

8   Do not remember the iniquities of *our* forefathers against us;
     Let Your compassion come quickly to meet us,
     For we are brought very low.
9   Help us, O God of our salvation, for the glory of Your name;
     And deliver us and forgive our sins for Your name's sake.
10   Why should the nations say, "Where is their God?"
     Let there be known among the nations in our sight,
     Vengeance for the blood of Your servants which has been shed.
11   Let the groaning of the prisoner come before You;
     According to the greatness of Your power preserve those who are doomed
          to die.
12   And return to our neighbors sevenfold into their bosom
     The reproach with which they have reproached You, O Lord.
13   So we Your people and the sheep of Your pasture
     Will give thanks to You forever;
     To all generations we will tell of Your praise.

Praying Psalm 79

*Asaph prays for God to forgive the sins of His people and to
deliver them from their captivity to their enemies.*

O God, give me compassion for those who suffer, even if their suffering is due to their sins (vv. 1–4).

God, You said this would happen and it did (vv. 1–3; cf. Deut. 28–29). Please help me to fully believe that everything You say will come to pass just as You have said. Let that belief lead me to obey You.

Even now, many in Your covenant nation do not believe in Your Son. Draw them to their Messiah, Father. He will remove all reproach and bring justice. Then all generations will proclaim Your praise and we will give thanks to You forever (vv. 4–13).

Lord, establish Your justice in the chaos of horrific times (vv. 5–6, 12).

Father, forgive my sins against You (v. 8).

Lord Jesus, help me to give You thanks, even when circumstances might not make me feel like it (v. 13).

How Jesus could be interceding for you: You sent Me to the lost sheep of the house of Israel, dear Father (Matt. 10:6). Redeem Israel (Rom. 11:26–27), and cause sinners to confess their sins and to thank and praise You forever (2 Chron. 7:13–14; 2 Cor. 4:15; Col. 1:12).

Psalm 80

God Implored to Rescue His People from Their Calamities.

For the choir director; set to El Shoshannim; Eduth. A Psalm of Asaph.

1   Oh, give ear, Shepherd of Israel,
You who lead Joseph like a flock;
You who are enthroned *above* the cherubim, shine forth!

2   Before Ephraim and Benjamin and Manasseh, stir up Your power
And come to save us!

3   O God, restore us
And cause Your face to shine *upon us,* and we will be saved.

4   O Lord God *of* hosts,
How long will You be angry with the prayer of Your people?

5   You have fed them with the bread of tears,
And You have made them to drink tears in large measure.

6   You make us an object of contention to our neighbors,
And our enemies laugh among themselves.

7   O God *of* hosts, restore us
And cause Your face to shine *upon us,* and we will be saved.

8   You removed a vine from Egypt;
You drove out the nations and planted it.

9   You cleared *the ground* before it,
And it took deep root and filled the land.

10   The mountains were covered with its shadow,
And the cedars of God with its boughs.

11   It was sending out its branches to the sea
And its shoots to the River.

12   Why have You broken down its hedges,
So that all who pass *that* way pick its *fruit?*

13   A boar from the forest eats it away
And whatever moves in the field feeds on it.

14   O God *of* hosts, turn again now, we beseech You;
Look down from heaven and see, and take care of this vine,

15   Even the shoot which Your right hand has planted,
And on the son whom You have strengthened for Yourself.

Praying Psalm 80

Asaph pleads with God to answer the prayers of His
people and restore them to His favor.

Shepherd of Israel, restore and bless Your flock. Reveal Messiah Jesus, the Good Shepherd (vv. 1–7; cf. John 10).

Restore, revive Your people, dear Lord, and renew their fellowship with You (vv. 3, 7, 19).

Father, don't let all You have done for Israel be ineffective for Your people's ultimate blessing (vv. 8–15).

While I work in my garden or watch others working in theirs, remind me, Lord, of the illustration of the vine You transplanted and nurtured—Israel. And, teach me that I too am a branch of my Savior's vine (vv. 8–13; cf. John 15:1–11).

Look upon Your vine and care for it, Father (v. 14).

16   It is burned with fire, it is cut down;
      They perish at the rebuke of Your countenance.
17   Let Your hand be upon the man of Your right hand,
      Upon the son of man whom You made strong for Yourself.
18   Then we shall not turn back from You;
      Revive us, and we will call upon Your name.
19   O Lord God of hosts, restore us;
      Cause Your face to shine *upon us,* and we will be saved.

Great Shepherd, restore and bless Your people through Messiah Jesus, the ultimate Son of Man (vv. 16–19).

Lord Jesus, revive us and cause us to serve and praise You for our salvation (v. 18).

How Jesus could be interceding for you: Almighty Father and Shepherd of Your people, hear My prayer for those whose fellowship with You has been broken by their sins (1 John 1:6–9). Restore, heal, and bless Your people again through My obedience even unto death on their behalf (Rom. 5:19; Phil. 2:8; Heb. 5:8–10).

Psalm 81

God's Goodness and Israel's Waywardness.

For the choir director; on the Gittith. A Psalm *of Asaph.*

1   Sing for joy to God our strength;
    Shout joyfully to the God of Jacob.
2   Raise a song, strike the timbrel,
    The sweet sounding lyre with the harp.
3   Blow the trumpet at the new moon,
    At the full moon, on our feast day.
4   For it is a statute for Israel,
    An ordinance of the God of Jacob.
5   He established it for a testimony in Joseph
    When he went throughout the land of Egypt.
    I heard a language that I did not know:

6   "I relieved his shoulder of the burden,
    His hands were freed from the basket.
7   "You called in trouble and I rescued you;
    I answered you in the hiding place of thunder;
    I proved you at the waters of Meribah.   *Selah.*
8   "Hear, O My people, and I will admonish you;
    O Israel, if you would listen to Me!
9   "Let there be no strange god among you;
    Nor shall you worship any foreign god.
10 "I, the Lord, am your God,
    Who brought you up from the land of Egypt;
    Open your mouth wide and I will fill it.

11 "But My people did not listen to My voice,
    And Israel did not obey Me.
12 "So I gave them over to the stubbornness of their heart,
    To walk in their own devices.
13 "Oh that My people would listen to Me,
    That Israel would walk in My ways!
14 "I would quickly subdue their enemies
    And turn My hand against their adversaries.
15 "Those who hate the Lord would pretend obedience to Him,
    And their time *of punishment* would be forever.
16 "But I would feed you with the finest of the wheat,
    And with honey from the rock I would satisfy you."

Praying Psalm 81

*Asaph's prayer may have been composed for the Feast of
Tabernacles. Rabbinic tradition identifies it as the psalm sung
in the daily services in the Temple on Thursdays.*

It is hard to fathom, Father, that You have fellowship with me—yet You are the God
of the Exodus. Teach me to trust You and find my satisfaction in You (vv. 1–10).

Lord, thank You for being my strength (v. 1).

How I praise You for freeing me from my slavery to sin (v.6)!

Father, help me listen to You and to Your Word (v. 8).

Lord, train my heart to listen to and obey You. Don't give me over to myself
(vv. 11–16).

Defeat my stubborn heart and my pride, Lord Jesus (v. 12).

Thank You, God, for providing me with an abundance of food (v. 16).

How Jesus could be interceding for you: Father, enable Your people to rejoice and
to celebrate all Your gifts to them (John 15:10–11; 17:13; Rom. 15:13). Through My
example of obedience, teach them to walk in Your ways (John 13:15; 1 Pet. 2:21).

Psalm 82

Unjust Judgments Rebuked.

A Psalm of Asaph.

1   God takes His stand in His own congregation;
     He judges in the midst of the rulers.
2   How long will you judge unjustly
     And show partiality to the wicked?   *Selah.*
3   Vindicate the weak and fatherless;
     Do justice to the afflicted and destitute.
4   Rescue the weak and needy;
     Deliver *them* out of the hand of the wicked.

5   They do not know nor do they understand;
     They walk about in darkness;
     All the foundations of the earth are shaken.
6   I said, "You are gods,
     And all of you are sons of the Most High.
7   "Nevertheless you will die like men
     And fall like *any* one of the princes."
8   Arise, O God, judge the earth!
     For it is You who possesses all the nations.

Praying Psalm 82

Due to rampant injustice, Asaph prays for God to administer justice.

Lord Jesus, You are the true Son of the Living God. The wicked rulers—who sat as gods among the people—did not recognize You. Lord, turn me away from injustice and partiality in whatever ways You have me lead others (vv. 1–6).

⚜⚜⚜

Cause the rulers of my nation to act with justice, Lord (v. 2).

⚜⚜⚜

Father, give me wisdom to act justly with those in need (vv. 3–4).

⚜⚜⚜

Arise, God, judge the earth. May Your Kingdom come, Lord—so that Your will may be done on earth as it is in heaven (vv. 7–8).

How Jesus could be interceding for you: Judge of all the earth (Heb. 12:23), grant Your people's prayer for justice in their land (Deut. 10:17–18; Luke 18:7–8). Prepare their hearts for the Kingdom I will bring when I return to establish righteousness and truth over all the earth (Acts 17:31; Heb. 1:8–9; Rev. 19:11).

Psalm 83

God Implored to Confound His Enemies.

A Song, a Psalm of Asaph.

1 O God, do not remain quiet;
Do not be silent and, O God, do not be still.
2 For behold, Your enemies make an uproar,
And those who hate You have exalted themselves.
3 They make shrewd plans against Your people,
And conspire together against Your treasured ones.
4 They have said, "Come, and let us wipe them out as a nation,
That the name of Israel be remembered no more."
5 For they have conspired together with one mind;
Against You they make a covenant:
6 The tents of Edom and the Ishmaelites,
Moab and the Hagrites;
7 Gebal and Ammon and Amalek,
Philistia with the inhabitants of Tyre;
8 Assyria also has joined with them;
They have become a help to the children of Lot.   *Selah.*

9 Deal with them as with Midian,
As with Sisera *and* Jabin at the torrent of Kishon,
10 Who were destroyed at En-dor,
Who became as dung for the ground.
11 Make their nobles like Oreb and Zeeb
And all their princes like Zebah and Zalmunna,
12 Who said, "Let us possess for ourselves
The pastures of God."
13 O my God, make them like the whirling dust,
Like chaff before the wind.
14 Like fire that burns the forest
And like a flame that sets the mountains on fire,
15 So pursue them with Your tempest
And terrify them with Your storm.
16 Fill their faces with dishonor,
That they may seek Your name, O Lord.
17 Let them be ashamed and dismayed forever,
And let them be humiliated and perish,
18 That they may know that You alone, whose name is the Lord,
Are the Most High over all the earth.

Praying Psalm 83

*Asaph penned this community prayer calling upon
God to bring their enemies to know Him.*

God of Abraham, Isaac, and Jacob—over and over again through the centuries nations and peoples have sought to destroy Your covenant nation Israel. You have been faithful to preserve Your people. Your Kingdom will surely come. I wait for it, Lord Jesus (vv. 1–12).

Father, please don't remain silent—answer my prayer (v. 1)!

Protect Your people, O God (v. 3)!

Lord Jesus, when I feel like everyone is against me, help me to remember it is because they first hated You (vv. 2–8).

Turn the hearts of those who would oppose You and Your people to seek Your name, dear Lord. Make all people everywhere know that You are the Most High God (vv. 13–18).

Father, turn Your enemies from hating You to seeking You (v. 16).

Lord, put Your enemies to shame (v. 17).

Make unbelievers understand that You are the Most High God (v. 18).

How Jesus could be interceding for you: O Father of the oppressed and persecuted (Matt. 5:10), instill in Your people the conviction that the world hated Me before it hated them (Luke 21:17; John 15:18, 20). Just as You, by Your Spirit, turn Your enemies into Your children (Rom. 5:10), use the testimony of Your children to bring the message of mercy and salvation to their enemies (Luke 6:27–36).

Psalm 84

Longing for the Temple Worship.

For the choir director; on the Gittith. A Psalm of the sons of Korah.

1   How lovely are Your dwelling places,
     O Lord of hosts!
2   My soul longed and even yearned for the courts of the Lord;
     My heart and my flesh sing for joy to the living God.
3   The bird also has found a house,
     And the swallow a nest for herself, where she may lay her young,
     Even Your altars, O Lord of hosts,
     My King and my God.
4   How blessed are those who dwell in Your house!
     They are ever praising You.   *Selah.*

5   How blessed is the man whose strength is in You,
     In whose heart are the highways *to Zion!*
6   Passing through the valley of Baca they make it a spring;
     The early rain also covers it with blessings.
7   They go from strength to strength,
     Every one of them appears before God in Zion.

8   O Lord God of hosts, hear my prayer;
     Give ear, O God of Jacob!   *Selah.*
9   Behold our shield, O God,
     And look upon the face of Your anointed.
10   For a day in Your courts is better than a thousand *outside.*
     I would rather stand at the threshold of the house of my God
     Than dwell in the tents of wickedness.
11   For the Lord God is a sun and shield;
     The Lord gives grace and glory;
     No good thing does He withhold from those who walk uprightly.
12   O Lord of hosts,
     How blessed is the man who trusts in You!

Praying Psalm 84

*The descendants of Korah prayerfully express their longing for
God's presence among His people when they worship Him.*

I have found my joy and my rest in You, the Lord of hosts. You are my King and my
God. Praise the Lord (vv. 1–4).

O Lord, how I long to be in Your presence (vv. 1–2)!

Father, bless everyone who loves to gather in Your assembly for worship (v. 4).

I am truly blessed in You, O God. You turn even my tears into good things (vv. 5–7).

Continue to give me the joy of joining others in giving You praise (vv. 5–7).

You are our Source of life, our protection, and the Giver of every good and perfect
gift. How truly satisfied is the one who trusts in You, Father (vv. 8–12).

Lord Jesus, keep me from "the tents of wickedness" (v. 10).

Above all else, Lord, teach me to trust You completely (v. 12).

How Jesus could be interceding for you: Living Father, increase Your children's
desire for Our fellowship (Matt. 5:8; 1 John 1:6–9) and for dwelling in Our presence
(John 14:1–3; 17:24; 2 Cor. 5:8). Pour out all spiritual blessings upon those who trust
You (Eph. 1:3–4).

Psalm 85

Prayer for God's Mercy upon the Nation.

For the choir director. A Psalm of the sons of Korah.

1   O Lord, You showed favor to Your land;
    You restored the captivity of Jacob.
2   You forgave the iniquity of Your people;
    You covered all their sin.   *Selah.*
3   You withdrew all Your fury;
    You turned away from Your burning anger.

4   Restore us, O God of our salvation,
    And cause Your indignation toward us to cease.
5   Will You be angry with us forever?
    Will You prolong Your anger to all generations?
6   Will You not Yourself revive us again,
    That Your people may rejoice in You?
7   Show us Your lovingkindness, O Lord,
    And grant us Your salvation.

8   I will hear what God the Lord will say;
    For He will speak peace to His people, to His godly ones;
    But let them not turn back to folly.
9   Surely His salvation is near to those who fear Him,
    That glory may dwell in our land.
10 Lovingkindness and truth have met together;
    Righteousness and peace have kissed each other.
11 Truth springs from the earth,
    And righteousness looks down from heaven.
12 Indeed, the Lord will give what is good,
    And our land will yield its produce.
13 Righteousness will go before Him
    And will make His footsteps into a way.

Praying Psalm 85

This prayer by Korah's descendants praises God for His
loyal love in restoring the joy of their salvation.

Thank You, Father, that You forgive and restore Your people. Open the hearts of the covenant nation to receive Your Messiah, Your love, and their salvation (vv. 1–7).

Lord, thank You for covering my sin and forgiving my iniquity (v. 2).

Father, prevent me from causing You any displeasure (v. 4).

May I always rejoice in You, my God (v. 6).

Show me and my family Your amazing loyal love (v. 7).

Love and truth, righteousness and peace, have come together in Your Son, the Lord Jesus. Praise be to our Savior (vv. 8–13).

Lord Jesus, keep me from turning back to my folly (v. 8).

May all praise be to You, Lord, for salvation filled with Your favor, forgiveness, joy, love, truth, peace, goodness, and righteousness (vv. 9–12).

How Jesus could be interceding for you: Faithful and loving Father, fill the hearts and lives of Your children with the abundance of the fruit of the Spirit (Gal. 5:22–24) in the salvation You provided them through My sacrificial death and My resurrection (Acts 4:9–12).

Psalm 86

A Psalm of Supplication and Trust.

A Prayer of David.

1   Incline Your ear, O Lᴏʀᴅ, *and* answer me;
    For I am afflicted and needy.
2   Preserve my soul, for I am a godly man;
    O You my God, save Your servant who trusts in You.
3   Be gracious to me, O Lord,
    For to You I cry all day long.
4   Make glad the soul of Your servant,
    For to You, O Lord, I lift up my soul.
5   For You, Lord, are good, and ready to forgive,
    And abundant in lovingkindness to all who call upon You.
6   Give ear, O Lᴏʀᴅ, to my prayer;
    And give heed to the voice of my supplications!
7   In the day of my trouble I shall call upon You,
    For You will answer me.
8   There is no one like You among the gods, O Lord,
    Nor are there any works like Yours.
9   All nations whom You have made shall come and worship before You, O Lord,
    And they shall glorify Your name.
10 For You are great and do wondrous deeds;
    You alone are God.
11 Teach me Your way, O Lᴏʀᴅ;
    I will walk in Your truth;
    Unite my heart to fear Your name.
12 I will give thanks to You, O Lord my God, with all my heart,
    And will glorify Your name forever.
13 For Your lovingkindness toward me is great,
    And You have delivered my soul from the depths of Sheol.
14 O God, arrogant men have risen up against me,
    And a band of violent men have sought my life,
    And they have not set You before them.
15 But You, O Lord, are a God merciful and gracious,
    Slow to anger and abundant in lovingkindness and truth.
16 Turn to me, and be gracious to me;
    Oh grant Your strength to Your servant,
    And save the son of Your handmaid.
17 Show me a sign for good,
    That those who hate me may see *it* and be ashamed,
    Because You, O Lᴏʀᴅ, have helped me and comforted me.

Praying Psalm 86

In this second psalm titled "Prayer of David"
(cf. Ps. 17), David prays for help and guidance.

Indeed, there is no one like You, Lord. You never forsake those who trust in You. You hear our cry. You are good, ready to forgive, and full of love. There is no one like You (vv. 1–10).

God, I am totally dependent upon You (v. 1).

You alone are my God—I trust in You and only You (v. 2).

Father, You are good, forgiving, and faithful to me (v. 5).

Lord, please give me an undivided heart that fears You always. Your love and salvation are my life (vv. 11–13).

Lord Jesus, teach me how to walk in Your ways (v. 11).

Give me an undivided heart of faith and allegiance to You (v. 11).

Again, Lord Jesus, I am reminded of the injustice and arrogance You suffered in the incarnation. The Father saved, helped, and comforted You. I am Yours. I too am saved, helped, and comforted (vv. 14–17).

Gracious and merciful Father, give me strength to be Your servant (v. 16).

How Jesus could be interceding for you: In the time of My distress, I called upon You and You answered, Father (Matt. 26:33–36; Luke 12:50; Heb. 5:7). Pour out Your abundant grace upon Your children (Rom. 5:17; 2 Cor. 9:8) and strengthen them so they might serve You faithfully (Rom. 16:25–27; Eph. 3:14–16; 1 Pet. 4:11).

Psalm 87

The Privileges of Citizenship in Zion.

A Psalm of the sons of Korah. A Song.

1   His foundation is in the holy mountains.
2   The Lord loves the gates of Zion
      More than all the *other* dwelling places of Jacob.
3   Glorious things are spoken of you,
      O city of God.   *Selah.*
4   "I shall mention Rahab and Babylon among those who know Me;
      Behold, Philistia and Tyre with Ethiopia:
      'This one was born there.' "
5   But of Zion it shall be said, "This one and that one were born in her";
      And the Most High Himself will establish her.
6   The Lord will count when He registers the peoples,
      "This one was born there."   *Selah.*
7   Then those who sing as well as those who play the flutes *shall say,*
      "All my springs *of joy* are in you."

Praying Psalm 87

Having experienced amazing grace, the descendants of Korah offer praise to the Lord Who gives new birth and an abundance of joy even to Gentiles.

God of Israel, come and reign in Zion. Let the nations know and see Your glory, Lord Jesus. The city that refused to be gathered to You will one day be exalted in Your grace (vv. 1–7).

Bring peace to Jerusalem, Almighty and gracious God (v. 2; 122:6)!

Praise the Lord for all who know Him in many nations (v. 4).

Father, help people understand that spiritual birth is the truly important issue (vv. 4–6).

May I always find my greatest joy in You, Lord Jesus (v. 7).

How Jesus could be interceding for you: Just as this prayer of praise indicates, Father, You sent Me to gather sheep outside the fold of Israel and You love Me because I laid down My life for them also (John 10:16–17). Gather all Your sheep to Mount Zion by means of their new birth (John 3:5–7) accomplished through My sacrifice (Heb. 12:22–24).

Psalm 88

A Petition to Be Saved from Death.

A Song. A Psalm of the sons of Korah. For the choir director; according to Mahalath Leannoth. A Maskil of Heman the Ezrahite.

1 O LORD, the God of my salvation,
I have cried out by day and in the night before You.
2 Let my prayer come before You;
Incline Your ear to my cry!
3 For my soul has had enough troubles,
And my life has drawn near to Sheol.
4 I am reckoned among those who go down to the pit;
I have become like a man without strength,
5 Forsaken among the dead,
Like the slain who lie in the grave,
Whom You remember no more,
And they are cut off from Your hand.
6 You have put me in the lowest pit,
In dark places, in the depths.
7 Your wrath has rested upon me,
And You have afflicted me with all Your waves.   *Selah.*
8 You have removed my acquaintances far from me;
You have made me an object of loathing to them;
I am shut up and cannot go out.
9 My eye has wasted away because of affliction;
I have called upon You every day, O LORD;
I have spread out my hands to You.
10 Will You perform wonders for the dead?
Will the departed spirits rise *and* praise You?   *Selah.*
11 Will Your lovingkindness be declared in the grave,
Your faithfulness in Abaddon?
12 Will Your wonders be made known in the darkness?
And Your righteousness in the land of forgetfulness?
13 But I, O LORD, have cried out to You for help,
And in the morning my prayer comes before You.
14 O LORD, why do You reject my soul?
Why do You hide Your face from me?

Praying Psalm 88

Heman lays before the Lord his despair in the midst of his suffering.

Hear I am again, Lord. I'm weak. I feel like I'm dying. I'm rejected by people. I need You. Hear me, Lord (vv. 1–9).

How I praise You, Lord, for being the God of my salvation (v. 1).

Father, when everyone forsakes me, hear my prayer (vv. 5, 8, 18).

How I thank You, O God, that I am no longer a child of Your wrath (vv. 7, 16)!

If I die, will it bring You glory? I'm crying out. Please hear. Have You rejected me (vv. 10–18)?

Lord Jesus, allow me to praise you in life and in death (vv. 10–12).

Lord Jesus, for me You were forsaken. You experienced abandonment by men and felt the fury of the Father. Thank You for taking my place. I want to live for You, no matter what I feel (vv. 13–18).

15   I was afflicted and about to die from my youth on;
      I suffer Your terrors; I am overcome.
16   Your burning anger has passed over me;
      Your terrors have destroyed me.
17   They have surrounded me like water all day long;
      They have encompassed me altogether.
18   You have removed lover and friend far from me;
      My acquaintances are *in* darkness.

Father, teach me that the greatest terror would be to suffer as an unbeliever, separated from You and subject to Your full wrath (vv. 15–16).

In the dark hopelessness of Heman's prayer, O God, remind me of the Light of the world and the joy I experience in Him (v. 18; John 8:12).

How Jesus could be interceding for you: Let My intercession come before You, Father, on behalf of this troubled soul who cries out to You in his/her despair (Rom. 8:34). I went down into the pit, to the grave, for them (John 19:41–42; Rom. 10:7) and I defeated death and the grave that Your children might enjoy Your help and hope (1 Cor. 15:54–57).

Psalm 89

The Lord's Covenant with David, and Israel's Afflictions.

A Maskil of Ethan the Ezrahite.

1 I will sing of the lovingkindness of the Lord forever;
To all generations I will make known Your faithfulness with my mouth.
2 For I have said, "Lovingkindness will be built up forever;
In the heavens You will establish Your faithfulness."
3 "I have made a covenant with My chosen;
I have sworn to David My servant,
4 I will establish your seed forever
And build up your throne to all generations."   *Selah.*

5 The heavens will praise Your wonders, O Lord;
Your faithfulness also in the assembly of the holy ones.
6 For who in the skies is comparable to the Lord?
Who among the sons of the mighty is like the Lord,
7 A God greatly feared in the council of the holy ones,
And awesome above all those who are around Him?
8 O Lord God of hosts, who is like You, O mighty Lord?
Your faithfulness also surrounds You.
9 You rule the swelling of the sea;
When its waves rise, You still them.
10 You Yourself crushed Rahab like one who is slain;
You scattered Your enemies with Your mighty arm.
11 The heavens are Yours, the earth also is Yours;
The world and all it contains, You have founded them.
12 The north and the south, You have created them;
Tabor and Hermon shout for joy at Your name.
13 You have a strong arm;
Your hand is mighty, Your right hand is exalted.
14 Righteousness and justice are the foundation of Your throne;
Lovingkindness and truth go before You.
15 How blessed are the people who know the joyful sound!
O Lord, they walk in the light of Your countenance.
16 In Your name they rejoice all the day,
And by Your righteousness they are exalted.

Praying Psalm 89

At the close of Book Three, Ethan prays that God might fulfill His promises to David before the psalmist's death.

Kindle a song in my heart, Father, to sing of Your love and faithfulness forever. The Son of David is Lord—now and forever (vv. 1–4).

Lord, You have always been faithful to me, just as You have been faithful to David (v. 1).

There is no one like You—mighty in strength. No angel or even all the hosts of angels can compare to You (vv. 5–8).

O God, no one is like You in heaven and earth—let me seek no other (v. 6).

You are the great Sovereign, the Creator, the Almighty, the Savior, and the Refuge of Your people (vv. 9–18).

Thank You, O Triune God, for blessing me with Your presence (v. 15).

17 For You are the glory of their strength,
   And by Your favor our horn is exalted.
18 For our shield belongs to the LORD,
   And our king to the Holy One of Israel.
19 Once You spoke in vision to Your godly ones,
   And said, "I have given help to one who is mighty;
   I have exalted one chosen from the people.
20 "I have found David My servant;
   With My holy oil I have anointed him,
21 With whom My hand will be established;
   My arm also will strengthen him.
22 "The enemy will not deceive him,
   Nor the son of wickedness afflict him.
23 "But I shall crush his adversaries before him,
   And strike those who hate him.
24 "My faithfulness and My lovingkindness will be with him,
   And in My name his horn will be exalted.
25 "I shall also set his hand on the sea
   And his right hand on the rivers.
26 "He will cry to Me, 'You are my Father,
   My God, and the rock of my salvation.'
27 "I also shall make him *My* firstborn,
   The highest of the kings of the earth.
28 "My lovingkindness I will keep for him forever,
   And My covenant shall be confirmed to him.
29 "So I will establish his descendants forever
   And his throne as the days of heaven.

30 "If his sons forsake My law
   And do not walk in My judgments,
31 If they violate My statutes
   And do not keep My commandments,
32 Then I will punish their transgression with the rod
   And their iniquity with stripes.
33 "But I will not break off My lovingkindness from him,
   Nor deal falsely in My faithfulness.
34 "My covenant I will not violate,
   Nor will I alter the utterance of My lips.
35 "Once I have sworn by My holiness;
   I will not lie to David.

Exalted is the Lord! Father, You have chosen David's Seed, the Lord Jesus Christ. He is the Firstborn. He is King. Praise be to the Lord Jesus Christ, Son of David, Son of God (vv. 19–29).

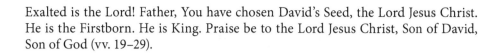

Thank You, Father, that Your covenant with David cannot be broken (vv. 20–37).

Fill my mind and heart with the theme of this psalm: Your faithfulness and steadfast love. In times of doubt, distress, and difficulty, cause me to remember You are always present and You never fail to fulfill Your promises (vv. 24, 33).

How good and gracious You are, Lord, to patiently repeat Your promises to one of little faith (vv. 28–33; 2 Sam. 7:11–16).

36 "His descendants shall endure forever
    And his throne as the sun before Me.
37 "It shall be established forever like the moon,
    And the witness in the sky is faithful."   *Selah.*
38 But You have cast off and rejected,
    You have been full of wrath against Your anointed.
39 You have spurned the covenant of Your servant;
    You have profaned his crown in the dust.
40 You have broken down all his walls;
    You have brought his strongholds to ruin.
41 All who pass along the way plunder him;
    He has become a reproach to his neighbors.
42 You have exalted the right hand of his adversaries;
    You have made all his enemies rejoice.
43 You also turn back the edge of his sword
    And have not made him stand in battle.
44 You have made his splendor to cease
    And cast his throne to the ground.
45 You have shortened the days of his youth;
    You have covered him with shame.   *Selah.*
46 How long, O LORD?
    Will You hide Yourself forever?
    Will Your wrath burn like fire?
47 Remember what my span of life is;
    For what vanity You have created all the sons of men!
48 What man can live and not see death?
    Can he deliver his soul from the power of Sheol?   *Selah.*
49 Where are Your former lovingkindnesses, O Lord,
    Which You swore to David in Your faithfulness?
50 Remember, O Lord, the reproach of Your servants;
    How I bear in my bosom *the reproach of* all the many peoples,
51 With which Your enemies have reproached, O LORD,
    With which they have reproached the footsteps of Your anointed.
52 Blessed be the LORD forever!
    Amen and Amen.

Remind me, dear Savior, to look at the sun and moon above and to know that as long as they exist, You are accomplishing Your plan of Kingdom and redemption in this world (vv. 36–37).

The descendants of David went into exile and no king in Israel has ruled since. Thank You for opening my eyes to see that Jesus is Son of David and He will fulfill Your promises. But how long, Lord? How long before He comes in His Kingdom glory? Don't let the enemy exalt over Your people (vv. 38–51).

O Lord God, teach me to praise You for Your perfect timing, rather than to complain about Your delays (v. 47).

Father, consider the brevity of my life and let me experience Your blessings now (v. 49).

Blessed be Yahweh forever! Amen and amen (v. 52).

How Jesus could be interceding for you: Faithful Father, I am the anointed King (Ps. 2:7; Luke 1:31–33), the greater Son of David (2 Sam. 7:11–16; Rev. 5:5). Heman did not see the fulfillment of Your promise before he died, and Your children still pray for Your Kingdom to come (Matt. 6:10). Preserve their hope for that Kingdom (Matt. 6:33; 2 Tim. 4:18; Jas. 2:5) until the time comes when You send Me back to establish the Kingdom (Matt. 26:29; Luke 19:15; Rev. 11:15).

Book 4

Psalm 90

God's Eternity and Man's Transitoriness.

A Prayer of Moses, the man of God.

1   Lord, You have been our dwelling place in all generations.
2   Before the mountains were born
Or You gave birth to the earth and the world,
Even from everlasting to everlasting, You are God.

3   You turn man back into dust
And say, "Return, O children of men."
4   For a thousand years in Your sight
Are like yesterday when it passes by,
Or *as* a watch in the night.
5   You have swept them away like a flood, they fall asleep;
In the morning they are like grass which sprouts anew.
6   In the morning it flourishes and sprouts anew;
Toward evening it fades and withers away.

7   For we have been consumed by Your anger
And by Your wrath we have been dismayed.
8   You have placed our iniquities before You,
Our secret *sins* in the light of Your presence.
9   For all our days have declined in Your fury;
We have finished our years like a sigh.
10   As for the days of our life, they contain seventy years,
Or if due to strength, eighty years,
Yet their pride is *but* labor and sorrow;
For soon it is gone and we fly away.
11   Who understands the power of Your anger
And Your fury, according to the fear that is due You?
12   So teach us to number our days,
That we may present to You a heart of wisdom.

Praying Psalm 90

Book Four opens with the oldest psalm of the Psalter with Moses praying for God to grant comfort for experiencing the brevity of life and the death of loved ones—a message of hope after the despair expressed in Ps. 89:46–51.

Everlasting Father, You are the Source of life for every generation that has ever lived. You remain, but generation after generation of mankind returns to dust. Thank You for reminding me of the brevity of this life and the need for a relationship with the One Who is eternal life (vv. 1–6).

Thank You for being my dwelling place, my place of refuge now and forever (v. 1).

Lord, teach me to use whatever time You have allotted for me on this earth for Your glory and not for things that anger and grieve You (vv. 7–12).

Lord Jesus, thank You for delivering me from God's wrath for my sins (vv. 7–8).

Father, teach me how to redeem the time You grant me to live in this world. Give me wisdom to live according to Your Word and Your will in this brief life (vv. 9–12).

13　Do return, O LORD; how long *will it be?*
　　And be sorry for Your servants.
14　O satisfy us in the morning with Your lovingkindness,
　　That we may sing for joy and be glad all our days.
15　Make us glad according to the days You have afflicted us,
　　And the years we have seen evil.
16　Let Your work appear to Your servants
　　And Your majesty to their children.
17　Let the favor of the Lord our God be upon us;
　　And confirm for us the work of our hands;
　　Yes, confirm the work of our hands.

Have mercy on those who are afflicted. Spirit of the eternal God, fill us with joy. Show us Your love. Rain down Your favor upon Your people, Lord (vv. 13–17).

Father, satisfy me with Your steadfast, loyal love (v. 14).

O God, make me glad even in the midst of life's afflictions (v. 15).

Establish the work of my hands to Your glory, Lord (v. 17).

How Jesus could be interceding for you: I bore Your righteous wrath to provide salvation from sin for Your people, dear Father (Matt. 1:21; John 3:36). Give to Your people comfort and hope as they learn the brevity of life and experience the deaths of their loved ones and friends (Matt. 5:4).

Psalm 91

Security of the One Who Trusts in the Lord.

1 He who dwells in the shelter of the Most High
   Will abide in the shadow of the Almighty.
2 I will say to the Lord, "My refuge and my fortress,
   My God, in whom I trust!"
3 For it is He who delivers you from the snare of the trapper
   And from the deadly pestilence.
4 He will cover you with His pinions,
   And under His wings you may seek refuge;
   His faithfulness is a shield and bulwark.

5 You will not be afraid of the terror by night,
   Or of the arrow that flies by day;
6 Of the pestilence that stalks in darkness,
   Or of the destruction that lays waste at noon.
7 A thousand may fall at your side
   And ten thousand at your right hand,
   But it shall not approach you.
8 You will only look on with your eyes
   And see the recompense of the wicked.
9 For you have made the Lord, my refuge,
   Even the Most High, your dwelling place.
10 No evil will befall you,
   Nor will any plague come near your tent.
11 For He will give His angels charge concerning you,
   To guard you in all your ways.
12 They will bear you up in their hands,
   That you do not strike your foot against a stone.
13 You will tread upon the lion and cobra,
   The young lion and the serpent you will trample down.

14 "Because he has loved Me, therefore I will deliver him;
   I will set him *securely* on high, because he has known My name.
15 "He will call upon Me, and I will answer him;
   I will be with him in trouble;
   I will rescue him and honor him.
16 "With a long life I will satisfy him
   And let him see My salvation."

Praying Psalm 91

An anonymous believer speaks to God about trusting Him for refuge and protection.

Your throne, O God, is a throne of protection as well as grace. Thank you for Your powerful, protecting grace (vv. 1–4).

Thank You, Lord, that no evil can ultimately overtake those upon whom You have set Your love. Though now for a little while Your children are distressed and persecuted, keep our hearts set on Your coming Kingdom (vv. 5–10).

Father, remove my fear of circumstances and problems (v. 5).

Lord Jesus, thank You for overcoming the evil one as he tempted You in the desert with this psalm. You trusted Your Father, therefore You will crush the head of the serpent. I trust in You, so I too will have victory and see the salvation of Yahweh (vv. 11–16).

Thank You, Lord, for protecting me with Your angels when it is necessary (v. 11).

Give me a consuming passion for You, O God, in Whom I trust (v. 14).

How Jesus could be interceding for you: Yes, sovereign Father, this prayer became My prayer in the wilderness, even while Satan tried to use it to tempt Me (Matt. 4:5–7). Now, teach Your children to trust You completely for their deliverance and satisfaction (Luke 12:27–31).

Psalm 92

Praise for the Lord's Goodness.

A Psalm, a Song for the Sabbath day.

1 It is good to give thanks to the Lord
And to sing praises to Your name, O Most High;
2 To declare Your lovingkindness in the morning
And Your faithfulness by night,
3 With the ten-stringed lute and with the harp,
With resounding music upon the lyre.
4 For You, O Lord, have made me glad by what You have done,
I will sing for joy at the works of Your hands.

5 How great are Your works, O Lord!
Your thoughts are very deep.
6 A senseless man has no knowledge,
Nor does a stupid man understand this:
7 That when the wicked sprouted up like grass
And all who did iniquity flourished,
It *was only* that they might be destroyed forevermore.
8 But You, O Lord, are on high forever.
9 For, behold, Your enemies, O Lord,
For, behold, Your enemies will perish;
All who do iniquity will be scattered.
10 But You have exalted my horn like *that of* the wild ox;
I have been anointed with fresh oil.
11 And my eye has looked *exultantly* upon my foes,
My ears hear of the evildoers who rise up against me.
12 The righteous man will flourish like the palm tree,
He will grow like a cedar in Lebanon.
13 Planted in the house of the Lord,
They will flourish in the courts of our God.
14 They will still yield fruit in old age;
They shall be full of sap and very green,
15 To declare that the Lord is upright;
He is my rock, and there is no unrighteousness in Him.

Praying Psalm 92

In the post-exilic Temple this prayer was assigned for the morning worship on each Sabbath (Saturday).

How I praise You, Father, for the gift of song and music. You are worthy to be praised with gladness (vv. 1–4).

How I praise You, Father, for the gift of song and music. You are worthy to be praised with gladness (vv. 1–4).

Lord, thank You for being steadfastly loving and faithful to me (vv. 1–2).

I shout for joy because of all You have done for me, my Lord and Savior (v. 4).

Thank You, Jesus, that You too had to deal with the seeming prosperity of the wicked. You too learned to see their future based on Your Father's promises. Teach me to live in faith and hope—trusting in Your righteousness, O God (vv. 5–15).

Lord, keep me from being insensitive and dull about spiritual things (v. 6).

Father, grant me the privilege of serving You even in my old age (v. 14).

How Jesus could be interceding for you: Exalted Father, thanking You was My joy on earth (Matt. 11:25; Luke 10:21; John 11:41). You have given Me the authority to judge (John 5:22–23) and to make Your people's enemies My footstool (Acts 2:33–36). Cause the righteous to flourish in Your service (Matt. 13:23; John 15:1–5).

Psalm 93

The Majesty of the LORD.

1   The LORD reigns, He is clothed with majesty;
     The LORD has clothed and girded Himself with strength;
     Indeed, the world is firmly established, it will not be moved.
2   Your throne is established from of old;
     You are from everlasting.

3   The floods have lifted up, O LORD,
     The floods have lifted up their voice,
     The floods lift up their pounding waves.
4   More than the sounds of many waters,
     Than the mighty breakers of the sea,
     The LORD on high is mighty.
5   Your testimonies are fully confirmed;
     Holiness befits Your house,
     O LORD, forevermore.

Praying Psalm 93

*In the post-exilic Temple, this prayer of praise was assigned
for the morning worship on each Friday.*

Yours is the Kingdom, and the power and the glory, Lord. You reign in majesty. Reveal that majesty to this dark world (vv. 1–2).

Almighty Lord of creation, You are in control of all things (v. 1).

The roaring waters of Victoria Falls or the incessant pounding of the waves of the sea are but small echoes of Your power and might. Your Word witnesses to Your unique grandeur, power, and holiness—thank You for Your testimonies. As they come from You, they are my life (vv. 3–5).

Father, I thank You that Your Word is dependable and trustworthy (v. 5).

How Jesus could be interceding for you: Glorious and majestic Father, You have clothed Me with majesty, authority, and power to reign over Your Kingdom (Matt. 28:18; Luke 9:43; 2 Pet. 1:16). Fulfill My words and confirm their truth and power to Your servants (Matt. 7:24; 24:35; John 8:31–32; 15:7).

Psalm 94

The Lord Implored to Avenge His People.

1   O Lord, God of vengeance,
    God of vengeance, shine forth!
2   Rise up, O Judge of the earth,
    Render recompense to the proud.
3   How long shall the wicked, O Lord,
    How long shall the wicked exult?
4   They pour forth *words,* they speak arrogantly;
    All who do wickedness vaunt themselves.
5   They crush Your people, O Lord,
    And afflict Your heritage.
6   They slay the widow and the stranger
    And murder the orphans.
7   They have said, "The Lord does not see,
    Nor does the God of Jacob pay heed."

8   Pay heed, you senseless among the people;
    And when will you understand, stupid ones?
9   He who planted the ear, does He not hear?
    He who formed the eye, does He not see?
10 He who chastens the nations, will He not rebuke,
    Even He who teaches man knowledge?
11 The Lord knows the thoughts of man,
    That they are a *mere* breath.
12 Blessed is the man whom You chasten, O Lord,
    And whom You teach out of Your law;
13 That You may grant him relief from the days of adversity,
    Until a pit is dug for the wicked.
14 For the Lord will not abandon His people,
    Nor will He forsake His inheritance.
15 For judgment will again be righteous,
    And all the upright in heart will follow it.
16 Who will stand up for me against evildoers?
    Who will take his stand for me against those who do wickedness?
17 If the Lord had not been my help,
    My soul would soon have dwelt in *the abode of* silence.

Praying Psalm 94

In the post-exilic Temple this prayer of praise was assigned for the morning worship on each Wednesday.

Lord, some of Your people suffer severely for Your name's sake. Vindicate their faith in You. Rise up and judge Your enemies—and ours. Either grant them repentance or repay them for their torture of Your children (vv. 1–11).

Give justice to Your people, Lord God (vv. 1–5).

Thank You, God, for seeing everything that happens to me and to care for me (vv. 7–9).

Lord Jesus, teach me from Your Word (v. 12).

Thank You for never forsaking Your people (v. 14).

Father, teach me to stand up against evil and evildoers (v. 16).

You are the help of Your people—eternal, infinite, Almighty God is our Helper! Your love will uphold us. There is no unrighteousness with You, Lord. We take refuge in You, and You will bring justice to this earth (vv. 17–23).

18 If I should say, "My foot has slipped,"
    Your lovingkindness, O LORD, will hold me up.
19 When my anxious thoughts multiply within me,
    Your consolations delight my soul.
20 Can a throne of destruction be allied with You,
    One which devises mischief by decree?
21 They band themselves together against the life of the righteous
    And condemn the innocent to death.
22 But the LORD has been my stronghold,
    And my God the rock of my refuge.
23 He has brought back their wickedness upon them
    And will destroy them in their evil;
    The LORD our God will destroy them.

Father, teach me to delight in Your comfort when my mind is troubled (v. 19).

Praise God! You stand like a great rock wall to preserve me and to confound the plans of those who would harm me (v. 22).

Righteous Father, bring upon the wicked the destruction You have planned for them and uphold justice by Your highest standards (v. 23).

How Jesus could be interceding for you: Vengeance belongs to You, righteous Father (Rom. 12:19). Bring down the arrogant wicked who persecute Your children and bring the full penalty for their wickedness upon them (1 Cor. 3:16–17; Phil. 3:18–19). Send forth Your justice through Me and give help to Your children (2 Thess. 1:8; Rev. 19:1–2).

Psalm 95

Praise to the Lord, and Warning against Unbelief.

1 O come, let us sing for joy to the Lord,
   Let us shout joyfully to the rock of our salvation.
2 Let us come before His presence with thanksgiving,
   Let us shout joyfully to Him with psalms.
3 For the Lord is a great God
   And a great King above all gods,
4 In whose hand are the depths of the earth,
   The peaks of the mountains are His also.
5 The sea is His, for it was He who made it,
   And His hands formed the dry land.

6 Come, let us worship and bow down,
   Let us kneel before the Lord our Maker.
7 For He is our God,
   And we are the people of His pasture and the sheep of His hand.
   Today, if you would hear His voice,
8 Do not harden your hearts, as at Meribah,
   As in the day of Massah in the wilderness,
9 "When your fathers tested Me,
   They tried Me, though they had seen My work.
10 "For forty years I loathed *that* generation,
   And said they are a people who err in their heart,
   And they do not know My ways.
11 "Therefore I swore in My anger,
   Truly they shall not enter into My rest."

Praying Psalm 95

Traditionally, this prayer begins the evening service on the Sabbath in the synagogue. In the New Testament, this prayer forms the text for the sermon in Hebrews 3:7–4:13.

You are worthy, my King—the great King—of songs of joy and worship. You are our Creator and our Caretaker. I love You. Thank You for loving us (vv. 1–7).

Praise the Lord! He is the rock of my salvation (v. 1).

Lord, You are a great, great God (v. 2)!

Father, I bow down before You, because You are my Maker (v. 6).

Lord Jesus, help me to obey You today (v. 7).

God, help me to learn from the wilderness wanderings of Israel. I rest in Jesus. Help me to hear His voice and follow Him (vv. 8–11).

Teach me Your ways, Lord (v. 10).

How Jesus could be interceding for you: You sent Me as Israel's Rock, gracious Father (Rom. 9:33; 1 Cor. 10:4). May the sheep of Your pasture truly worship their Creator (Col. 1:15–16). Give them an abundant entrance into Your rest (Matt. 11:28–30; Heb. 4:9–10).

Psalm 96

A Call to Worship the Lord the Righteous Judge.

1   Sing to the Lord a new song;
    Sing to the Lord, all the earth.
2   Sing to the Lord, bless His name;
    Proclaim good tidings of His salvation from day to day.
3   Tell of His glory among the nations,
    His wonderful deeds among all the peoples.
4   For great is the Lord and greatly to be praised;
    He is to be feared above all gods.
5   For all the gods of the peoples are idols,
    But the Lord made the heavens.
6   Splendor and majesty are before Him,
    Strength and beauty are in His sanctuary.

7   Ascribe to the Lord, O families of the peoples,
    Ascribe to the Lord glory and strength.
8   Ascribe to the Lord the glory of His name;
    Bring an offering and come into His courts.
9   Worship the Lord in holy attire;
    Tremble before Him, all the earth.
10 Say among the nations, "The Lord reigns;
    Indeed, the world is firmly established, it will not be moved;
    He will judge the peoples with equity."
11 Let the heavens be glad, and let the earth rejoice;
    Let the sea roar, and all it contains;
12 Let the field exult, and all that is in it.
    Then all the trees of the forest will sing for joy
13 Before the Lord, for He is coming,
    For He is coming to judge the earth.
    He will judge the world in righteousness
    And the peoples in His faithfulness.

Praying Psalm 96

An anonymous prayer ascribes all praise, honor, and glory to Almighty God as King.

Living God, Savior of the world, You are worthy of every tongue singing Your praises (vv. 1–2).

I praise You, O Lord, because You saved me (vv. 1–2).

You are great and I give You all my praise, dear Lord (v. 4).

Forgive me, Father, that my spiritual senses are still tainted and dulled, so that I struggle to grasp the significance of words like splendor, majesty, and beauty as they describe You (v. 6).

O Lord Jesus, I ask that all people might praise You (v. 7).

Teach me to tremble now as I see You with eyes of faith, anticipating the day when all the earth will tremble before You at Your appearing, Lord Jesus (v. 9).

Set Your creation free of its bondage, O God (vv. 11–12).

Lord hasten the day when the phrase "He is coming" will be changed to "He has come" (v. 13).

How Jesus could be interceding for you: Father, Your children pray for Your Kingdom to come and Your will to be done on earth as it is in heaven (Matt. 6:10). Bring it to pass so Your praise and glory might be multiplied through My reign as Your King (Matt. 25:31; Luke 10:37–40; Phil. 2:9–11; Rev. 5:13).

Psalm 97

The LORD's Power and Dominion.

1   The LORD reigns, let the earth rejoice;
    Let the many islands be glad.
2   Clouds and thick darkness surround Him;
    Righteousness and justice are the foundation of His throne.
3   Fire goes before Him
    And burns up His adversaries round about.
4   His lightnings lit up the world;
    The earth saw and trembled.
5   The mountains melted like wax at the presence of the LORD,
    At the presence of the Lord of the whole earth.
6   The heavens declare His righteousness,
    And all the peoples have seen His glory.

7   Let all those be ashamed who serve graven images,
    Who boast themselves of idols;
    Worship Him, all you gods.
8   Zion heard *this* and was glad,
    And the daughters of Judah have rejoiced
    Because of Your judgments, O LORD.
9   For You are the LORD Most High over all the earth;
    You are exalted far above all gods.
10 Hate evil, you who love the LORD,
    Who preserves the souls of His godly ones;
    He delivers them from the hand of the wicked.
11 Light is sown *like seed* for the righteous
    And gladness for the upright in heart.
12 Be glad in the LORD, you righteous ones,
    And give thanks to His holy name.

Praying Psalm 97

The gathering crescendo of praise-filled prayers continues with this focus on God's righteousness.

What an awesome and terrifyingly glorious day it will be, Lord, when You come back in the clouds to reign. What a privilege it is that You are my King, my God, and my Savior. Thank You for having mercy on me (vv. 1–6).

Lord Jesus, prepare me for Your return (vv. 1–6).

Father, use me to take Your Word to those who do not believe (v. 7).

I do hate evil, but not as much as I should. Help me hate it more—especially the sin in me. I love You, Lord. Thank You for the joy of praising You (vv. 10–12).

Thank You, Father, for providing light and joy for me (vv. 11–12).

How Jesus could be interceding for you: O righteous and holy Father, increase the praise and rejoicing of Your people as they await My return to establish the Kingdom (Luke 19:11–15; 2 Tim. 4:18; Rev. 22:20). Cause many to abandon the idols of their hearts and to love You (1 Thess. 1:9–10). Establish joy for those waiting for my imminent return (John 16:22; 1 Pet. 4:13).

Psalm 98

A Call to Praise the Lord for His Righteousness.

A Psalm.

1   O sing to the Lord a new song,
    For He has done wonderful things,
    His right hand and His holy arm have gained the victory for Him.
2   The Lord has made known His salvation;
    He has revealed His righteousness in the sight of the nations.
3   He has remembered His lovingkindness and His faithfulness to the house
        of Israel;
    All the ends of the earth have seen the salvation of our God.

4   Shout joyfully to the Lord, all the earth;
    Break forth and sing for joy and sing praises.
5   Sing praises to the Lord with the lyre,
    With the lyre and the sound of melody.
6   With trumpets and the sound of the horn
    Shout joyfully before the King, the Lord.

7   Let the sea roar and all it contains,
    The world and those who dwell in it.
8   Let the rivers clap their hands,
    Let the mountains sing together for joy
9   Before the Lord, for He is coming to judge the earth;
    He will judge the world with righteousness
    And the peoples with equity.

Praying Psalm 98

*This anonymous prayer of joyful praise provided the catalyst
for the Christmas carol "Joy to the World."*

Your people long for this great day, Lord. Restore Israel in faith and let all the nations see Your salvation, O Lord Jesus (vv. 1–3).

I praise You for Your wonderful works, O God (v. 1).

Father, thank You for allowing me to see Your faithfulness to Israel (v. 3).

Every tongue will sing to You, Lord Messiah. All creation will be set free from its futility and praise You. Come and judge the world with perfect justice. Come, Lord (vv. 4–9).

My Lord and God, thank You for wonderful music with which to praise You (vv. 4–6).

Come quickly, Lord Jesus (v. 9; Rev. 22:20)!

How Jesus could be interceding for you: Glorious Father, fill Your children's hearts with joy-filled praise for their salvation (Luke 2:10–11; 1 Pet. 1:8–9) and for My imminent return to reign as King (Luke 1:31–33; 1 Tim. 6:13–16) to judge the world with righteousness (Acts 17:31; 2 Tim. 4:8).

Psalm 99

Praise to the Lord for His Fidelity to Israel.

1   The Lord reigns, let the peoples tremble;
    He is enthroned *above* the cherubim, let the earth shake!
2   The Lord is great in Zion,
    And He is exalted above all the peoples.
3   Let them praise Your great and awesome name;
    Holy is He.
4   The strength of the King loves justice;
    You have established equity;
    You have executed justice and righteousness in Jacob.
5   Exalt the Lord our God
    And worship at His footstool;
    Holy is He.

6   Moses and Aaron were among His priests,
    And Samuel was among those who called on His name;
    They called upon the Lord and He answered them.
7   He spoke to them in the pillar of cloud;
    They kept His testimonies
    And the statute that He gave them.
8   O Lord our God, You answered them;
    You were a forgiving God to them,
    And *yet* an avenger of their *evil* deeds.
9   Exalt the Lord our God
    And worship at His holy hill,
    For holy is the Lord our God.

Praying Psalm 99

Another anonymous believer offers a prayer of praise to God for His holiness.

Living Lord, You are holy—unique and perfect, without any defect of character. Loving justice and establishing righteousness, may Your Spirit enlighten the eyes of the hearts of Your people to see Your glory in the Person of Your Son. You are worthy of our worship. You are holy (vv. 1–5).

You are holy, O Lord, therefore I praise You (v. 3).

Enable me to worship You without reservation, Father (v. 5).

Moses, Aaron, and Samuel were sinners saved by grace. You accepted their worship, Lord. You forgave their sin. Receive my worship, Father. Be exalted, O God. You are holy (vv. 6–9).

Dear Jesus, teach me to pray like Moses, Aaron, and Samuel (v. 6).

Thank You, Lord, for forgiving my sins (v. 8).

How Jesus could be interceding for you: Holy Father (John 17:11), fill Your people with a full awareness of Your holiness so that they turn away from their sins and run to You for forgiveness (John 17:17; 1 Pet. 3:15; Rev. 4:8). Forgive this sinner on the basis of My finished work of redemption (1 Cor. 1:30; Heb. 10:10).

Psalm 100

All Men Exhorted to Praise God.

A Psalm for Thanksgiving.

1   Shout joyfully to the Lᴏʀᴅ, all the earth.
2   Serve the Lᴏʀᴅ with gladness;
     Come before Him with joyful singing.
3   Know that the Lᴏʀᴅ Himself is God;
     It is He who has made us, and not we ourselves;
     We are His people and the sheep of His pasture.

4   Enter His gates with thanksgiving
     And His courts with praise.
     Give thanks to Him, bless His name.
5   For the Lᴏʀᴅ is good;
     His lovingkindness is everlasting
     And His faithfulness to all generations.

Praying Psalm 100

An unknown believer prays with thanksgiving while entering the place of worship.

Your sheep hear Your voice, Lord Jesus. May our voices shout joyfully to You—especially in the day Your Kingdom comes to earth. People of every language will give You the honor You are due (vv. 1–4).

⋘⋘

Help me serve and worship You with gladness, Lord (v. 2).

⋘⋘

Thank You, Father, for all You have done and are doing for me (v. 4).

⋘⋘

It's true. You are good; Your love is for forever, and Your faithfulness never ends (v. 5).

How Jesus could be interceding for you: You are worthy of all worship and service, dear Father (Matt. 4:10). Here is one of Your sheep bringing You their offering of thanksgiving (Eph. 5:18–21; Col. 2:6–7). Accept this offering and bless this dear saint (Rom. 12:1; Phil. 4:18–20; Heb. 12:28).

Psalm 101

The Psalmist's Profession of Uprightness.

A Psalm of David.

1   I will sing of lovingkindness and justice,
To You, O LORD, I will sing praises.
2   I will give heed to the blameless way.
When will You come to me?
I will walk within my house in the integrity of my heart.
3   I will set no worthless thing before my eyes;
I hate the work of those who fall away;
It shall not fasten its grip on me.
4   A perverse heart shall depart from me;
I will know no evil.
5   Whoever secretly slanders his neighbor, him I will destroy;
No one who has a haughty look and an arrogant heart will I endure.

6   My eyes shall be upon the faithful of the land, that they may dwell with me;
He who walks in a blameless way is the one who will minister to me.
7   He who practices deceit shall not dwell within my house;
He who speaks falsehood shall not maintain his position before me.
8   Every morning I will destroy all the wicked of the land,
So as to cut off from the city of the LORD all those who do iniquity.

Praying Psalm 101

*David praises God in this prayer as he commits himself to live
with righteousness on his throne and in his home.*

O just and loving God, let me sing Your praises (v. 1).

When I think of the words "love" and "justice," I think of You, Lord Jesus—and Your cross. At Your cross justice was accomplished and love to sinners poured out. Praise Your name (v. 1).

Father, teach me to hate sin and depart from it. Teach me to love humility, truth, and integrity (vv. 2–8).

Lord Jesus, thank You that You lived these things perfectly and are my righteous Defender and righteous Defense (vv. 2–8).

Fill me with the ability to live blamelessly for You in my home, Lord (v. 2).

Father, help me control my eyes and choose carefully what I watch (v. 3).

Lord Jesus, keep me from slander and arrogance, deceit and lying (vv. 5, 7).

How Jesus could be interceding for you: Father, here is a sheep of Your pasture who desires to serve you blamelessly in private and in public (Eph. 1:4; Phil. 2:15–16; Jude 24–25). Lead them to faithfully assemble with other like-minded believers who will pray for them and encourage living a godly life (Heb. 10:24–25).

Psalm 102

Prayer of an Afflicted Man for Mercy on Himself and on Zion.

A Prayer of the Afflicted when he is faint and pours out
his complaint before the LORD.

1   Hear my prayer, O LORD!
    And let my cry for help come to You.
2   Do not hide Your face from me in the day of my distress;
    Incline Your ear to me;
    In the day when I call answer me quickly.
3   For my days have been consumed in smoke,
    And my bones have been scorched like a hearth.
4   My heart has been smitten like grass and has withered away,
    Indeed, I forget to eat my bread.
5   Because of the loudness of my groaning
    My bones cling to my flesh.
6   I resemble a pelican of the wilderness;
    I have become like an owl of the waste places.
7   I lie awake,
    I have become like a lonely bird on a housetop.

8   My enemies have reproached me all day long;
    Those who deride me have used my *name* as a curse.
9   For I have eaten ashes like bread
    And mingled my drink with weeping
10   Because of Your indignation and Your wrath,
    For You have lifted me up and cast me away.
11   My days are like a lengthened shadow,
    And I wither away like grass.
12   But You, O LORD, abide forever,
    And Your name to all generations.
13   You will arise *and* have compassion on Zion;
    For it is time to be gracious to her,
    For the appointed time has come.
14   Surely Your servants find pleasure in her stones
    And feel pity for her dust.
15   So the nations will fear the name of the LORD
    And all the kings of the earth Your glory.

Praying Psalm 102

A person afflicted with illness and anxiety prays for relief and comfort.

As I await Your return, Lord, I too am sometimes filled with grief and an over-whelming sense of oppression in this world. Hear my prayer and do not hide Your face in the day of my distress (vv. 1–11).

When I am sick, Father, please hear my prayer and relieve me from the illness (vv. 1–5).

As I lie awake at night, filled with anxiety for my problems, help me to focus on You, Lord (v. 7).

O God, I feel abandoned, forgotten, and uncomforted. My tears mix with what little food I can stomach. My days stretch to the sunset of my life as I wither away. Focus my attention and You the way the writer of this psalm does (vv. 8–11).

Throughout the years, Father, You heard the prayers of Your suffering people in every circumstance. You will fulfill Your covenant promises because You abide for-ever and Your character does not change (vv. 12–17).

Lord, bring the nations and their leaders to You (v. 15).

16　For the LORD has built up Zion;
　　He has appeared in His glory.
17　He has regarded the prayer of the destitute
　　And has not despised their prayer.
18　This will be written for the generation to come,
　　That a people yet to be created may praise the LORD.
19　For He looked down from His holy height;
　　From heaven the LORD gazed upon the earth,
20　To hear the groaning of the prisoner,
　　To set free those who were doomed to death,
21　That *men* may tell of the name of the LORD in Zion
　　And His praise in Jerusalem,
22　When the peoples are gathered together,
　　And the kingdoms, to serve the LORD.
23　He has weakened my strength in the way;
　　He has shortened my days.
24　I say, "O my God, do not take me away in the midst of my days,
　　Your years are throughout all generations.
25　"Of old You founded the earth,
　　And the heavens are the work of Your hands.
26　"Even they will perish, but You endure;
　　And all of them will wear out like a garment;
　　Like clothing You will change them and they will be changed.
27　"But You are the same,
　　And Your years will not come to an end.
28　"The children of Your servants will continue,
　　And their descendants will be established before You."

In Your Kingdom, Lord, all peoples will know of Your faithfulness and compassion. Help me to make it known now (vv. 18–22).

❦

Thank You, Spirit of the Living God, for inspiring, preserving, and illuminating the Scriptures (v. 18).

❦

God, thank You for eternal life and the new creation to come. Jesus, Messiah, Savior—You are the everlasting Lord who brings this to pass (vv. 23–28).

❦

I praise you, Lord, because You never change (vv. 26–27).

❦

"Eternal God, help me to feel Your presence when dark shadows fall upon me. When my own weakness and the storms of life hide You from my sight, help me to know that You have not deserted me. Uphold me with the comfort of Your love."—A modern Jewish prayer.

How Jesus could be interceding for you: Loving and merciful Father, Your child calls out to You for help, for relief from illness, pain, and anxiety (Phil. 4:4–7; 2 Cor. 1:3–5). They feel like Job and do not understand why they suffer so (Jas. 5:11). They feel abandoned and forgotten, passing all too quickly through their brief life without their prayers being answered (Matt. 5:3–6). Bring relief, Father, and comfort, as well as the peace of mind and heart that removes anxiety (2 Cor. 7:6; Phil. 4:7).

Psalm 103

Praise for the Lord's Mercies.

A Psalm of David.

1 Bless the Lord, O my soul,
   And all that is within me, *bless* His holy name.
2 Bless the Lord, O my soul,
   And forget none of His benefits;
3 Who pardons all your iniquities,
   Who heals all your diseases;
4 Who redeems your life from the pit,
   Who crowns you with lovingkindness and compassion;
5 Who satisfies your years with good things,
   So that your youth is renewed like the eagle.

6 The Lord performs righteous deeds
   And judgments for all who are oppressed.
7 He made known His ways to Moses,
   His acts to the sons of Israel.
8 The Lord is compassionate and gracious,
   Slow to anger and abounding in lovingkindness.
9 He will not always strive *with us,*
   Nor will He keep *His anger* forever.
10 He has not dealt with us according to our sins,
    Nor rewarded us according to our iniquities.
11 For as high as the heavens are above the earth,
    So great is His lovingkindness toward those who fear Him.
12 As far as the east is from the west,
    So far has He removed our transgressions from us.
13 Just as a father has compassion on *his* children,
    So the Lord has compassion on those who fear Him.
14 For He Himself knows our frame;
    He is mindful that we are *but* dust.
15 As for man, his days are like grass;
    As a flower of the field, so he flourishes.
16 When the wind has passed over it, it is no more,
    And its place acknowledges it no longer.

Praying Psalm 103

David praises the Lord for His many blessings upon those who serve Him.

Thank You, Lord, for the privilege of praising You. It is my highest joy (v. 1)!

Father, help me by Your Spirit to remember all You've done for me (v. 2).

Thank You for the forgiveness of sins and eternal life. I praise You for Your love and compassion, and being the satisfaction of my soul (vv. 3–14).

Lord Jesus, thank You for redeeming me and delivering me from death's power (v. 4).

Teach me, Father, how to count my many blessings because I've been delivered from Your wrath (vv. 9–10).

Lord God, thank You for considering my frailty and being merciful to me (v. 14).

17   But the lovingkindness of the LORD is from everlasting to everlasting on
          those who fear Him,
     And His righteousness to children's children,
18   To those who keep His covenant
     And remember His precepts to do them.
19   The LORD has established His throne in the heavens,
     And His sovereignty rules over all.
20   Bless the LORD, you His angels,
     Mighty in strength, who perform His word,
     Obeying the voice of His word!
21   Bless the LORD, all you His hosts,
     You who serve Him, doing His will.
22   Bless the LORD, all you works of His,
     In all places of His dominion;
     Bless the LORD, O my soul!

Enable me to pass to my children, grandchildren, and great-grandchildren my witness to Your loyal love and righteousness (v. 17).

⟨⟨⟨⟨⟩

Thank You for being sovereign—ruling all, free to do anything that is good and right in accordance with Your character (v. 19).

⟨⟨⟨⟨⟩

You are worthy of the praise of everyone and everything, everywhere. Bless the Lord, O my soul (vv. 20–22)!

How Jesus could be interceding for you: Father of all blessing, mercy, and grace, You have not dealt with mankind according to their sins, but according to Your grace (Rom. 3:25; 5:15). Continue to deal compassionately with Your children (Heb. 4:16; Jas. 5:11) and pour out on them those blessings that result in more praise to You (Eph. 1:3–4; Heb. 13:15).

Psalm 104

The LORD's Care over All His Works.

1 Bless the LORD, O my soul!
   O LORD my God, You are very great;
   You are clothed with splendor and majesty,

2 Covering Yourself with light as with a cloak,
   Stretching out heaven like a *tent* curtain.

3 He lays the beams of His upper chambers in the waters;
   He makes the clouds His chariot;
   He walks upon the wings of the wind;

4 He makes the winds His messengers,
   Flaming fire His ministers.

5 He established the earth upon its foundations,
   So that it will not totter forever and ever.

6 You covered it with the deep as with a garment;
   The waters were standing above the mountains.

7 At Your rebuke they fled,
   At the sound of Your thunder they hurried away.

8 The mountains rose; the valleys sank down
   To the place which You established for them.

9 You set a boundary that they may not pass over,
   So that they will not return to cover the earth.

10 He sends forth springs in the valleys;
    They flow between the mountains;

11 They give drink to every beast of the field;
    The wild donkeys quench their thirst.

12 Beside them the birds of the heavens dwell;
    They lift up *their* voices among the branches.

13 He waters the mountains from His upper chambers;
    The earth is satisfied with the fruit of His works.

14 He causes the grass to grow for the cattle,
    And vegetation for the labor of man,
    So that he may bring forth food from the earth,

15 And wine which makes man's heart glad,
    So that he may make *his* face glisten with oil,
    And food which sustains man's heart.

Praying Psalm 104

*An anonymous psalmist prays to the Creator and
offers praise for all His wondrous works.*

In the beginning, O God, You created the heavens and its angels—and You created the earth, separating the waters from the dry land. Thank You, Lord (vv. 1–9).

O Lord, You are very great and majestic—worthy of all praise and thanks (v. 1).

Teach me from Your creation to know You more fully and to give praise to You (vv. 5–13).

You alone satisfy and sustain creation and its needs by Your grace (vv. 10–23).

Thank You, O Creator of heaven and earth, for the food I eat by Your gracious provision (v. 14).

16 The trees of the Lord drink their fill,
    The cedars of Lebanon which He planted,
17 Where the birds build their nests,
    And the stork, whose home is the fir trees.
18 The high mountains are for the wild goats;
    The cliffs are a refuge for the shephanim.
19 He made the moon for the seasons;
    The sun knows the place of its setting.
20 You appoint darkness and it becomes night,
    In which all the beasts of the forest prowl about.
21 The young lions roar after their prey
    And seek their food from God.
22 *When* the sun rises they withdraw
    And lie down in their dens.
23 Man goes forth to his work
    And to his labor until evening.
24 O Lord, how many are Your works!
    In wisdom You have made them all;
    The earth is full of Your possessions.
25 There is the sea, great and broad,
    In which are swarms without number,
    Animals both small and great.
26 There the ships move along,
    And Leviathan, which You have formed to sport in it.
27 They all wait for You
    To give them their food in due season.
28 You give to them, they gather *it* up;
    You open Your hand, they are satisfied with good.
29 You hide Your face, they are dismayed;
    You take away their spirit, they expire
    And return to their dust.
30 You send forth Your Spirit, they are created;
    And You renew the face of the ground.
31 Let the glory of the Lord endure forever;
    Let the Lord be glad in His works;
32 He looks at the earth, and it trembles;
    He touches the mountains, and they smoke.
33 I will sing to the Lord as long as I live;
    I will sing praise to my God while I have my being.
34 Let my meditation be pleasing to Him;
    As for me, I shall be glad in the Lord.
35 Let sinners be consumed from the earth
    And let the wicked be no more.
    Bless the Lord, O my soul.
    Praise the Lord!

Father, thank You for giving me work by which I might care for myself and those around me (v. 23).

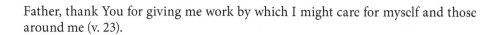

Everything everywhere is dependent on You—Your power, Your compassion, Your wisdom. You are glorious beyond our full comprehension. Yet You reveal Yourself in Your Word so we might know You. Praise God (vv. 24–30)!

Let my thoughts, my words, my songs—let everything I am and all that I have, bring honor to You, O Living God (vv. 31–35).

Lord Jesus, since You created all things, make my meditation on Your creation pleasing to You (v. 34).

How Jesus could be interceding for you: All-wise and all-powerful Father, may Your glory endure forever (Rom. 16:27; Jude 25). Rejoice in Your works and accept the praise of Your people (Heb. 13:15). Enable Your people to see Your splendor, might, and wisdom in all creation (Job 12:7–10; Rom. 1:20).

Psalm 105

The Lord's Wonderful Works in Behalf of Israel.

1   Oh give thanks to the Lord, call upon His name;
    Make known His deeds among the peoples.
2   Sing to Him, sing praises to Him;
    Speak of all His wonders.
3   Glory in His holy name;
    Let the heart of those who seek the Lord be glad.
4   Seek the Lord and His strength;
    Seek His face continually.
5   Remember His wonders which He has done,
    His marvels and the judgments uttered by His mouth,
6   O seed of Abraham, His servant,
    O sons of Jacob, His chosen ones!
7   He is the Lord our God;
    His judgments are in all the earth.

8   He has remembered His covenant forever,
    The word which He commanded to a thousand generations,
9   *The covenant* which He made with Abraham,
    And His oath to Isaac.
10   Then He confirmed it to Jacob for a statute,
    To Israel as an everlasting covenant,
11   Saying, "To you I will give the land of Canaan
    As the portion of your inheritance,"
12   When they were only a few men in number,
    Very few, and strangers in it.
13   And they wandered about from nation to nation,
    From *one* kingdom to another people.
14   He permitted no man to oppress them,
    And He reproved kings for their sakes:
15   "Do not touch My anointed ones,
    And do My prophets no harm."
16   And He called for a famine upon the land;
    He broke the whole staff of bread.
17   He sent a man before them,
    Joseph, *who* was sold as a slave.

Praying Psalm 105

This prayer of thanksgiving and praise calls upon all God's people to praise Him and be glad when they consider the way He has dealt with His people Israel historically.

Father, You chose to make a covenant with Abraham and his offspring. You made that one man into a nation too many to count. You protected a tiny nation of 70 in Egypt through Joseph—the beloved son, rejected by his brothers. You prospered them in Egypt and they grew to be a mighty nation. You delivered them through the plagues. You sustained them in the wilderness. Fulfill Your word, O Father, to Abraham and Your covenant with Israel. In grace, draw Israel to faith and obedience to her Messiah Jesus (vv. 1–45).

Thank You, Lord, for all that You have done for me (v. 1).

O God, give me Your strength (v. 4).

Because You fulfill Your promises to Israel, I know you will fulfill Your promises to me. Thank You, Father (vv. 8–12).

Lord, You always protect Your own even while they pass through times of severe trial. You never forget Your people and You never abandon them no matter how small a number they might be. Thank You for being our Protector (vv. 12–15).

18 They afflicted his feet with fetters,
    He himself was laid in irons;
19 Until the time that his word came to pass,
    The word of the LORD tested him.
20 The king sent and released him,
    The ruler of peoples, and set him free.
21 He made him lord of his house
    And ruler over all his possessions,
22 To imprison his princes at will,
    That he might teach his elders wisdom.
23 Israel also came into Egypt;
    Thus Jacob sojourned in the land of Ham.
24 And He caused His people to be very fruitful,
    And made them stronger than their adversaries.
25 He turned their heart to hate His people,
    To deal craftily with His servants.
26 He sent Moses His servant,
    And Aaron, whom He had chosen.
27 They performed His wondrous acts among them,
    And miracles in the land of Ham.
28 He sent darkness and made *it* dark;
    And they did not rebel against His words.
29 He turned their waters into blood
    And caused their fish to die.
30 Their land swarmed with frogs
    Even in the chambers of their kings.
31 He spoke, and there came a swarm of flies
    And gnats in all their territory.
32 He gave them hail for rain,
    And flaming fire in their land.
33 He struck down their vines also and their fig trees,
    And shattered the trees of their territory.
34 He spoke, and locusts came,
    And young locusts, even without number,
35 And ate up all vegetation in their land,
    And ate up the fruit of their ground.
36 He also struck down all the firstborn in their land,
    The first fruits of all their vigor.
37 Then He brought them out with silver and gold,
    And among His tribes there was not one who stumbled.

Just as You orchestrated Joseph's removal to Egypt through famine and betrayal, direct my life in ways that will result in Your doing good to others through me (vv. 16–22).

Lord Jesus, help me to remain faithful and obedient to You even in suffering (v. 19).

When people turn against me because of my faith, help me to realize, Lord, that You may do that for my good as well as for Your glory (v. 25).

Almighty God, You indeed are a God of miracles and wonders. All praise be to You alone (vv. 26–36).

Thank You, Jesus, for saving me in the Father's timing (vv. 37–42).

38   Egypt was glad when they departed,
      For the dread of them had fallen upon them.
39   He spread a cloud for a covering,
      And fire to illumine by night.
40   They asked, and He brought quail,
      And satisfied them with the bread of heaven.
41   He opened the rock and water flowed out;
      It ran in the dry places *like* a river.
42   For He remembered His holy word
      With Abraham His servant;
43   And He brought forth His people with joy,
      His chosen ones with a joyful shout.
44   He gave them also the lands of the nations,
      That they might take possession of *the fruit of* the peoples' labor,
45   So that they might keep His statutes
      And observe His laws,
      Praise the LORD!

You never fail to fulfill Your promises, O God. The truth and dependability of Your spoken word and written Word bring joy (vv. 42–43).

~~~~~

Guide me, Father, in the ways I might rejoice in the salvation You have provided to me (v. 43).

~~~~~

My responsibility continues to be obedience to You and Your Word, Lord Jesus. Enable me to remain faithful and filled with praise to You (v. 45).

How Jesus could be interceding for you: You indeed are the God of all history and the great Father of Your people (Hos. 11:1; Isa. 43:5–7; Matt. 5:44–45). As Your people read this prayer of praise for Your faithful love, may You turn their hearts to worship and obey only You and to accept Me as their promised Messiah and Savior (Matt. 12:16–21; Luke 4:16–21; Acts 3:17–26).

Psalm 106

Israel's Rebelliousness and the Lord's Deliverances.

1 Praise the Lord!
Oh give thanks to the Lord, for He is good;
For His lovingkindness is everlasting.

2 Who can speak of the mighty deeds of the Lord,
Or can show forth all His praise?

3 How blessed are those who keep justice,
Who practice righteousness at all times!

4 Remember me, O Lord, in *Your* favor toward Your people;
Visit me with Your salvation,

5 That I may see the prosperity of Your chosen ones,
That I may rejoice in the gladness of Your nation,
That I may glory with Your inheritance.

6 We have sinned like our fathers,
We have committed iniquity, we have behaved wickedly.

7 Our fathers in Egypt did not understand Your wonders;
They did not remember Your abundant kindnesses,
But rebelled by the sea, at the Red Sea.

8 Nevertheless He saved them for the sake of His name,
That He might make His power known.

9 Thus He rebuked the Red Sea and it dried up,
And He led them through the deeps, as through the wilderness.

10 So He saved them from the hand of the one who hated *them,*
And redeemed them from the hand of the enemy.

11 The waters covered their adversaries;
Not one of them was left.

12 Then they believed His words;
They sang His praise.

13 They quickly forgot His works;
They did not wait for His counsel,

14 But craved intensely in the wilderness,
And tempted God in the desert.

15 So He gave them their request,
But sent a wasting disease among them.

Praying Psalm 106

*In yet another anonymous prayer of praise, the psalmist confesses
the sins of God's people while telling more about God's dealings with
His people Israel. This prayer closes Book Four of the Psalter.*

Lord, You are good, and Your lovingkindness lasts forever. Remember Your people
Lord. Bring salvation to Your people and once again set Your favor upon the Jewish
nation. Bring the promised repentance and faith (vv. 1–6; cf. Zech. 13).

Gracious Father, thank You for Your goodness and faithfulness upon a people
undeserving of Your favor (v. 1).

Lord, give me wisdom and strength to practice Your righteousness (v. 3).

Give me joy in contemplating the salvation of Your people, O God (v. 5).

Teach me, Holy Spirit, how to flee from sin (vv. 6–39; 1 Cor. 10:6, 11–13).

Thank you for Your patience and for disciplining Your wayward people. Praise You,
Father, for being faithful to Your covenant. People are faithless and treacherous—
and I know I can be as well. Forgive me, O God (vv. 7–46).

Father, do not allow me to forgot Your works You have accomplished for me (v. 13).

16 When they became envious of Moses in the camp,
And of Aaron, the holy one of the LORD,

17 The earth opened and swallowed up Dathan,
And engulfed the company of Abiram.

18 And a fire blazed up in their company;
The flame consumed the wicked.

19 They made a calf in Horeb
And worshiped a molten image.

20 Thus they exchanged their glory
For the image of an ox that eats grass.

21 They forgot God their Savior,
Who had done great things in Egypt,

22 Wonders in the land of Ham
And awesome things by the Red Sea.

23 Therefore He said that He would destroy them,
Had not Moses His chosen one stood in the breach before Him,
To turn away His wrath from destroying *them.*

24 Then they despised the pleasant land;
They did not believe in His word,

25 But grumbled in their tents;
They did not listen to the voice of the LORD.

26 Therefore He swore to them
That He would cast them down in the wilderness,

27 And that He would cast their seed among the nations
And scatter them in the lands.

28 They joined themselves also to Baal-peor,
And ate sacrifices offered to the dead.

29 Thus they provoked *Him* to anger with their deeds,
And the plague broke out among them.

30 Then Phinehas stood up and interposed,
And so the plague was stayed.

31 And it was reckoned to him for righteousness,
To all generations forever.

32 They also provoked *Him* to wrath at the waters of Meribah,
So that it went hard with Moses on their account;

33 Because they were rebellious against His Spirit,
He spoke rashly with his lips.

34 They did not destroy the peoples,
As the LORD commanded them,

Deliver my heart from envy, Father. Teach me to accept the role You have given me in service for You (vv. 16–17).

Remove from my heart and mind anything that I've allowed to take Your place in my life, Lord God (vv. 19–20).

Spirit of God, never let me forget God my Savior (v. 21).

Father, bend my heart and mind to Your Word, that I might not forget it, but would believe it and act upon Your promises (vv. 24–25).

Keep me from despising Your gifts and disbelieving Your promises, dear Lord (v. 24).

Jesus, give me the courage to stand up for You, even when it is difficult (vv. 30–31).

Holy Spirit, keep me from rebelling against You and from speaking rashly and irreverently (v. 33).

35   But they mingled with the nations
     And learned their practices,
36   And served their idols,
     Which became a snare to them.
37   They even sacrificed their sons and their daughters to the demons,
38   And shed innocent blood,
     The blood of their sons and their daughters,
     Whom they sacrificed to the idols of Canaan;
     And the land was polluted with the blood.
39   Thus they became unclean in their practices,
     And played the harlot in their deeds.
40   Therefore the anger of the LORD was kindled against His people
     And He abhorred His inheritance.
41   Then He gave them into the hand of the nations,
     And those who hated them ruled over them.
42   Their enemies also oppressed them,
     And they were subdued under their power.
43   Many times He would deliver them;
     They, however, were rebellious in their counsel,
     And *so* sank down in their iniquity.
44   Nevertheless He looked upon their distress
     When He heard their cry;
45   And He remembered His covenant for their sake,
     And relented according to the greatness of His lovingkindness.
46   He also made them *objects* of compassion
     In the presence of all their captors.
47   Save us, O LORD our God,
     And gather us from among the nations,
     To give thanks to Your holy name
     And glory in Your praise.
48   Blessed be the LORD, the God of Israel,
     From everlasting even to everlasting.
     And let all the people say, "Amen."
     Praise the LORD!

Remove from me my idols, my rebellion, and my impure thoughts and deeds, Lord. Teach me to live in accord with Your commands to live a godly life (vv. 34–39).

Father, thank You for answering my prayer when I am in distress (vv. 44–45).

Your Kingdom come, dear Yahweh, so that all people may praise You forever (vv. 47–48).

How Jesus could be interceding for you: Faithful Father, forgive the sins of Your people and show them the fullness of Your grace and mercy (Luke 11:4). My work of redemption opened the way for them to come to You without any other mediator (1 Tim. 2:5) to whom they must confess their sins and ask for mercy (Luke 18:13; Rom. 11:30–32). Gather Your people and fulfill Your covenants through My sacrifice (Matt. 26:26–28; Heb. 6:13–20; 10:10–18).

Psalm 107

The LORD Delivers Men from Manifold Troubles.

1   Oh give thanks to the LORD, for He is good,
     For His lovingkindness is everlasting.
2   Let the redeemed of the LORD say *so,*
     Whom He has redeemed from the hand of the adversary
3   And gathered from the lands,
     From the east and from the west,
     From the north and from the south.

4   They wandered in the wilderness in a desert region;
     They did not find a way to an inhabited city.
5   *They were* hungry and thirsty;
     Their soul fainted within them.
6   Then they cried out to the LORD in their trouble;
     He delivered them out of their distresses.
7   He led them also by a straight way,
     To go to an inhabited city.
8   Let them give thanks to the LORD for His lovingkindness,
     And for His wonders to the sons of men!
9   For He has satisfied the thirsty soul,
     And the hungry soul He has filled with what is good.
10   There were those who dwelt in darkness and in the shadow of death,
     Prisoners in misery and chains,
11   Because they had rebelled against the words of God
     And spurned the counsel of the Most High.
12   Therefore He humbled their heart with labor;
     They stumbled and there was none to help.
13   Then they cried out to the LORD in their trouble;
     He saved them out of their distresses.
14   He brought them out of darkness and the shadow of death
     And broke their bands apart.
15   Let them give thanks to the LORD for His lovingkindness,
     And for His wonders to the sons of men!

Praying Psalm 107

*At the start of Book Five, an anonymous psalmist presents a prayer
of thanks including examples of circumstances in which people ought
to give thanks to God for His loyal love and faithfulness.*

Praise belongs to You, our Redeemer. You are good and Your love is forever! You have and will deliver Your people (vv. 1–3).

Lord, help me to speak out about my redemption (v. 2).

Blessed is the God who promises that all who call upon the name of the Lord will be saved (v. 6; cf. Rom. 10:12–13).

Blessed are You, dear Lord, who satisfies those who hunger and thirst for You (vv. 8–9; cf. Matt. 5:6).

Thank You, for being faithful to me in Your loyal love (v. 8).

Thank You, Father, for humbling my heart and opening my eyes to the misery of my rebellion, which led me to cry to You for mercy and deliverance. You are good and Your lovingkindness is everlasting (vv. 10–22).

Humble my heart, if I ever rebel against Your Word (vv. 11–12).

You are my Deliverer—You set me free from my bondage to sin and its consequences, Lord God (vv. 14–17).

16   For He has shattered gates of bronze
    And cut bars of iron asunder.

17   Fools, because of their rebellious way,
    And because of their iniquities, were afflicted.

18   Their soul abhorred all kinds of food,
    And they drew near to the gates of death.

19   Then they cried out to the LORD in their trouble;
    He saved them out of their distresses.

20   He sent His word and healed them,
    And delivered *them* from their destructions.

21   Let them give thanks to the LORD for His lovingkindness,
    And for His wonders to the sons of men!

22   Let them also offer sacrifices of thanksgiving,
    And tell of His works with joyful singing.

23   Those who go down to the sea in ships,
    Who do business on great waters;

24   They have seen the works of the LORD,
    And His wonders in the deep.

25   For He spoke and raised up a stormy wind,
    Which lifted up the waves of the sea.

26   They rose up to the heavens, they went down to the depths;
    Their soul melted away in *their* misery.

27   They reeled and staggered like a drunken man,
    And were at their wits' end.

28   Then they cried to the LORD in their trouble,
    And He brought them out of their distresses.

29   He caused the storm to be still,
    So that the waves of the sea were hushed.

30   Then they were glad because they were quiet,
    So He guided them to their desired haven.

31   Let them give thanks to the LORD for His lovingkindness,
    And for His wonders to the sons of men!

32   Let them extol Him also in the congregation of the people,
    And praise Him at the seat of the elders.

33   He changes rivers into a wilderness
    And springs of water into a thirsty ground;

34   A fruitful land into a salt waste,
    Because of the wickedness of those who dwell in it.

35   He changes a wilderness into a pool of water
    And a dry land into springs of water;

Lord Jesus, You accomplished these deeds. You are the Lord Who calmed the seas and rescued His distressed disciples. Thank You, that they did extol You in the congregation of people and we have the report preserved in the Spirit-inspired Word of God (vv. 23–32; cf. Mark 4:35–41).

When I face the storms of this world, disoriented, and fearful, deliver me, dear Lord (vv. 26–30).

Bring Your glorious Kingdom, dear Lord. Transform creation and vindicate Your name and Your people (vv. 33–43).

How I praise You, O God, for blessing Your people when they keep Your covenant (vv. 33–41).

36 And there He makes the hungry to dwell,
   So that they may establish an inhabited city,
37 And sow fields and plant vineyards,
   And gather a fruitful harvest.
38 Also He blesses them and they multiply greatly,
   And He does not let their cattle decrease.
39 When they are diminished and bowed down
   Through oppression, misery and sorrow,
40 He pours contempt upon princes
   And makes them wander in a pathless waste.
41 But He sets the needy securely on high away from affliction,
   And makes *his* families like a flock.
42 The upright see it and are glad;
   But all unrighteousness shuts its mouth.
43 Who is wise? Let him give heed to these things,
   And consider the lovingkindnesses of the LORD.

Thank You for making me glad when I see Your favor on the righteous, Lord God (v. 42).

Give me Your wisdom, Lord (v. 43).

How Jesus could be interceding for you: Merciful and loving Father, give the bread of life to the hungry (John 6:35–36), the water of life to the thirsty (John 4:10–14), strength to the weak (Matt. 11:28–30), help to the helpless (Matt. 9:36), healing to the sick (Matt. 8:16–17), peace to the troubled (John 14:1, 27), and deliverance to those near death (Mark 5:22–42).

Psalm 108

God Praised and Supplicated to Give Victory.

A Song, a Psalm of David.

1   My heart is steadfast, O God;
    I will sing, I will sing praises, even with my soul.
2   Awake, harp and lyre;
    I will awaken the dawn!
3   I will give thanks to You, O LORD, among the peoples,
    And I will sing praises to You among the nations.
4   For Your lovingkindness is great above the heavens,
    And Your truth *reaches* to the skies.
5   Be exalted, O God, above the heavens,
    And Your glory above all the earth.
6   That Your beloved may be delivered,
    Save with Your right hand, and answer me!

7   God has spoken in His holiness:
    "I will exult, I will portion out Shechem
    And measure out the valley of Succoth.
8   "Gilead is Mine, Manasseh is Mine;
    Ephraim also is the helmet of My head;
    Judah is My scepter.
9   "Moab is My washbowl;
    Over Edom I shall throw My shoe;
    Over Philistia I will shout aloud."
10 Who will bring me into the besieged city?
    Who will lead me to Edom?
11 Have not You Yourself, O God, rejected us?
    And will You not go forth with our armies, O God?
12 Oh give us help against the adversary,
    For deliverance by man is in vain.
13 Through God we will do valiantly,
    And it is He who shall tread down our adversaries.

Praying Psalm 108

*David offers praise-filled prayer to the Lord, borrowing
from previous prayers in Psalms 57 and 60.*

God, I am confident Your Kingdom will come. You will be exalted among the nations. Grant me a greater passion to sing Your praises and tell others now of Your glory (vv. 1–6).

Let me sing Your praises, O God—even during the night (v. 1).

Father, Your steadfast love is great—thank You (v. 4).

O Lord, answer my prayer; deliver me (v. 6).

You will be victorious, Lord Messiah. You will deliver Your people. The Kingdom will come in Israel and You will destroy the adversaries of Your people. Return, dear Savior (vv. 7–13).

Lord, teach me to trust You, rather than my fellow human beings (v. 12).

How Jesus could be interceding for you: I give thanks to You, Father, for Your great glory (Matt. 16:27; John 17:5). Bring Your people into My Kingdom, a kingdom not of this world (Matt. 6:10; John 18:36).

Psalm 109

Vengeance Invoked upon Adversaries.

For the choir director. A Psalm of David.

1   O God of my praise,
Do not be silent!
2   For they have opened the wicked and deceitful mouth against me;
They have spoken against me with a lying tongue.
3   They have also surrounded me with words of hatred,
And fought against me without cause.
4   In return for my love they act as my accusers;
But I am *in* prayer.
5   Thus they have repaid me evil for good
And hatred for my love.

6   Appoint a wicked man over him,
And let an accuser stand at his right hand.
7   When he is judged, let him come forth guilty,
And let his prayer become sin.
8   Let his days be few;
Let another take his office.
9   Let his children be fatherless
And his wife a widow.
10   Let his children wander about and beg;
And let them seek *sustenance* far from their ruined homes.
11   Let the creditor seize all that he has,
And let strangers plunder the product of his labor.
12   Let there be none to extend lovingkindness to him,
Nor any to be gracious to his fatherless children.
13   Let his posterity be cut off;
In a following generation let their name be blotted out.
14   Let the iniquity of his fathers be remembered before the Lord,
And do not let the sin of his mother be blotted out.
15   Let them be before the Lord continually,
That He may cut off their memory from the earth;
16   Because he did not remember to show lovingkindness,
But persecuted the afflicted and needy man,
And the despondent in heart, to put *them* to death.

Praying Psalm 109

David prayerfully pleads with God for justice.

God, defend Your slandered and oppressed children. The enemy twists and maligns and tries to sow seeds of doubt and a focus on self that does not lead to repentance and faith, but rather condemnation and fear. Lord Jesus, thank You that You know what this is like to an infinite degree, because You are sinless and holy—yet You were slandered and accused. You loved sinners and hatred was Your reward. Thank You, Savior, for being our faithful High Priest (vv. 1–5).

O Lord, be my praise at all times and in all circumstances (v. 1).

Father, help me to do good to my enemies and to love them (v. 5).

O Father, Your Son stood before wicked accusers and endured the betrayal of Judas. David knew the betrayal of Ahithophel. All of Your people know the hostility of the great enemy of our souls—even the accuser, Satan. Let the full force of Your justice be poured out on all those who will not take refuge in Jesus Christ, the Son of God (vv. 6–20).

17 He also loved cursing, so it came to him;
And he did not delight in blessing, so it was far from him.

18 But he clothed himself with cursing as with his garment,
And it entered into his body like water
And like oil into his bones.

19 Let it be to him as a garment with which he covers himself,
And for a belt with which he constantly girds himself.

20 Let this be the reward of my accusers from the LORD,
And of those who speak evil against my soul.

21 But You, O GOD, the Lord, deal *kindly* with me for Your name's sake;
Because Your lovingkindness is good, deliver me;

22 For I am afflicted and needy,
And my heart is wounded within me.

23 I am passing like a shadow when it lengthens;
I am shaken off like the locust.

24 My knees are weak from fasting,
And my flesh has grown lean, without fatness.

25 I also have become a reproach to them;
When they see me, they wag their head.

26 Help me, O LORD my God;
Save me according to Your lovingkindness.

27 And let them know that this is Your hand;
You, LORD, have done it.

28 Let them curse, but You bless;
When they arise, they shall be ashamed,
But Your servant shall be glad.

29 Let my accusers be clothed with dishonor,
And let them cover themselves with their own shame as with a robe.

30 With my mouth I will give thanks abundantly to the LORD;
And in the midst of many I will praise Him.

31 For He stands at the right hand of the needy,
To save him from those who judge his soul.

Cause me to delight in blessing others as well as to enjoy Your blessings, O God (v. 17).

Master, deal with me according to Your love—even the love You showed to Your Son Christ Jesus. You vindicated Him with resurrection, and You will put His accusers to shame. In this hope I too will endure. You stand at the right hand of those who know their poverty so You might save them from those who condemn them. Thank You, Lord (vv. 21–31).

Lord Jesus, I'm afflicted, weak, exhausted, and feeling quite alone and rejected. Deliver me (vv. 22–26).

Save me from the evil deeds of those who falsely accuse me (v. 31).

How Jesus could be interceding for you: On the cross, surrounded by the hatred of those I loved (Luke 19:14; John 3:16; 7:7) and betrayed by one of My disciples (Matt. 10:2–4), Father, I cried out to You (Luke 23:34, 46). Now I intercede on behalf of all people that they might believe in Me (John 17:20) and that believers might receive Our kindness, mercy, and comfort (Matt. 5:4; Rom. 2:4; Titus 3:4).

Psalm 110

The Lord Gives Dominion to the King.

A Psalm of David.

1   The Lord says to my Lord:
"Sit at My right hand
Until I make Your enemies a footstool for Your feet."
2   The Lord will stretch forth Your strong scepter from Zion, *saying,*
"Rule in the midst of Your enemies."
3   Your people will volunteer freely in the day of Your power;
In holy array, from the womb of the dawn,
Your youth are to You *as* the dew.

4   The Lord has sworn and will not change His mind,
"You are a priest forever
According to the order of Melchizedek."
5   The Lord is at Your right hand;
He will shatter kings in the day of His wrath.
6   He will judge among the nations,
He will fill *them* with corpses,
He will shatter the chief men over a broad country.
7   He will drink from the brook by the wayside;
Therefore He will lift up *His* head.

Praying Psalm 110

David's psalm of praise for the coming Messiah.

From suffering Servant, accused and slandered, to exalted Lord—King and everlasting Priest. Praise be to Jesus Christ (vv. 1–4)!

O Lord, come and rule over Your enemies (vv. 1–2).

Help me volunteer to serve You even today (v. 3).

Thank You, Lord Jesus, for being my High Priest (v. 4).

May Your Kingdom come and let justice reign on the earth (vv. 5–7).

How Jesus could be interceding for you: As Your Spirit has testified through David, many will serve Me, Father. Increase their numbers and make them holy—sanctify them to My service (Ps. 110:3; John 17:17). Dear Father, draw the hearts of the young to Me (1 Tim. 4:12). As their Priest and their King, I intercede for them (Ps. 110:4; Heb. 7:15–25).

Psalm 111

The Lord Praised for His Goodness.

1   Praise the Lord!
    I will give thanks to the Lord with all *my* heart,
    In the company of the upright and in the assembly.
2   Great are the works of the Lord;
    They are studied by all who delight in them.
3   Splendid and majestic is His work,
    And His righteousness endures forever.
4   He has made His wonders to be remembered;
    The Lord is gracious and compassionate.
5   He has given food to those who fear Him;
    He will remember His covenant forever.
6   He has made known to His people the power of His works,
    In giving them the heritage of the nations.

7   The works of His hands are truth and justice;
    All His precepts are sure.
8   They are upheld forever and ever;
    They are performed in truth and uprightness.
9   He has sent redemption to His people;
    He has ordained His covenant forever;
    Holy and awesome is His name.
10 The fear of the Lord is the beginning of wisdom;
    A good understanding have all those who do *His commandments;*
    His praise endures forever.

Praying Psalm 111

*Throughout Church history believers have sung this
psalm when observing the Lord's Supper.*

I long for the day when my praise is perfect and without defect in Your presence (cf. 1 John 3:1–3). I will give thanks to You, Lord, with my whole heart now and a perfect heart then—in the company of the redeemed. We will spend eternity meditating on Your glorious attributes and Your wondrous works that reveal those attributes (vv. 1–6).

With all my heart, Lord, I give thanks to You (v. 1).

Father, enable me to see Your works and to delight in them (v. 2).

O God, You are gracious and compassionate (v. 4).

Thank You for Your perfect Word and faithful promises. Teach me to fear You more, because You truly are holy and awesome (vv. 7–10).

Lord Jesus, make me a doer of Your precepts and not just a hearer (v. 10; Jas. 1:22).

How Jesus could be interceding for you: Father, thank You for sending Me to provide redemption for Your people (Gal. 4:4–5). Give them their daily food according to Your gracious provision (Matt. 6:11), and cause them to delight in Your Word and Your works even as I have (Pss. 40:8; 119:174; Heb. 10:7).

Psalm 112

Prosperity of the One Who Fears the LORD.

1   Praise the LORD!
How blessed is the man who fears the LORD,
Who greatly delights in His commandments.

2   His descendants will be mighty on earth;
The generation of the upright will be blessed.

3   Wealth and riches are in his house,
And his righteousness endures forever.

4   Light arises in the darkness for the upright;
He is gracious and compassionate and righteous.

5   It is well with the man who is gracious and lends;
He will maintain his cause in judgment.

6   For he will never be shaken;
The righteous will be remembered forever.

7   He will not fear evil tidings;
His heart is steadfast, trusting in the LORD.

8   His heart is upheld, he will not fear,
Until he looks *with satisfaction* on his adversaries.

9   He has given freely to the poor,
His righteousness endures forever;
His horn will be exalted in honor.

10   The wicked will see it and be vexed,
He will gnash his teeth and melt away;
The desire of the wicked will perish.

Praying Psalm 112

An anonymous prayer praising God for His blessing upon the godly.

Again, blessed be the One who blesses us with His Word to delight in and His promises in which to put our hope. But Father, the prophets like Jeremiah, or the apostles like Paul, and especially Jesus Your Son, did not experience temporal wealth and riches. Help my heart to be steadfast in hope, trusting in You until faith becomes sight and Your Kingdom blessings are fully realized (vv. 1–10).

Thank You, Lord Jesus, for giving me a righteousness that lasts forever (v. 4).

Encourage my heart, O God, so that I will not be afraid (v. 8).

How Jesus could be interceding for you: Righteous Father, may Your people praise You for providing My sacrifice as the means of bringing them everlasting righteousness (Rom. 5:19–21). Enable Your people to act with kindness and compassion (Col. 3:12); remove fear from their heart and grant them a steadfast trust in You (2 Tim. 1:7; Heb. 13:6).

Psalm 113

The LORD Exalts the Humble.

1 Praise the LORD!
Praise, O servants of the LORD,
Praise the name of the LORD.

2 Blessed be the name of the LORD
From this time forth and forever.

3 From the rising of the sun to its setting
The name of the LORD is to be praised.

4 The LORD is high above all nations;
His glory is above the heavens.

5 Who is like the LORD our God,
Who is enthroned on high,

6 Who humbles Himself to behold
The things that are in heaven and in the earth?

7 He raises the poor from the dust
And lifts the needy from the ash heap,

8 To make *them* sit with princes,
With the princes of His people.

9 He makes the barren woman abide in the house
As a joyful mother of children.
Praise the LORD!

Praying Psalm 113

At Passover the Jewish community sings this psalm before the Passover meal.

I praise You, Lord. I am Your servant. Praise be to Your holy name forever and ever in every place, everywhere (vv. 1–4).

There is none like You, dear God. You are exalted far beyond all, yet You care for the lowly and bless creatures made of dust. Praise Yahweh—the living God—our Savior, Redeemer, and Friend (vv. 5–9).

O God, there is no one like You (v. 5)!

How I praise You, Father, for Your care and provisions (v. 7).

Dear Lord, thank You for giving me the joy of a spouse and children (v. 9).

How Jesus could be interceding for you: You are incomparable, Father—You are worthy of all praise (Luke 19:37; Phil. 1:11). Provide relief for the poor and the needy (Matt. 5:3; 2 Cor. 9:9). Give children to the barren woman so she might rejoice in Your gift (Luke 1:36–37).

Psalm 114

God's Deliverance of Israel from Egypt.

1   When Israel went forth from Egypt,
    The house of Jacob from a people of strange language,
2   Judah became His sanctuary,
    Israel, His dominion.

3   The sea looked and fled;
    The Jordan turned back.
4   The mountains skipped like rams,
    The hills, like lambs.
5   What ails you, O sea, that you flee?
    O Jordan, that you turn back?
6   O mountains, that you skip like rams?
    O hills, like lambs?

7   Tremble, O earth, before the Lord,
    Before the God of Jacob,
8   Who turned the rock into a pool of water,
    The flint into a fountain of water.

Praying Psalm 114

The Jewish community also sings this psalm before the Passover meal.

Thank You, Father for the reminder of Your power, Your salvation, Your faithfulness to Your people (vv. 1–6).

Lord, You alone deliver Your people (v. 1).

Father, You rule over all the elements of Your creation (vv. 3–6).

Redeem creation, Lord. May all tremble before You in faith-filled awe and holy fear (vv. 7–8).

Create in me a godly sense of awe at Your great Power and Presence (v. 7).

Thank You, Savior, for providing for Your people in unexpected ways (v. 8).

How Jesus could be interceding for you: You delivered Your people out of Egypt and into the land You promised to give them, Father. Now, for this child of Yours who longs for deliverance from sin's power and presence (Rom. 7:17–20; 1 John 1:8–10), fulfill all You promised to provide him/her through My death and resurrection (Rom. 6:4; Eph. 2:4–10).

Psalm 115

Heathen Idols Contrasted with the Lord.

1   Not to us, O Lord, not to us,
    But to Your name give glory
    Because of Your lovingkindness, because of Your truth.
2   Why should the nations say,
    "Where, now, is their God?"
3   But our God is in the heavens;
    He does whatever He pleases.
4   Their idols are silver and gold,
    The work of man's hands.
5   They have mouths, but they cannot speak;
    They have eyes, but they cannot see;
6   They have ears, but they cannot hear;
    They have noses, but they cannot smell;
7   They have hands, but they cannot feel;
    They have feet, but they cannot walk;
    They cannot make a sound with their throat.
8   Those who make them will become like them,
    Everyone who trusts in them.

9   O Israel, trust in the Lord;
    He is their help and their shield.
10   O house of Aaron, trust in the Lord;
    He is their help and their shield.
11   You who fear the Lord, trust in the Lord;
    He is their help and their shield.
12   The Lord has been mindful of us; He will bless *us;*
    He will bless the house of Israel;
    He will bless the house of Aaron.
13   He will bless those who fear the Lord,
    The small together with the great.
14   May the Lord give you increase,
    You and your children.
15   May you be blessed of the Lord,
    Maker of heaven and earth.

Praying Psalm 115

Psalms 115–118 are sung after the Passover meal in Jewish communities—perhaps also sung by Jesus and His disciples (Matt. 26:30).

Sovereign Lord, Living God, for the sake of Your own glory—for the sake of Your love and Your faithfulness—reveal the idols of our world for what they are. Reveal our prosperity, our pleasures, all that feeds our pride as dead and damning (vv. 1–8).

I am so thankful that You sit in the heavens and do whatever You please, because You are good and You always do what will ultimately work together for the good of Your people and Your glory (v. 3).

Father, I praise You because You speak, You see, You hear, You feel, and You move (vv. 5–7).

Thank You, Father, that You help those who trust in You. You protect those who put their faith in Your Son (vv. 9–11).

Increase my trust in You, Lord Jesus (v. 11).

Bless us, Lord, that we may praise Your name forever (vv. 12–18).

Thank You for Your many blessings upon me, Lord God (v. 15).

16   The heavens are the heavens of the LORD,
     But the earth He has given to the sons of men.
17   The dead do not praise the LORD,
     Nor *do* any who go down into silence;
18   But as for us, we will bless the LORD
     From this time forth and forever.
     Praise the LORD!

Father, what a beautiful earth You have given to us in which to make our home and to live in service for You—thank You (v. 16).

Give me the breath to praise You and to declare Your wondrous grace and mercy throughout all my life (vv. 17–18).

How Jesus could be interceding for you: Loving Father, help Your people and shield them from all harm (Heb. 2:16–18; 6:17–20). Pour out blessing upon those who have placed their faith in Me as their Savior and Lord (Eph. 1:3).

Psalm 116

Thanksgiving for Deliverance from Death.

1 I love the Lord, because He hears
My voice *and* my supplications.
2 Because He has inclined His ear to me,
Therefore I shall call *upon Him* as long as I live.
3 The cords of death encompassed me
And the terrors of Sheol came upon me;
I found distress and sorrow.
4 Then I called upon the name of the Lord:
"O Lord, I beseech You, save my life!"

5 Gracious is the Lord, and righteous;
Yes, our God is compassionate.
6 The Lord preserves the simple;
I was brought low, and He saved me.
7 Return to your rest, O my soul,
For the Lord has dealt bountifully with you.
8 For You have rescued my soul from death,
My eyes from tears,
My feet from stumbling.
9 I shall walk before the Lord
In the land of the living.
10 I believed when I said,
"I am greatly afflicted."
11 I said in my alarm,
"All men are liars."
12 What shall I render to the Lord
For all His benefits toward me?
13 I shall lift up the cup of salvation
And call upon the name of the Lord.
14 I shall pay my vows to the Lord,
Oh *may it be* in the presence of all His people.
15 Precious in the sight of the Lord
Is the death of His godly ones.
16 O Lord, surely I am Your servant,
I am Your servant, the son of Your handmaid,
You have loosed my bonds.

Praying Psalm 116

*A prayer of praise to be sung after the Passover meal, just
as Jesus and His disciples did (Matt. 26:30).*

I love You, Lord. Thank You for hearing my prayers (vv. 1–2).

Gracious, righteous, compassionate—You, O Lord, have indeed dealt bountifully with my soul (vv. 5–7).

You have rescued me, dear Lord. When I could not trust others, You honored my faith and listened to my complaint (vv. 8–11)

Lord Jesus, enable me to live a life of consistent faith and obedience (v.9).

My heart's desire is to obey You and make You known, dear God. Thank You for saving me and all who call upon the name of Jesus (vv. 12–19).

What a joy, O God, to know that the death of Your servants is precious in Your sight (vv. 15–16).

17 To You I shall offer a sacrifice of thanksgiving,
  And call upon the name of the Lord.
18 I shall pay my vows to the Lord,
  Oh *may it be* in the presence of all His people,
19 In the courts of the Lord's house,
  In the midst of you, O Jerusalem.
  Praise the Lord!

Lord, I offer You all my thanks in the presence of Your people (vv. 17–18).

No matter where I am, enable me to offer You worship and praise. Father, preserve worship and praise in the assemblies of believers around the world (v. 19).

How Jesus could be interceding for you: When I cried out to You, dear Father, You responded and raised Me from the dead (Acts 2:24–28). Show Your compassion and care for this afflicted believer (2 Cor. 1:3–5); preserve his/her life (Luke 12:22–27). The life of one of Our sheep is indeed precious to Us and I ask that this one might be with Us forever because I died and rose again for him/her (John 14:1–3; 17:24).

Psalm 117

A Psalm of Praise.

1   Praise the LORD, all nations;
     Laud Him, all peoples!
2   For His lovingkindness is great toward us,
     And the truth of the LORD is everlasting.
     Praise the LORD!

Praying Psalm 117

The shortest prayer of praise in the Psalter.

Father, hasten the day when every knee in every nation bows before Your Son and gives due honor to Him as Lord (vv. 1–2).

Lord, enable me to be a faithful witness to You through my praise (v. 1).

How Jesus could be interceding for you: Exalted Father, magnify Your love and Your truth in the lives of all Your people through Me (John 1:14; 3:16; 14:6; 16:27).

Psalm 118

Thanksgiving for the Lord's Saving Goodness.

1   Give thanks to the Lord, for He is good;
     For His lovingkindness is everlasting.
2   Oh let Israel say,
     "His lovingkindness is everlasting."
3   Oh let the house of Aaron say,
     "His lovingkindness is everlasting."
4   Oh let those who fear the Lord say,
     "His lovingkindness is everlasting."

5   From *my* distress I called upon the Lord;
     The Lord answered me *and set me* in a large place.
6   The Lord is for me; I will not fear;
     What can man do to me?
7   The Lord is for me among those who help me;
     Therefore I will look *with satisfaction* on those who hate me.
8   It is better to take refuge in the Lord
     Than to trust in man.
9   It is better to take refuge in the Lord
     Than to trust in princes.
10   All nations surrounded me;
     In the name of the Lord I will surely cut them off.
11   They surrounded me, yes, they surrounded me;
     In the name of the Lord I will surely cut them off.
12   They surrounded me like bees;
     They were extinguished as a fire of thorns;
     In the name of the Lord I will surely cut them off.
13   You pushed me violently so that I was falling,
     But the Lord helped me.
14   The Lord is my strength and song,
     And He has become my salvation.
15   The sound of joyful shouting and salvation is in the tents of the righteous;
     The right hand of the Lord does valiantly.
16   The right hand of the Lord is exalted;
     The right hand of the Lord does valiantly.
17   I will not die, but live,
     And tell of the works of the Lord.

Praying Psalm 118

A prayer of thanks to the Lord sung at Passover and by Jesus and His disciples following the Last Supper.

Thank You, Lord. You are good, and You are love eternal (vv. 1–4, 29).

I trust You, Father. Help me to trust You more and to fully understand that man can do nothing to separate me from You. You are my refuge (vv. 6–9).

Lord Jesus, You will intervene for Your people and cut off their enemies. You are our strength and our song (vv. 10–14).

When I feel like I'm surrounded by trouble and enemies, You, Lord, are my strength and my song (vv. 10–14).

You will be faithful to Your covenant nation, Lord. Save Israel, dear God, to the praise of Your glory (vv. 15–21).

Father, help me tell of Your works as long as I live (v. 17).

18 The LORD has disciplined me severely,
    But He has not given me over to death.
19 Open to me the gates of righteousness;
    I shall enter through them, I shall give thanks to the LORD.
20 This is the gate of the LORD;
    The righteous will enter through it.
21 I shall give thanks to You, for You have answered me,
    And You have become my salvation.
22 The stone which the builders rejected
    Has become the chief corner *stone.*
23 This is the LORD's doing;
    It is marvelous in our eyes.
24 This is the day which the LORD has made;
    Let us rejoice and be glad in it.
25 O LORD, do save, we beseech You;
    O LORD, we beseech You, do send prosperity!
26 Blessed is the one who comes in the name of the LORD;
    We have blessed you from the house of the LORD.
27 The LORD is God, and He has given us light;
    Bind the festival sacrifice with cords to the horns of the altar.
28 You are my God, and I give thanks to You;
    You are my God, I extol You.
29 Give thanks to the LORD, for He is good;
    For His lovingkindness is everlasting.

Thank You for loving me enough to discipline me when I need it to be ready to serve You (v. 18).

※※※

Lord Jesus, You are the Cornerstone, once rejected now exalted forever. Save, dear Lord. Let the nation cry out: "Blessed is He who comes in the name of the Lord!" (vv. 22–26).

※※※

O loving Father, enable me to celebrate all You have done for me through Christ (v. 27).

※※※

You are my God—I give all praise and thanks to You (v. 28).

How Jesus could be interceding for you: When I was rejected by mankind, You helped Me by Your loyal love (Matt. 21:42). O Father of all mercies, give aid and refuge to those for whom I died (Acts 4:11–12). Join Your people into a single holy temple for Our dwelling (Eph. 2:19–22; 1 Pet. 2:4–10).

Psalm 119

Meditations and Prayers Relating to the Law of God.

א

Aleph.

1   How blessed are those whose way is blameless,
Who walk in the law of the Lord.

2   How blessed are those who observe His testimonies,
Who seek Him with all *their* heart.

3   They also do no unrighteousness;
They walk in His ways.

4   You have ordained Your precepts,
That we should keep *them* diligently.

5   Oh that my ways may be established
To keep Your statutes!

6   Then I shall not be ashamed
When I look upon all Your commandments.

7   I shall give thanks to You with uprightness of heart,
When I learn Your righteous judgments.

8   I shall keep Your statutes;
Do not forsake me utterly!

ב

Beth.

9   How can a young man keep his way pure?
By keeping *it* according to Your word.

10   With all my heart I have sought You;
Do not let me wander from Your commandments.

11   Your word I have treasured in my heart,
That I may not sin against You.

12   Blessed are You, O Lord;
Teach me Your statutes.

13   With my lips I have told of
All the ordinances of Your mouth.

14   I have rejoiced in the way of Your testimonies,
As much as in all riches.

Praying Psalm 119

*The longest prayer in Scripture emphasizes the anonymous
psalmist's love for the Lord and His Word.*

Abiding by the LORD's Law (vv. 1–8)

Enable me, Lord Jesus, to seek You with all my heart (v. 2).

Establish my ways, O God, that I might keep Your Word (v. 5).

Thank You, Father, for helping me to learn Your Word (v. 7).

Lord, I will keep Your Word. I need You, Spirit of the Living God, to will and to
work in me for Your good pleasure and the glory of Christ (v. 8).

Behaving according to the LORD's Word (vv. 9–16)

I will seek You in Your Word, Father—day after day. Keep me by Your grace. Do not
let me wander from Your Word (v. 10).

Teach me Your Word, O God (v. 12).

Lord, keep Your Word upon my lips, in all my speech (v. 13).

15   I will meditate on Your precepts
      And regard Your ways.
16   I shall delight in Your statutes;
      I shall not forget Your word.

ג

Gimel.

17   Deal bountifully with Your servant,
      That I may live and keep Your word.
18   Open my eyes, that I may behold
      Wonderful things from Your law.
19   I am a stranger in the earth;
      Do not hide Your commandments from me.
20   My soul is crushed with longing
      After Your ordinances at all times.
21   You rebuke the arrogant, the cursed,
      Who wander from Your commandments.
22   Take away reproach and contempt from me,
      For I observe Your testimonies.
23   Even though princes sit *and* talk against me,
      Your servant meditates on Your statutes.
24   Your testimonies also are my delight;
      They are my counselors.

ד

Daleth.

25   My soul cleaves to the dust;
      Revive me according to Your word.
26   I have told of my ways, and You have answered me;
      Teach me Your statutes.
27   Make me understand the way of Your precepts,
      So I will meditate on Your wonders.
28   My soul weeps because of grief;
      Strengthen me according to Your word.
29   Remove the false way from me,
      And graciously grant me Your law.
30   I have chosen the faithful way;
      I have placed Your ordinances *before me.*

Give me a delight in Your Word so I never forget it (v. 16).

Contemplating the LORD's commandments (vv. 17-24)

Help me to see Your glory revealed in Your Word and humble my heart before You (vv. 18, 20–21).

Father, when I feel lost, lonely, and a victim of evil, increase my delight in Your Word (vv. 19, 22–24).

Directing one's way by the LORD's precepts (vv. 25-32)

Thank You, my God, for answering my prayer when I told You all my needs (v. 26).

I need You, Lord. I sense my weakness and my sin and your grace all mixed together. Strengthen me in Your Word (v. 28).

Dear Spirit of God, help me to remain faithful to my God and my Savior (v. 30).

31   I cling to Your testimonies;
       O Lord, do not put me to shame!
32   I shall run the way of Your commandments,
       For You will enlarge my heart.

ה

He.

33   Teach me, O Lord, the way of Your statutes,
       And I shall observe it to the end.
34   Give me understanding, that I may observe Your law
       And keep it with all *my* heart.
35   Make me walk in the path of Your commandments,
       For I delight in it.
36   Incline my heart to Your testimonies
       And not to *dishonest* gain.
37   Turn away my eyes from looking at vanity,
       And revive me in Your ways.
38   Establish Your word to Your servant,
       As that which produces reverence for You.
39   Turn away my reproach which I dread,
       For Your ordinances are good.
40   Behold, I long for Your precepts;
       Revive me through Your righteousness.

ו

Vav.

41   May Your lovingkindnesses also come to me, O Lord,
       Your salvation according to Your word;
42   So I will have an answer for him who reproaches me,
       For I trust in Your word.
43   And do not take the word of truth utterly out of my mouth,
       For I wait for Your ordinances.
44   So I will keep Your law continually,
       Forever and ever.
45   And I will walk at liberty,
       For I seek Your precepts.
46   I will also speak of Your testimonies before kings
       And shall not be ashamed.

Free my heart from the fetters of my sin, dear Lord (v. 32)!

Educating a believer in the Lord's Law (vv. 33–40)

Oh how I desire to understand Your Word, Father, so I might obey it completely (v. 34)!

Lord Jesus, turn my eyes away from worthless things (v. 37).

Use the Scriptures to produce in me more and more reverence for You, my Savior and my God (v. 38).

Freeing a believer by the Lord's Word (vv. 41–48)

Loving Father, thank You for loving me and saving me just as You said You would in Your Word (v. 41).

Lord, when I walk in Your Word, I walk in freedom. I love the Scriptures. They delight my soul. Praise the Lord (vv. 45, 47–48)!

Give me the wisdom and the courage to speak Your Word to influential and powerful leaders (v. 46).

47   I shall delight in Your commandments,
       Which I love.
48   And I shall lift up my hands to Your commandments,
       Which I love;
       And I will meditate on Your statutes.

ז

Zayin.

49   Remember the word to Your servant,
       In which You have made me hope.
50   This is my comfort in my affliction,
       That Your word has revived me.
51   The arrogant utterly deride me,
       Yet I do not turn aside from Your law.
52   I have remembered Your ordinances from of old, O LORD,
       And comfort myself.
53   Burning indignation has seized me because of the wicked,
       Who forsake Your law.
54   Your statutes are my songs
       In the house of my pilgrimage.
55   O LORD, I remember Your name in the night,
       And keep Your law.
56   This has become mine,
       That I observe Your precepts.

ח

Heth.

57   The LORD is my portion;
       I have promised to keep Your words.
58   I sought Your favor with all *my* heart;
       Be gracious to me according to Your word.
59   I considered my ways
       And turned my feet to Your testimonies.
60   I hastened and did not delay
       To keep Your commandments.
61   The cords of the wicked have encircled me,
       But I have not forgotten Your law.
62   At midnight I shall rise to give thanks to You
       Because of Your righteous ordinances.

Generating a memory of the LORD's Law (vv. 49–56)

Thank You for the comfort of Your commandments and precepts. They fill my heart and deliver me from the emptiness that fills this world (vv. 49–56).

Thank You, Father, for comfort, hope, and life through Your Word (vv. 49–50).

O Lord Jesus, make Your Word my song to sing all the days of my life on earth (v. 54).

When I obey Your Word, Lord, You pour out Your blessings upon me. Thank You (v. 56).

Hastening to keep the LORD's Word (vv. 57–64)

So many times I have promised to obey Your Word—enable me to fulfill those promises (v. 57).

Spirit, empower me to be quick to obey the Word (v. 60).

Even in the middle of the night, cause me to praise You for Your Word (v. 62).

63   I am a companion of all those who fear You,
     And of those who keep Your precepts.
64   The earth is full of Your lovingkindness, O Lord;
     Teach me Your statutes.

ט

Teth.

65   You have dealt well with Your servant,
     O Lord, according to Your word.
66   Teach me good discernment and knowledge,
     For I believe in Your commandments.
67   Before I was afflicted I went astray,
     But now I keep Your word.
68   You are good and do good;
     Teach me Your statutes.
69   The arrogant have forged a lie against me;
     With all *my* heart I will observe Your precepts.
70   Their heart is covered with fat,
     But I delight in Your law.
71   It is good for me that I was afflicted,
     That I may learn Your statutes.
72   The law of Your mouth is better to me
     Than thousands of gold and silver *pieces*.

י

Yodh.

73   Your hands made me and fashioned me;
     Give me understanding, that I may learn Your commandments.
74   May those who fear You see me and be glad,
     Because I wait for Your word.
75   I know, O Lord, that Your judgments are righteous,
     And that in faithfulness You have afflicted me.
76   O may Your lovingkindness comfort me,
     According to Your word to Your servant.
77   May Your compassion come to me that I may live,
     For Your law is my delight.
78   May the arrogant be ashamed, for they subvert me with a lie;
     But I shall meditate on Your precepts.

Father, thank You for friends who love and obey Your Word (v. 63).

Increasing good by the LORD's Word (vv. 65–72)

Give me discernment, knowledge, and faith by Your Word (v. 66).

Dear God, thank You for the trials that seem to come so often, because they keep me closer to You than when things are easy (vv. 67, 71).

As I open my Bible today, Lord Jesus, make Your Word more valuable to me than millions of dollars in gold and silver (v. 72).

Judging situations by the LORD's Word (vv. 73–80)

Father, increase my faith and hope in Your Word, so others see and rejoice (v. 74).

Turn my eyes, my mind, and my heart to Your Word and away from offenses committed against me (v. 78).

79 May those who fear You turn to me,
    Even those who know Your testimonies.
80 May my heart be blameless in Your statutes,
    So that I will not be ashamed.

כ

Kaph.

81 My soul languishes for Your salvation;
    I wait for Your word.
82 My eyes fail *with longing* for Your word,
    While I say, "When will You comfort me?"
83 Though I have become like a wineskin in the smoke,
    I do not forget Your statutes.
84 How many are the days of Your servant?
    When will You execute judgment on those who persecute me?
85 The arrogant have dug pits for me,
    Men who are not in accord with Your law.
86 All Your commandments are faithful;
    They have persecuted me with a lie; help me!
87 They almost destroyed me on earth,
    But as for me, I did not forsake Your precepts.
88 Revive me according to Your lovingkindness,
    So that I may keep the testimony of Your mouth.

ל

Lamedh.

89 Forever, O Lord,
    Your word is settled in heaven.
90 Your faithfulness *continues* throughout all generations;
    You established the earth, and it stands.
91 They stand this day according to Your ordinances,
    For all things are Your servants.
92 If Your law had not been my delight,
    Then I would have perished in my affliction.
93 I will never forget Your precepts,
    For by them You have revived me.
94 I am Yours, save me;
    For I have sought Your precepts.

I want to obey You in every way, dear Savior (v. 80).

Keeping oriented according to the LORD's Word (vv. 81–88)

Even when I feel overwhelmed and oppressed, I will look to Your Word and wait for Your comfort through it. Revive me in Your love, so that I may fellowship with You (vv. 81–88).

Holy Spirit, seal Your Word deep in my heart so that I neither forget nor forsake Your precepts (vv. 83, 87).

Help me, Lord, to seek truth, integrity, and security in Your Word rather than from human beings (v. 86).

Living by means of the LORD's precepts (vv. 89–96)

I offer You my praise for Your wonderful works in creating the heavens and the earth by Your Word (vv. 89–91).

Savior, You not only created all things, You gave me life. Thank You (v. 93).

95   The wicked wait for me to destroy me;
      I shall diligently consider Your testimonies.
96   I have seen a limit to all perfection;
      Your commandment is exceedingly broad.

מ

Mem.

97   O how I love Your law!
      It is my meditation all the day.
98   Your commandments make me wiser than my enemies,
      For they are ever mine.
99   I have more insight than all my teachers,
      For Your testimonies are my meditation.
100   I understand more than the aged,
      Because I have observed Your precepts.
101   I have restrained my feet from every evil way,
      That I may keep Your word.
102   I have not turned aside from Your ordinances,
      For You Yourself have taught me.
103   How sweet are Your words to my taste!
      Yes, sweeter than honey to my mouth!
104   From Your precepts I get understanding;
      Therefore I hate every false way.

נ

Nun.

105   Your word is a lamp to my feet
      And a light to my path.
106   I have sworn and I will confirm it,
      That I will keep Your righteous ordinances.
107   I am exceedingly afflicted;
      Revive me, O Lord, according to Your word.
108   O accept the freewill offerings of my mouth, O Lord,
      And teach me Your ordinances.
109   My life is continually in my hand,
      Yet I do not forget Your law.
110   The wicked have laid a snare for me,
      Yet I have not gone astray from Your precepts.

In the end, though all else falls short and will not fulfill, Your Word satisfies and sustains me. Praise God (v. 96).

Mastering understanding through the LORD's precepts (vv. 97–104)

I really do love Your law. Help me to love and obey it more and more each day. Fellowship with You in Your Word is sweet. Truly, nothing else in life even comes close to it (vv. 97–104).

Thank You, Lord, for wisdom from Your Word (vv. 98–100).

Keep me from the path of sin and disobedience, Lord, by enabling me to keep Your Word (vv. 101–102)

Negating affliction by the LORD's ordinances (vv. 105–112)

I so often feel like I'm being chased by enemies—on the run with nothing to cling to except Your Word. Thank You for Your precious Word (vv. 105–112).

Enable me to fulfill my promise to You, Lord Jesus, to obey all Your instruction (v. 106).

111 I have inherited Your testimonies forever,
For they are the joy of my heart.

112 I have inclined my heart to perform Your statutes
Forever, *even* to the end.

ס

Samekh.

113 ˙ I hate those who are double-minded,
But I love Your law.

114 You are my hiding place and my shield;
I wait for Your word.

115 Depart from me, evildoers,
That I may observe the commandments of my God.

116 Sustain me according to Your word, that I may live;
And do not let me be ashamed of my hope.

117 Uphold me that I may be safe,
That I may have regard for Your statutes continually.

118 You have rejected all those who wander from Your statutes,
For their deceitfulness is useless.

119 You have removed all the wicked of the earth *like* dross;
Therefore I love Your testimonies.

120 My flesh trembles for fear of You,
And I am afraid of Your judgments.

ע

Ayin.

121 I have done justice and righteousness;
Do not leave me to my oppressors.

122 Be surety for Your servant for good;
Do not let the arrogant oppress me.

123 My eyes fail *with longing* for Your salvation
And for Your righteous word.

124 Deal with Your servant according to Your lovingkindness
And teach me Your statutes.

125 I am Your servant; give me understanding,
That I may know Your testimonies.

126 It is time for the LORD to act,
For they have broken Your law.

Lord Jesus, keep my heart inclined to obey Your Word every day (v. 112).

Obtaining comfort through the Lord's statutes (vv. 113–120)

Father, create in me a greater hatred for sin and an ever-increasing love for Your law (v. 113).

Don't let me be ashamed of my hope in You, Lord Jesus, and in Your Word (v. 116).

Dear God, teach me to distrust my own cunning and to hold fast to Your Word (v. 118).

Teach me to fear You and Your judgment with a holy and righteous love for You and Your Word (v. 120).

Praying in accord with the Lord's Word (vv. 121–128)

Lord, You know I love You and Your Word. I have walked uprightly—not in perfection, but with genuine faith. Don't let the enemies of my soul have the satisfaction of seeing my faith falter. Help, Father (vv. 121–128).

Oh how I look forward to seeing all Your promises fulfilled in the eternal outcomes of the salvation You have so graciously provided (v. 123).

Lord, take action now to preserve your servant and to uphold Your Word (v. 126).

127   Therefore I love Your commandments
       Above gold, yes, above fine gold.
128   Therefore I esteem right all *Your* precepts concerning everything,
       I hate every false way.

 פ

Pe.

129   Your testimonies are wonderful;
       Therefore my soul observes them.
130   The unfolding of Your words gives light;
       It gives understanding to the simple.
131   I opened my mouth wide and panted,
       For I longed for Your commandments.
132   Turn to me and be gracious to me,
       After Your manner with those who love Your name.
133   Establish my footsteps in Your word,
       And do not let any iniquity have dominion over me.
134   Redeem me from the oppression of man,
       That I may keep Your precepts.
135   Make Your face shine upon Your servant,
       And teach me Your statutes.
136   My eyes shed streams of water,
       Because they do not keep Your law.

צ

Tsadhe.

137   Righteous are You, O Lord,
       And upright are Your judgments.
138   You have commanded Your testimonies in righteousness
       And exceeding faithfulness.
139   My zeal has consumed me,
       Because my adversaries have forgotten Your words.
140   Your word is very pure,
       Therefore Your servant loves it.
141   I am small and despised,
       Yet I do not forget Your precepts.
142   Your righteousness is an everlasting righteousness,
       And Your law is truth.

Quenching one's thirst with the LORD's Word (vv. 129–136)

The testimony You have given of Your Son in Your Spirit-inspired Word is more wonderful than my words can describe. Oh that all people might love Your law (v. 129).

Teach me to desire Your Word with all my being (v. 131).

Bless me, Lord. Teach me Your Word and enable me to grieve over those who disobey it (vv. 135–136).

Revealing the LORD's righteousness by His Word (vv. 137–144)

Thank You, O God, for being righteous and faithful (vv. 137–138).

I confess to my own failure to fulfill my promises when I see that You always fulfill Yours (v. 140).

Your Word is truth. Sanctify me in the truth, dear Father (v. 142).

143   Trouble and anguish have come upon me,
       Yet Your commandments are my delight.
144   Your testimonies are righteous forever;
       Give me understanding that I may live.

ק

Qoph.

145   I cried with all my heart; answer me, O Lord!
       I will observe Your statutes.
146   I cried to You; save me
       And I shall keep Your testimonies.
147   I rise before dawn and cry for help;
       I wait for Your words.
148   My eyes anticipate the night watches,
       That I may meditate on Your word.
149   Hear my voice according to Your lovingkindness;
       Revive me, O Lord, according to Your ordinances.
150   Those who follow after wickedness draw near;
       They are far from Your law.
151   You are near, O Lord,
       And all Your commandments are truth.
152   Of old I have known from Your testimonies
       That You have founded them forever.

ר

Resh.

153   Look upon my affliction and rescue me,
       For I do not forget Your law.
154   Plead my cause and redeem me;
       Revive me according to Your word.
155   Salvation is far from the wicked,
       For they do not seek Your statutes.
156   Great are Your mercies, O Lord;
       Revive me according to Your ordinances.
157   Many are my persecutors and my adversaries,
       Yet I do not turn aside from Your testimonies.
158   I behold the treacherous and loathe *them*,
       Because they do not keep Your word.

Seeking the LORD's help according to His Word (vv. 145–152)

Make my heart fully devoted to obeying Your Word, Lord (v. 145).

Increase my longing to know You through Your Word (v. 147).

Father, cause me to meditate on and keep Your Word day and night (vv. 147–148).

Thank You, dear Jesus, that You are always near me (v. 151).

Tossing oneself on the LORD's mercy by His Word (vv. 153–160)

Help me, Lord. I feel overwhelmed and surrounded again. Be my Advocate and defense as You have promised (v. 154).

O God, revive my heart through Your Word (vv. 154, 156, 159).

O Lord, how great are Your mercies to me (v. 156)!

159   Consider how I love Your precepts;
      Revive me, O Lᴏʀᴅ, according to Your lovingkindness.

160   The sum of Your word is truth,
      And every one of Your righteous ordinances is everlasting.

ש

Shin.

161   Princes persecute me without cause,
      But my heart stands in awe of Your words.

162   I rejoice at Your word,
      As one who finds great spoil.

163   I hate and despise falsehood,
      But I love Your law.

164   Seven times a day I praise You,
      Because of Your righteous ordinances.

165   Those who love Your law have great peace,
      And nothing causes them to stumble.

166   I hope for Your salvation, O Lᴏʀᴅ,
      And do Your commandments.

167   My soul keeps Your testimonies,
      And I love them exceedingly.

168   I keep Your precepts and Your testimonies,
      For all my ways are before You.

ת

Tav.

169   Let my cry come before You, O Lᴏʀᴅ;
      Give me understanding according to Your word.

170   Let my supplication come before You;
      Deliver me according to Your word.

171   Let my lips utter praise,
      For You teach me Your statutes.

172   Let my tongue sing of Your word,
      For all Your commandments are righteousness.

173   Let Your hand be ready to help me,
      For I have chosen Your precepts.

174   I long for Your salvation, O Lᴏʀᴅ,
      And Your law is my delight.

175   Let my soul live that it may praise You,
      And let Your ordinances help me.

176   I have gone astray like a lost sheep; seek Your servant,
      For I do not forget Your commandments.

Uniting hope with love for the LORD's Word (vv. 161–168)

No matter who opposes me or what I face in life, I stand in awe of and rejoice in Your Word (vv. 161–162).

Thank You for the peace that comes to me as I fellowship with You in Your Word (v. 165).

Look upon all my life and deeds, dear God, and increase my hope (vv. 166–168).

Voicing one's plea according to the LORD's Word (vv. 169–176)

I love Your Word. I long for Your salvation. I need Your grace, Lord. I still go astray so often. Seek Your servant (vv. 169–176).

Teach my tongue to sing of Your wonderful Word, Lord Jesus (v. 172)!

Forgive me, Father, for going astray like a lost sheep (v. 176).

How Jesus could be interceding for you: Father, I am Your incarnate Word sent to bring light, grace, and truth to the world (John 1:1–18). Fulfill Your Word for Your people whom You have given the new birth by that Word (1 Pet. 1:23). Bring Your Word to their hearts and minds in times of distress (John 14:18–24; 17:6–16). Sanctify them by Your Word (John 17:17).

Psalm 120

Prayer for Deliverance from the Treacherous.

A Song of Ascents.

1 In my trouble I cried to the LORD,
And He answered me.
2 Deliver my soul, O LORD, from lying lips,
From a deceitful tongue.
3 What shall be given to you, and what more shall be done to you,
You deceitful tongue?
4 Sharp arrows of the warrior,
With the *burning* coals of the broom tree.

5 Woe is me, for I sojourn in Meshech,
For I dwell among the tents of Kedar!
6 Too long has my soul had its dwelling
With those who hate peace.
7 I am *for* peace, but when I speak,
They are for war.

Praying Psalm 120

The fifteen Psalms of Ascents (Pss. 120–134) consist of the prayers of pilgrims to Jerusalem for the feasts of Passover, Pentecost, and Booths.

Father, please keep me from lying and deception, and keep me from those who are marked by lying and deception. You are truth, dear God (vv. 1–7).

Dear Lord, I leave retribution of the wicked in Your hands—execute justice as well as mercy (vv. 2–3).

Protect me and keep me in a hostile world and make me a person of peace (vv. 5–7).

How Jesus could be interceding for you: Gracious Father, give My peace (John 14:27) to this believer surrounded by a sin-darkened world filled with perversion and deceit (Luke 1:76–79; Phil. 2:14–16).

Psalm 121

The L<small>ORD</small> the Keeper of Israel.

A Song of Ascents.

1   I will lift up my eyes to the mountains;
     From where shall my help come?
2   My help *comes* from the L<small>ORD</small>,
     Who made heaven and earth.
3   He will not allow your foot to slip;
     He who keeps you will not slumber.
4   Behold, He who keeps Israel
     Will neither slumber nor sleep.

5   The L<small>ORD</small> is your keeper;
     The L<small>ORD</small> is your shade on your right hand.
6   The sun will not smite you by day,
     Nor the moon by night.
7   The L<small>ORD</small> will protect you from all evil;
     He will keep your soul.
8   The L<small>ORD</small> will guard your going out and your coming in
     From this time forth and forever.

Praying Psalm 121

This pilgrim prayer has become known as the "Traveler's Psalm."

Helper of Israel, You are Keeper, Protector, Guardian, and Savior of Your people. Thank You. Please keep me, protect me, keep watch over me, and save me for Your Son's sake (vv. 1–8).

~~~

O Maker of heaven and earth, thank You for being my help (vv. 1–2).

~~~

O God, You never sleep—You are my ever present Protector wherever I go (vv. 3–8).

How Jesus could be interceding for you: Keeper of Your people (Jude 24–25), You remain always alert to provide help in their time of need (Heb. 4:16; 1 Pet. 3:12). Deliver them from all evil by My death and resurrection on their behalf (Matt. 6:13; Gal. 1:3–5).

Psalm 122

Prayer for the Peace of Jerusalem.

A Song of Ascents, of David.

1   I was glad when they said to me,
      "Let us go to the house of the LORD."
2   Our feet are standing
      Within your gates, O Jerusalem,
3   Jerusalem, that is built
      As a city that is compact together;
4   To which the tribes go up, even the tribes of the LORD—
      An ordinance for Israel—
      To give thanks to the name of the LORD.
5   For there thrones were set for judgment,
      The thrones of the house of David.

6   Pray for the peace of Jerusalem:
      "May they prosper who love you.
7   "May peace be within your walls,
      And prosperity within your palaces."
8   For the sake of my brothers and my friends,
      I will now say, "May peace be within you."
9   For the sake of the house of the LORD our God,
      I will seek your good.

Praying Psalm 122

As a pilgrim, David prays for Jerusalem's peace in the midst of a hostile world.

Father, I do pray for the peace of Jerusalem—the day when the Prince of Peace, Messiah Jesus, the Son of God rules the world from the throne of David in its midst (vv. 1–9).

Lord, help me encourage others to attend assemblies of believers to worship You (v. 1).

Enable me always to seek Your good for the sake of others (vv. 8–9).

How Jesus could be interceding for you: Grant Jerusalem peace, gracious Father. Bring the time when I will finally gather her people to find refuge in Me (Matt. 23:37–38). Once again, as at the beginning of the church, multiply believers in Jerusalem (Acts 6:7).

Psalm 123

Prayer for the Lord's Help.

A Song of Ascents.

1   To You I lift up my eyes,
     O You who are enthroned in the heavens!
2   Behold, as the eyes of servants *look* to the hand of their master,
     As the eyes of a maid to the hand of her mistress,
     So our eyes *look* to the Lord our God,
     Until He is gracious to us.

3   Be gracious to us, O Lord, be gracious to us,
     For we are greatly filled with contempt.
4   Our soul is greatly filled
     With the scoffing of those who are at ease,
     And with the contempt of the proud.

Praying Psalm 123

A pilgrim prays for God's grace while experiencing scoffing and antagonism.

You give grace to the humble, Father. Humble my heart to look to You for grace and to live for You always. Be gracious to us, O Lord; be gracious to us (vv. 1–4).

~~~

Lord Jesus, I'm unworthy of Your grace—we are all undeserving—help us (vv. 3–4).

How Jesus could be interceding for you: From Your heavenly throne You rule over all Your creation, Father (Heb. 8:1). Pour out Your grace upon Your people (Heb. 4:16) and guard them from the scoffers, the arrogant, and false teachers (2 Pet. 3:1–7; Jude 18–23).

Psalm 124

Praise for Rescue from Enemies.

A Song of Ascents, of David.

1 "Had it not been the LORD who was on our side,"
   Let Israel now say,
2 "Had it not been the LORD who was on our side
   When men rose up against us,
3 Then they would have swallowed us alive,
   When their anger was kindled against us;
4 Then the waters would have engulfed us,
   The stream would have swept over our soul;
5 Then the raging waters would have swept over our soul."

6 Blessed be the LORD,
   Who has not given us to be torn by their teeth.
7 Our soul has escaped as a bird out of the snare of the trapper;
   The snare is broken and we have escaped.
8 Our help is in the name of the LORD,
   Who made heaven and earth.

Praying Psalm 124

As a pilgrim, David again prays for the Lord's protection from hostile people.

Lord, thank You for Your promises to save Your people no matter the opposition they face. Your plan for Israel will be fulfilled. Your plan for me will be fulfilled. Blessed be the living God who will not allow His people to be destroyed (vv. 1–8).

Help me, Father, to keep my head above the "raging waters" of life (v. 5).

Thank You for setting me free from the traps of my enemies (v. 7).

How Jesus could be interceding for you: Father, deliver Your people from dangerous perils (Rom. 8:35–39). Seal in their hearts and minds that You are on their side (Matt. 6:8; 1 Pet. 5:6–7) and that We will never leave them nor forsake them (Heb. 13:5–6).

Psalm 125

The LORD Surrounds His People.

A Song of Ascents.

1 Those who trust in the LORD
   Are as Mount Zion, which cannot be moved but abides forever.
2 As the mountains surround Jerusalem,
   So the LORD surrounds His people
   From this time forth and forever.
3 For the scepter of wickedness shall not rest upon the land of the
      righteous,
   So that the righteous will not put forth their hands to do wrong.

4 Do good, O LORD, to those who are good
   And to those who are upright in their hearts.
5 But as for those who turn aside to their crooked ways,
   The LORD will lead them away with the doers of iniquity.
   Peace be upon Israel.

Praying Psalm 125

A pilgrim prays for God to dispense goodness to the
righteous and justice to the wicked.

I do trust You, Lord. Make my faith stronger. I want to stand firm in You and for
You (vv. 1–2).

How Jesus could be interceding for you: Surround the sheep of Our pasture with
love and make them aware of how secure they are in Us (John 10:7–11, 14–15, 27–30).

Psalm 126

Thanksgiving for Return from Captivity.

A Song of Ascents.

1   When the LORD brought back the captive ones of Zion,
    We were like those who dream.
2   Then our mouth was filled with laughter
    And our tongue with joyful shouting;
    Then they said among the nations,
    "The LORD has done great things for them."
3   The LORD has done great things for us;
    We are glad.

4   Restore our captivity, O LORD,
    As the streams in the South.
5   Those who sow in tears shall reap with joyful shouting.
6   He who goes to and fro weeping, carrying *his* bag of seed,
    Shall indeed come again with a shout of joy, bringing his sheaves *with him.*

Praying Psalm 126

At Thanksgiving and Advent many churches read this pilgrim prayer.

O Lord God, I am overwhelmed by all that You have done for me (vv. 1–2).

—

Give me perseverance to keep on laboring in Your harvest field, Lord Jesus (v. 5).

—

Faithful Father, encourage Your people to put their hope in You. Those who sow in tears will reap Your tender mercies and experience Kingdom joy (v. 6).

How Jesus could be interceding for you: Father, by Your will I proclaimed release to those who were captive and set free those oppressed by sin (Luke 4:17–21). Deliver them from Satan's dominion and sanctify them by faith in Me (Acts 26:15–18).

Psalm 127

Prosperity Comes from the Lord.

A Song of Ascents, of Solomon.

1   Unless the Lord builds the house,
They labor in vain who build it;
Unless the Lord guards the city,
The watchman keeps awake in vain.
2   It is vain for you to rise up early,
To retire late,
To eat the bread of painful labors;
For He gives to His beloved *even in his* sleep.

3   Behold, children are a gift of the Lord,
The fruit of the womb is a reward.
4   Like arrows in the hand of a warrior,
So are the children of one's youth.
5   How blessed is the man whose quiver is full of them;
They will not be ashamed
When they speak with their enemies in the gate.

Praying Psalm 127

*As a pilgrim, Solomon prays for the Lord's working
and His blessings upon his family.*

Lord Jesus, You called us to rest in You (cf. Matt. 11:28–30). Please build, when I labor for Your glory. Please guard, while I seek to be spiritually alert. Please help me to find my satisfaction in You (vv. 1–2).

Thank You, Father, for the children you have given to me (v. 3).

Provide me with confident faith as I live in a hostile world, Lord (v. 5).

How Jesus could be interceding for you: Father of the institution of marriage, keep this husband and wife united as one (Matt. 19:4–6). Father of families, bring Your blessing upon this home's parents and children as they obey You (Eph. 6:1–4).

Psalm 128

Blessedness of the Fear of the LORD.

A Song of Ascents.

1   How blessed is everyone who fears the LORD,
    Who walks in His ways.
2   When you shall eat of the fruit of your hands,
    You will be happy and it will be well with you.
3   Your wife shall be like a fruitful vine
    Within your house,
    Your children like olive plants
    Around your table.
4   Behold, for thus shall the man be blessed
    Who fears the LORD.

5   The LORD bless you from Zion,
    And may you see the prosperity of Jerusalem all the days of your life.
6   Indeed, may you see your children's children.
    Peace be upon Israel!

Praying Psalm 128

A pilgrim prays for a blessed and happy family life.

You always feared the Lord and walked in His ways, Lord Jesus. Come in Your Kingdom glory with Your bride, the Church, and enjoy the prosperity of Jerusalem, and see Your offspring live in peace (vv. 1–6).

O Lord God, how you have blessed me and my family beyond all measure (vv. 1, 4, 5).

If it be Your will, grant me the opportunity to enjoy the blessing of grandchildren (v. 6).

How Jesus could be interceding for you: Bless this family, Father, because they fear You—pour out Your mercy on them (Luke 1:50). Bless those who worship You in spirit and in truth (John 4:23–24).

Psalm 129

Prayer for the Overthrow of Zion's Enemies.

A Song of Ascents.

1   "Many times they have persecuted me from my youth up,"
    Let Israel now say,

2   "Many times they have persecuted me from my youth up;
    Yet they have not prevailed against me.

3   "The plowers plowed upon my back;
    They lengthened their furrows."

4   The LORD is righteous;
    He has cut in two the cords of the wicked.

5   May all who hate Zion
    Be put to shame and turned backward;

6   Let them be like grass upon the housetops,
    Which withers before it grows up;

7   With which the reaper does not fill his hand,
    Or the binder of sheaves his bosom;

8   Nor do those who pass by say,
    "The blessing of the LORD be upon you;
    We bless you in the name of the LORD."

Praying Psalm 129

A pilgrim thanks God for preserving His people despite their suffering persecution.

Thank You, God, for preserving me through suffering and trials (vv. 1–2).

Oo God, You alone are righteous in character and in deed (v. 4).

Father, may all those who do not delight in Your people bear their reproach and know no blessing from the God of Israel, the God and Father of our Lord Jesus Christ (vv. 5–8).

How Jesus could be interceding for you: These believers who have been persecuted for believing in Me belong in Our Kingdom, Father (Matt. 5:10–12). Give them such a portion of My love that they love their enemies and pray for them (Matt. 5:44).

Psalm 130

Hope in the LORD's Forgiving Love.

A Song of Ascents.

1   Out of the depths I have cried to You, O LORD.
2   Lord, hear my voice!
     Let Your ears be attentive
     To the voice of my supplications.
3   If You, LORD, should mark iniquities,
     O Lord, who could stand?
4   But there is forgiveness with You,
     That You may be feared.

5   I wait for the LORD, my soul does wait,
     And in His word do I hope.
6   My soul *waits* for the Lord
     More than the watchmen for the morning;
     Indeed, more than the watchmen for the morning.
7   O Israel, hope in the LORD;
     For with the LORD there is lovingkindness,
     And with Him is abundant redemption.
8   And He will redeem Israel
     From all his iniquities.

Praying Psalm 130

A pilgrim prays for forgiveness by means of the redemption that supplies hope.

It is true, dear Savior, there is forgiveness with You and it is awesome and fearful. You stood in my place and paid for my iniquities so I could stand in Your righteousness. I love You, Lord. Thank You for loving me (vv. 3–4).

I long to be with You in glory. I will wait in hope (vv. 5–6).

Thank You, Lord, for redeeming me fully from my sins (vv. 7–8).

How Jesus could be interceding for you: Dear Father, hear the supplications of each one who comes to Me by faith (Luke 18:1–8; Eph. 6:18). Grant each one Your forgiveness on the basis of My redemptive work for them (Eph. 1:7).

Psalm 131

Childlike Trust in the LORD.

A Song of Ascents, of David.

1   O LORD, my heart is not proud, nor my eyes haughty;
Nor do I involve myself in great matters,
Or in things too difficult for me.
2   Surely I have composed and quieted my soul;
Like a weaned child *rests* against his mother,
My soul is like a weaned child within me.
3   O Israel, hope in the LORD
From this time forth and forever.

Praying Psalm 131

As a pilgrim, David prays for Israel's hope.

I trust You Lord—Your wisdom, Your goodness, Your timing. Help me to call others to hope in You by how I love (vv. 1–3).

Teach me, O God, to find contentment in You alone (v. 2).

How Jesus could be interceding for you: Loving and merciful Father, enable this spiritual pilgrim to hope fully in Me and My work (Rom. 5:1–2; 15:13) with deep humility (Eph. 4:1–6).

Psalm 132

Prayer for the LORD's Blessing upon the Sanctuary.

A Song of Ascents.

1 Remember, O LORD, on David's behalf,
   All his affliction;
2 How he swore to the LORD
   And vowed to the Mighty One of Jacob,
3 "Surely I will not enter my house,
   Nor lie on my bed;
4 I will not give sleep to my eyes
   Or slumber to my eyelids,
5 Until I find a place for the LORD,
   A dwelling place for the Mighty One of Jacob."

6 Behold, we heard of it in Ephrathah,
   We found it in the field of Jaar.
7 Let us go into His dwelling place;
   Let us worship at His footstool.
8 Arise, O LORD, to Your resting place,
   You and the ark of Your strength.
9 Let Your priests be clothed with righteousness,
   And let Your godly ones sing for joy.
10 For the sake of David Your servant,
   Do not turn away the face of Your anointed.
11 The LORD has sworn to David
   A truth from which He will not turn back:
   "Of the fruit of your body I will set upon your throne.
12 "If your sons will keep My covenant
   And My testimony which I will teach them,
   Their sons also shall sit upon your throne forever."
13 For the LORD has chosen Zion;
   He has desired it for His habitation.
14 "This is My resting place forever;
   Here I will dwell, for I have desired it.
15 "I will abundantly bless her provision;
   I will satisfy her needy with bread.
16 "Her priests also I will clothe with salvation,
   And her godly ones will sing aloud for joy.
17 "There I will cause the horn of David to spring forth;
   I have prepared a lamp for Mine anointed.
18 "His enemies I will clothe with shame,
   But upon himself his crown shall shine."

Praying Psalm 132

A pilgrim praises the Lord for providing a place of worship.

Father, thank You for the Son of David, Messiah Jesus. May He rule from Jerusalem as You have said. May Your promises to David be fulfilled and the world know the blessing of the Son of God (vv. 1–18).

Enable me, Lord, to keep my vow to contribute from my earnings to a building for worshiping You (vv. 2–4).

Lord Jesus, clothe me with Your righteousness and enable me to joyfully sing Your praises (vv. 9, 16).

Help me to follow my Savior's example in caring for the needy (v. 15).

How Jesus could be interceding for you: Holy Father, each pilgrim believer is a priest before You (1 Pet. 2:9–12). Clothe them with righteousness and salvation (Eph. 4:20–24; 6:14–17). Fill their hearts with joy and their mouths with songs of praise (Rom. 14:17; Acts 16:25; Eph. 5:18–21).

Psalm 133

The Excellency of Brotherly Unity.

A Song of Ascents, of David.

1   Behold, how good and how pleasant it is
For brothers to dwell together in unity!
2   It is like the precious oil upon the head,
Coming down upon the beard,
Even Aaron's beard,
Coming down upon the edge of his robes.
3   It is like the dew of Hermon
Coming down upon the mountains of Zion;
For there the Lord commanded the blessing—life forever.

Praying Psalm 133

As a pilgrim, David prays for unity among true believers.

Bring the day, dear Lord, when unity is fully realized among Your people (vv. 1–3).

Use me, Father, to nurture and spread a spirit of unity (vv. 2–3).

How Jesus could be interceding for you: Through My atoning death and resurrection, Father, I have made all Your people one (Eph. 2:11–22). Make that unity a witness to the world about My saving work for them (John 17:20–23).

Psalm 134

Greetings of Night Watchers.

A Song of Ascents.

1   Behold, bless the Lord, all servants of the Lord,
     Who serve by night in the house of the Lord!
2   Lift up your hands to the sanctuary
     And bless the Lord.
3   May the Lord bless you from Zion,
     He who made heaven and earth.

Praying Psalm 134

A pilgrim prays for God's servants to lift up their
praise to God and for Him to bless them.

Thank You, Father, for the prophetic glimpses You give us in the Psalter. May all Your servants, whether in a future Temple or in the living temple of the church, praise You as the living God (vv. 1–3).

O Creator of heaven and earth, how I praise You for the many blessings You have given me (v. 3).

How Jesus could be interceding for you: Lift Your people's hands in praise to You, Father (1 Tim. 2:8). Grant them abundant blessing, even as I Myself have blessed them (Matt. 25:34; Luke 24:50; Eph. 1:3).

Psalm 135

Praise the Lord's Wonderful Works. Vanity of Idols.

1 Praise the Lord!
Praise the name of the Lord;
Praise *Him*, O servants of the Lord,
2 You who stand in the house of the Lord,
In the courts of the house of our God!
3 Praise the Lord, for the Lord is good;
Sing praises to His name, for it is lovely.
4 For the Lord has chosen Jacob for Himself,
Israel for His own possession.

5 For I know that the Lord is great
And that our Lord is above all gods.
6 Whatever the Lord pleases, He does,
In heaven and in earth, in the seas and in all deeps.
7 He causes the vapors to ascend from the ends of the earth;
Who makes lightnings for the rain,
Who brings forth the wind from His treasuries.

8 He smote the firstborn of Egypt,
Both of man and beast.
9 He sent signs and wonders into your midst, O Egypt,
Upon Pharaoh and all his servants.
10 He smote many nations
And slew mighty kings,
11 Sihon, king of the Amorites,
And Og, king of Bashan,
And all the kingdoms of Canaan;
12 And He gave their land as a heritage,
A heritage to Israel His people.
13 Your name, O Lord, is everlasting,
Your remembrance, O Lord, throughout all generations.
14 For the Lord will judge His people
And will have compassion on His servants.
15 The idols of the nations are *but* silver and gold,
The work of man's hands.
16 They have mouths, but they do not speak;

Praying Psalm 135

An anonymous psalmist offers a prayer of praise drawing on Scripture from all three major sections of the Hebrew Bible (Law, Prophets, and Writings).

Your name, Lord, is indeed lovely—it is life. Praise be to God (v. 3).

Thank You for this reminder that You are sovereign and do as You please—and it always pleases You to do good to Your children (vv. 5–6).

Israel's history clearly reveals You are the living Lord. We will trust in You, Father (vv. 8–18).

Father, preserve my remembrance of all Your mighty deeds (v. 13).

---

* For example: verse 4 (Exod. 19:5; Deut. 7:6), verses 6–7 (Pss. 115:3; 136:5–9), verse 7 (Jer. 10:13; 51:16). Note the three-fold division of the Hebrew Scriptures is referenced by Jesus in Luke 24:44.

They have eyes, but they do not see;
17 They have ears, but they do not hear,
 Nor is there any breath at all in their mouths.
18 Those who make them will be like them,
 Yes, everyone who trusts in them.
19 O house of Israel, bless the LORD;
 O house of Aaron, bless the LORD;
20 O house of Levi, bless the LORD;
 You who revere the LORD, bless the LORD.
21 Blessed be the LORD from Zion,
 Who dwells in Jerusalem.
 Praise the LORD!

Precious Savior, teach me how to trust You, and only You, in all things (v. 18).

Blessed be the Lord (vv. 19–21)!

How Jesus could be interceding for you: Great Father, Father of all goodness, Father of lights (Jas. 1:17), receive the praise of Your beloved people who come to You in My name (Phil. 1:8–11; Heb. 13:12–16).

Psalm 136

Thanks for the LORD's Goodness to Israel.

1   Give thanks to the LORD, for He is good,
    For His lovingkindness is everlasting.
2   Give thanks to the God of gods,
    For His lovingkindness is everlasting.
3   Give thanks to the Lord of lords,
    For His lovingkindness is everlasting.
4   To Him who alone does great wonders,
    For His lovingkindness is everlasting;
5   To Him who made the heavens with skill,
    For His lovingkindness is everlasting;
6   To Him who spread out the earth above the waters,
    For His lovingkindness is everlasting;
7   To Him who made *the* great lights,
    For His lovingkindness is everlasting:
8   The sun to rule by day,
    For His lovingkindness is everlasting,
9   The moon and stars to rule by night,
    For His lovingkindness is everlasting.
10 To Him who smote the Egyptians in their firstborn,
    For His lovingkindness is everlasting,
11 And brought Israel out from their midst,
    For His lovingkindness is everlasting,
12 With a strong hand and an outstretched arm,
    For His lovingkindness is everlasting.
13 To Him who divided the Red Sea asunder,
    For His lovingkindness is everlasting,
14 And made Israel pass through the midst of it,
    For His lovingkindness is everlasting;
15 But He overthrew Pharaoh and his army in the Red Sea,
    For His lovingkindness is everlasting.
16 To Him who led His people through the wilderness,
    For His lovingkindness is everlasting;
17 To Him who smote great kings,
    For His lovingkindness is everlasting,
18 And slew mighty kings,
    For His lovingkindness is everlasting:

Praying Psalm 136

Jewish worshipers sing Psalm 136 by itself, or with Psalm 135,
on the morning of every Sabbath, on Passover evening, and for
Hanukkah—perhaps sung by Jesus and His disciples (Matt. 26:30).

You are good—infinitely and perfectly good, Lord. Thank You for Your everlasting love (v. 1).

You are sovereign, almighty, holy, Creator of all—You are good, and Your love is eternal (vv. 2–9).

Thank You, God, for giving light for the earth (vv. 7–9).

Your judgment and wrath are good, Lord, and perfect in love (vv. 10–22).

Thank You, Almighty God, for Your mighty deeds on behalf of Your people (vv. 10–22).

Thank You, Lord, for judging evil when You deliver Your people (vv. 15, 17, 20).

19 Sihon, king of the Amorites,
    For His lovingkindness is everlasting,
20 And Og, king of Bashan,
    For His lovingkindness is everlasting,
21 And gave their land as a heritage,
    For His lovingkindness is everlasting,
22 Even a heritage to Israel His servant,
    For His lovingkindness is everlasting.
23 Who remembered us in our low estate,
    For His lovingkindness is everlasting,
24 And has rescued us from our adversaries,
    For His lovingkindness is everlasting;
25 Who gives food to all flesh,
    For His lovingkindness is everlasting.
26 Give thanks to the God of heaven,
    For His lovingkindness is everlasting.

You are the Savior of all men, especially believers. Thank You (vv. 23–26).

Thank You, God of heaven, for rescuing us (vv. 23, 26).

How Jesus could be interceding for you: O Father of Israel and God of Heaven, because You love humankind You sent Me to save from sin those who believe in Me (John 3:16). Just as I also have loved them, give them love for one another (John 13:34–35; 17:23–26).

Psalm 137

An Experience of the Captivity.

1   By the rivers of Babylon,
    There we sat down and wept,
    When we remembered Zion.
2   Upon the willows in the midst of it
    We hung our harps.
3   For there our captors demanded of us songs,
    And our tormentors mirth, *saying,*
    "Sing us one of the songs of Zion."

4   How can we sing the LORD's song
    In a foreign land?
5   If I forget you, O Jerusalem,
    May my right hand forget *her skill.*
6   May my tongue cling to the roof of my mouth
    If I do not remember you,
    If I do not exalt Jerusalem
    Above my chief joy.

7   Remember, O LORD, against the sons of Edom
    The day of Jerusalem,
    Who said, "Raze it, raze it
    To its very foundation."
8   O daughter of Babylon, you devastated one,
    How blessed will be the one who repays you
    With the recompense with which you have repaid us.
9   How blessed will be the one who seizes and dashes your little ones
    Against the rock.

Praying Psalm 137

*The Jewish captives in Babylon pray for God to bring
about justice by judging their oppressors.*

Lord, it is good, loving, and righteous for You to repay with affliction those who have afflicted Your children. You are faithful and just as well as merciful and kind. We look to You to do what is right (vv. 1–9).

Father, teach me to weep over the loss of fellowship with You because of my disobedience (v. 1).

Teach me songs to sing in all circumstances, O Spirit of the Living God (vv. 2–3).

Dear God, help me understand when my praise is dishonoring to You because of my sinful hypocrisy (v. 4).

Lord Jesus, make Your presence and Your people my chief joy (v. 6).

O Lord of all righteousness, teach me to leave all vengeance to You alone (vv. 7–9).

How Jesus could be interceding for you: Father, imprint Jerusalem upon the hearts of all Your people. Cause them to grieve with Me over her sin (Matt. 23:37) and to pray for her restoration through My redemptive work (Heb. 12:18–24).

Psalm 138

Thanksgiving for the Lord's Favor.

A Psalm *of David.*

1 I will give You thanks with all my heart;
   I will sing praises to You before the gods.
2 I will bow down toward Your holy temple
   And give thanks to Your name for Your lovingkindness and Your truth;
   For You have magnified Your word according to all Your name.
3 On the day I called, You answered me;
   You made me bold with strength in my soul.

4 All the kings of the earth will give thanks to You, O Lord,
   When they have heard the words of Your mouth.
5 And they will sing of the ways of the Lord,
   For great is the glory of the Lord.
6 For though the Lord is exalted,
   Yet He regards the lowly,
   But the haughty He knows from afar.

7 Though I walk in the midst of trouble, You will revive me;
   You will stretch forth Your hand against the wrath of my enemies,
   And Your right hand will save me.
8 The Lord will accomplish what concerns me;
   Your lovingkindness, O Lord, is everlasting;
   Do not forsake the works of Your hands.

Praying Psalm 138

David's prayer of praise and thanks for the covenant which God made with him.

Fill all of my being with thanks to You, Father—to sing the praises of Your love and faithfulness (vv. 1–2).

Thank You, Father, for the strength You gave me when I asked (v. 3).

May kings hear Your Word and sing Your praise (vv. 4–5)!

I praise You, Lord, that You care for the lowly of heart. Forgive me for my pride and grant me a truly humble heart. I want to walk with You more intimately (v. 6).

I believe that in love You will accomplish what concerns me (v. 8).

How Jesus could be interceding for you: Your promises to David will be fulfilled, faithful Father (Luke 1:32–33; Rom. 1:1–6). I am the greater Son of David, Who fulfills Your promises (Matt. 1:1; Rev. 22:16). With the same faithfulness, fulfill Your Word for all who have come to Me by faith for salvation (Acts 2:29–36; 2 Cor. 1:18–22; Titus 1:1–2).

Psalm 139

God's Omnipresence and Omniscience.

For the choir director. A Psalm of David.

1   O Lord, You have searched me and known *me.*

2   You know when I sit down and when I rise up;
    You understand my thought from afar.

3   You scrutinize my path and my lying down,
    And are intimately acquainted with all my ways.

4   Even before there is a word on my tongue,
    Behold, O Lord, You know it all.

5   You have enclosed me behind and before,
    And laid Your hand upon me.

6   *Such* knowledge is too wonderful for me;
    It is *too* high, I cannot attain to it.

7   Where can I go from Your Spirit?
    Or where can I flee from Your presence?

8   If I ascend to heaven, You are there;
    If I make my bed in Sheol, behold, You are there.

9   If I take the wings of the dawn,
    If I dwell in the remotest part of the sea,

10   Even there Your hand will lead me,
    And Your right hand will lay hold of me.

11   If I say, "Surely the darkness will overwhelm me,
    And the light around me will be night,"

12   Even the darkness is not dark to You,
    And the night is as bright as the day.
    Darkness and light are alike *to You.*

13   For You formed my inward parts;
    You wove me in my mother's womb.

14   I will give thanks to You, for I am fearfully and wonderfully made;
    Wonderful are Your works,
    And my soul knows it very well.

15   My frame was not hidden from You,
    When I was made in secret,
    And skillfully wrought in the depths of the earth;

Praying Psalm 139

*David's prayer expresses his trust in the Lord Who is
everywhere, all-knowing, and all-powerful.*

You know everything, Lord, and I'm glad—though it makes me tremble. I praise You for being an infinitely wise and omniscient Lord and Savior who knows everything about everything and everyone who has or will ever exist. Yet You care about me. Thank You, Father (vv. 1–6).

Omnipresent Spirit of God, thank You for being with Your people wherever they go. You never leave them nor forsake them (vv. 7–12).

Sovereign Creator, Who ordains all of my days—from the cradle of the womb to eternity—praise belongs to You from the moment of conception to the endless aeons of eternity (vv. 13–16).

16   Your eyes have seen my unformed substance;
     And in Your book were all written
     The days that were ordained *for me,*
     When as yet there was not one of them.

17   How precious also are Your thoughts to me, O God!
     How vast is the sum of them!

18   If I should count them, they would outnumber the sand.
     When I awake, I am still with You.

19   O that You would slay the wicked, O God;
     Depart from me, therefore, men of bloodshed.

20   For they speak against You wickedly,
     And Your enemies take *Your name* in vain.

21   Do I not hate those who hate You, O Lord?
     And do I not loathe those who rise up against You?

22   I hate them with the utmost hatred;
     They have become my enemies.

23   Search me, O God, and know my heart;
     Try me and know my anxious thoughts;

24   And see if there be any hurtful way in me,
     And lead me in the everlasting way.

God, how wonderful You are that You would think of me—even in my sleep, You think of Your people with thoughts of love and wisdom. Even when I sleep in death, I will awake to resurrection life in Your presence. Thank You, Lord (vv. 17–18)!

Grant to me a holy hatred for that which You hate, Lord. Search me and refine me for Yourself—and lead me in fellowship with Your Son, Who is the everlasting way (vv. 23–24).

How Jesus could be interceding for you: All wise Creator and Father of mankind, You are everywhere present and know everything about each person (Luke 8:17; 16:15; Rom. 8:27). Demonstrate to this believer that We are always near in every circumstance (Matt. 6:8; John 2:24–25; 21:17; Heb. 13:5–6).

Psalm 140

Prayer for Protection against the Wicked.

For the choir director. A Psalm of David.

1   Rescue me, O Lord, from evil men;
    Preserve me from violent men
2   Who devise evil things in *their* hearts;
    They continually stir up wars.
3   They sharpen their tongues as a serpent;
    Poison of a viper is under their lips.   *Selah.*

4   Keep me, O Lord, from the hands of the wicked;
    Preserve me from violent men
    Who have purposed to trip up my feet.
5   The proud have hidden a trap for me, and cords;
    They have spread a net by the wayside;
    They have set snares for me.   *Selah.*

6   I said to the Lord, "You are my God;
    Give ear, O Lord, to the voice of my supplications.
7   "O God the Lord, the strength of my salvation,
    You have covered my head in the day of battle.
8   "Do not grant, O Lord, the desires of the wicked;
    Do not promote his *evil* device, *that* they *not* be exalted. *Selah.*

9   "As for the head of those who surround me,
    May the mischief of their lips cover them.
10 "May burning coals fall upon them;
    May they be cast into the fire,
    Into deep pits from which they cannot rise.
11 "May a slanderer not be established in the earth;
    May evil hunt the violent man speedily."
12 I know that the Lord will maintain the cause of the afflicted
    And justice for the poor.
13 Surely the righteous will give thanks to Your name;
    The upright will dwell in Your presence.

Praying Psalm 140

*When Absalom's rebellion drives David from Jerusalem,
David prays for God's protection and preservation.*

Protect me, Lord, from people who want to destroy with their words and entrap me with their plans—keep me trusting in You (vv. 1–5).

Protect me, Lord, from people who want to destroy with their words and entrap me with their plans—keep me trusting in You (vv. 1–5).

You are my God, and in You is my strength and my salvation. Hear, dear Savior, and deliver me from the desire of evil people (vv. 6–8).

Provide me with Your grace—You are my God (v. 6).

Again I am reminded, Lord Jesus, of how You must have prayed in perfect holiness in the time of Your sojourn here on earth. Evil people constantly wanted to entrap and destroy You. May all who hate You and Your people be cast away from You forever (vv. 9–11).

Lord, let me dwell in Your presence forever and ever (v. 13).

How Jesus could be interceding for you: Father of all comfort (2 Cor. 1:3–5), take up the cause of the afflicted, and preserve them from violent people as they seek to serve Me (2 Cor. 1:8–11; 4:8–11; 2 Thess. 1:5–10).

Psalm 141

An Evening Prayer for Sanctification and Protection.

A Psalm of David.

1   O LORD, I call upon You; hasten to me!
    Give ear to my voice when I call to You!
2   May my prayer be counted as incense before You;
    The lifting up of my hands as the evening offering.
3   Set a guard, O LORD, over my mouth;
    Keep watch over the door of my lips.
4   Do not incline my heart to any evil thing,
    To practice deeds of wickedness
    With men who do iniquity;
    And do not let me eat of their delicacies.

5   Let the righteous smite me in kindness and reprove me;
    It is oil upon the head;
    Do not let my head refuse it,
    For still my prayer is against their wicked deeds.
6   Their judges are thrown down by the sides of the rock,
    And they hear my words, for they are pleasant.
7   As when one plows and breaks open the earth,
    Our bones have been scattered at the mouth of Sheol.

8   For my eyes are toward You, O GOD, the Lord;
    In You I take refuge; do not leave me defenseless.
9   Keep me from the jaws of the trap which they have set for me,
    And from the snares of those who do iniquity.
10   Let the wicked fall into their own nets,
    While I pass by safely.

Praying Psalm 141

*Perhaps as an evening prayer, David prays every
word of this psalm as his plea to God.*

Father, receive my prayer as the worship You deserve—sanctify my worship as it is offered in Christ (v. 2).

Lord, keep me from sin in thought and word and deed—and teach me to receive instruction and correction (vv. 3–5).

Send godly friends to reprove me and correct me as I need it, Lord (v. 5).

Dear God, vindicate me before my enemies who have brought me to death's door (vv. 6–7).

Help me, Lord Jesus—be my rock and my refuge against those who want to see me forsake You (vv. 8–10).

How Jesus could be interceding for you: Give ear, Father, to the prayers of Your people. Incline their heart in obedience to Our words (John 17:6–8) and deliver them from evil (Matt. 6:13). Enable them to accept Your discipline even from fellow believers (Rom. 15:14; Col. 3:16). Keep them safe from the enemy and his snares (Eph. 6:10–13; 1 Pet. 5:8).

Psalm 142

Prayer for Help in Trouble.

Maskil of David, when he was in the cave. A Prayer.

1   I cry aloud with my voice to the LORD;
     I make supplication with my voice to the LORD.
2   I pour out my complaint before Him;
     I declare my trouble before Him.
3   When my spirit was overwhelmed within me,
     You knew my path.
     In the way where I walk
     They have hidden a trap for me.
4   Look to the right and see;
     For there is no one who regards me;
     There is no escape for me;
     No one cares for my soul.

5   I cried out to You, O LORD;
     I said, "You are my refuge,
     My portion in the land of the living.
6   "Give heed to my cry,
     For I am brought very low;
     Deliver me from my persecutors,
     For they are too strong for me.
7   "Bring my soul out of prison,
     So that I may give thanks to Your name;
     The righteous will surround me,
     For You will deal bountifully with me."

Praying Psalm 142

When Saul seeks David's life, David prays this prayer while hiding in a cave.

I am coming to You, Lord, trusting that, even though I feel overwhelmed, You are with me. I plead for Your grace (vv. 1–3).

No one else cares or can help but You—my Savior and my satisfaction. Deliver me, Lord, from all that overwhelms my soul. I need You—You are all I need and desire (vv. 4–7).

How Jesus could be interceding for you: Caring Father, deal bountifully with this troubled believer. Demonstrate to him/her the extent of Our care (1 Pet. 5:6–7). As You heard My cries, hear theirs (Heb. 5:7).

Psalm 143

Prayer for Deliverance and Guidance.

A Psalm of David.

1   Hear my prayer, O Lord,
     Give ear to my supplications!
     Answer me in Your faithfulness, in Your righteousness!
2   And do not enter into judgment with Your servant,
     For in Your sight no man living is righteous.
3   For the enemy has persecuted my soul;
     He has crushed my life to the ground;
     He has made me dwell in dark places, like those who have long been dead.
4   Therefore my spirit is overwhelmed within me;
     My heart is appalled within me.

5   I remember the days of old;
     I meditate on all Your doings;
     I muse on the work of Your hands.
6   I stretch out my hands to You;
     My soul *longs* for You, as a parched land.   *Selah.*

7   Answer me quickly, O Lord, my spirit fails;
     Do not hide Your face from me,
     Or I will become like those who go down to the pit.
8   Let me hear Your lovingkindness in the morning;
     For I trust in You;
     Teach me the way in which I should walk;
     For to You I lift up my soul.
9   Deliver me, O Lord, from my enemies;
     I take refuge in You.
10 Teach me to do Your will,
     For You are my God;
     Let Your good Spirit lead me on level ground.
11 For the sake of Your name, O Lord, revive me.
     In Your righteousness bring my soul out of trouble.
12 And in Your lovingkindness, cut off my enemies
     And destroy all those who afflict my soul,
     For I am Your servant.

Praying Psalm 143

*Humbled by Absalom's rebellion, David confesses
his own sin and asks God's forgiveness.*

For Your own name's sake, hear my prayer, Father. You alone are faithful and righteous. Forgive me for my sins—known and unknown—for no person living is righteous apart from You (vv. 1–2).

Lord Jesus, I feel overwhelmed and weak. Lord, help me and deliver me from the evil one who wants to destroy those who love You (vv. 3–9).

Give me a deep longing for You, Lord—just like a plant in dry ground thirsting for water (v. 6).

O God, I place all my trust in You in the midst of all my troubles (v. 8).

Teach me Your ways and guide me by Your Spirit. I am Yours, Lord—I belong to You (vv. 10–12).

How Jesus could be interceding for you: Keep the minds and hearts of Your servants steadfastly upon You and upon the work You sent Me to accomplish on their behalf, dear Father (Col. 3:1–4; Heb. 12:1–3). Deliver them from persecution and renew their strength (2 Cor. 4:16–18; Phil. 4:12–13).

Psalm 144

Prayer for Rescue and Prosperity.

A Psalm *of David.*

1 Blessed be the LORD, my rock,
   Who trains my hands for war,
   And my fingers for battle;
2 My lovingkindness and my fortress,
   My stronghold and my deliverer,
   My shield and He in whom I take refuge,
   Who subdues my people under me.
3 O LORD, what is man, that You take knowledge of him?
   Or the son of man, that You think of him?
4 Man is like a mere breath;
   His days are like a passing shadow.

5 Bow Your heavens, O LORD, and come down;
   Touch the mountains, that they may smoke.
6 Flash forth lightning and scatter them;
   Send out Your arrows and confuse them.
7 Stretch forth Your hand from on high;
   Rescue me and deliver me out of great waters,
   Out of the hand of aliens
8 Whose mouths speak deceit,
   And whose right hand is a right hand of falsehood.

9 I will sing a new song to You, O God;
   Upon a harp of ten strings I will sing praises to You,
10 Who gives salvation to kings,
   Who rescues David His servant from the evil sword.
11 Rescue me and deliver me out of the hand of aliens,
   Whose mouth speaks deceit
   And whose right hand is a right hand of falsehood.
12 Let our sons in their youth be as grown-up plants,
   And our daughters as corner pillars fashioned as for a palace;
13 Let our garners be full, furnishing every kind of produce,
   And our flocks bring forth thousands and ten thousands in our fields;
14 Let our cattle bear
   Without mishap and without loss,
   Let there be no outcry in our streets!
15 How blessed are the people who are so situated;
   How blessed are the people whose God is the LORD!

Praying Psalm 144

David praises the Lord for rescuing him out of a time of severe distress and trouble.

Come, our Rock and our Refuge. Reclaim creation by Your powerful hand and bring righteousness to earth (vv. 1–8).

Thank You, Lord, for protecting me and my family in a time of trouble (v. 2).

Father, I stand amazed at Your loving care for me (v. 3).

Protect me from those who would deceive me and draw me away from You, Lord (v. 8).

All of Your redeemed will sing of Your glory. Let Your Kingdom come and bless Your people, Lord Jesus (vv. 9–15).

Dear God, fill my home with Your blessings for my family and bring peace to our land (vv. 12–14).

Oh how blessed we are to have You, O Lord, as our God (v. 15)!

How Jesus could be interceding for you: Father, You sent Me from heaven to deliver Your people (Luke 4:18–21; John 6:38–40). I came down to earth, and taking upon Me human flesh I purchased their salvation by My death (Phil. 2:5–11; Heb. 2:9–10). Give to them a new song of redemption (Rev. 5:9), and teach them how blessed they are to have Yahweh as their God (Matt. 25:34; Rom. 4:7–8).

Psalm 145

The Lord Extolled for His Goodness.

A Psalm of Praise, of David.

1   I will extol You, my God, O King,
    And I will bless Your name forever and ever.
2   Every day I will bless You,
    And I will praise Your name forever and ever.
3   Great is the Lord, and highly to be praised,
    And His greatness is unsearchable.
4   One generation shall praise Your works to another,
    And shall declare Your mighty acts.
5   On the glorious splendor of Your majesty
    And on Your wonderful works, I will meditate.
6   Men shall speak of the power of Your awesome acts,
    And I will tell of Your greatness.
7   They shall eagerly utter the memory of Your abundant goodness
    And will shout joyfully of Your righteousness.

8   The Lord is gracious and merciful;
    Slow to anger and great in lovingkindness.
9   The Lord is good to all,
    And His mercies are over all His works.
10 All Your works shall give thanks to You, O Lord,
    And Your godly ones shall bless You.
11 They shall speak of the glory of Your kingdom
    And talk of Your power;
12 To make known to the sons of men Your mighty acts
    And the glory of the majesty of Your kingdom.
13 Your kingdom is an everlasting kingdom,
    And Your dominion *endures* throughout all generations.
14 The Lord sustains all who fall
    And raises up all who are bowed down.
15 The eyes of all look to You,
    And You give them their food in due time.
16 You open Your hand
    And satisfy the desire of every living thing.
17 The Lord is righteous in all His ways
    And kind in all His deeds.

Praying Psalm 145

David's final prayer in the Psalter occurs three times in Jewish daily liturgy.
The Lord's Prayer echoes a number of the themes in this prayer of David.

Let me praise You every day, all day—for all eternity will not be enough to extol Your virtues, perfections, and beauty, my King and my God (vv. 1–7).

Our Father in heaven, may Your name be holy (vv. 1, 21).

Father, teach me to be my children's and my grandchildren's model for praising You (v. 4).

Lord, You are full of kindness and compassion, love and goodness, in all that You do. Teach me to praise You in the presence of others every day. Forgive me for not declaring Your excellencies as You deserve (vv. 8–13).

Forgive us our sins, Father (v. 8).

Your Kingdom come, Your will be done, on earth as in heaven (vv. 11, 13).

Thank You, Father, for keeping me from falling away and for drawing near to me. I want to draw nearer to You, Lord. I love You, dear God, because Your Spirit has poured Your love into my heart (vv. 14–21).

Give us our daily food, Lord (v. 16).

18 The LORD is near to all who call upon Him,
    To all who call upon Him in truth.
19 He will fulfill the desire of those who fear Him;
    He will also hear their cry and will save them.
20 The LORD keeps all who love Him,
    But all the wicked He will destroy.
21 My mouth will speak the praise of the LORD,
    And all flesh will bless His holy name forever and ever.

And deliver us from evil (v. 20).

For Yours is the Kingdom, the power, and the glory forever (vv. 11, 13)!

How Jesus could be interceding for you: I taught My disciples how they should pray to You, heavenly Father (Matt. 6:8–13). Hear the prayers of the sheep of Our pasture and let them experience how very near to them We remain (Phil. 4:5; Jas. 5:8–9; 1 Tim. 5:21). Send Me again to set up Your Kingdom (Matt. 6:10; Luke 19:11–15).

Psalm 146

The LORD an Abundant Helper.

1 Praise the LORD!
   Praise the LORD, O my soul!
2 I will praise the LORD while I live;
   I will sing praises to my God while I have my being.
3 Do not trust in princes,
   In mortal man, in whom there is no salvation.
4 His spirit departs, he returns to the earth;
   In that very day his thoughts perish.
5 How blessed is he whose help is the God of Jacob,
   Whose hope is in the LORD his God,
6 Who made heaven and earth,
   The sea and all that is in them;
   Who keeps faith forever;
7 Who executes justice for the oppressed;
   Who gives food to the hungry.
   The LORD sets the prisoners free.

8 The LORD opens *the eyes of* the blind;
   The LORD raises up those who are bowed down;
   The LORD loves the righteous;
9 The LORD protects the strangers;
   He supports the fatherless and the widow,
   But He thwarts the way of the wicked.
10 The LORD will reign forever,
   Your God, O Zion, to all generations.
   Praise the LORD!

Praying Psalm 146

This anonymous prayer begins the final five "Hallelujah" (meaning "Praise the LORD") psalms with a focus on God's trustworthiness.

Father, I trust You with all my being (vv. 1–2).

Ⓐ

I will trust in You, dear Lord, rather than mortal humans (vv. 3–4).

Ⓐ

Jesus is Lord! And You, Lord, will reign forever and ever. Praise the Lord (vv. 5–10)!

Ⓐ

Thank You for help and hope as Your blessings (v. 5).

Ⓐ

Lord, I praise You for creating all things, applying justice, helping the helpless, loving the righteous, and protecting the vulnerable (vv. 6–9).

———

How Jesus could be interceding for you: Father, You sent Me to be the Hope and the Help of Your people (Matt. 12:17–21; Rom. 15:12–13; Heb. 4:16). You sent Me to do Your works and to demonstrate Your love (John 13:1; 15:9–10; 17:23). Cause Your people to praise You for all I have done, am doing, and will do to Your glory (Phil. 1:8–11).

Psalm 147

Praise for Jerusalem's Restoration and Prosperity.

1   Praise the Lord!
    For it is good to sing praises to our God;
    For it is pleasant *and* praise is becoming.

2   The Lord builds up Jerusalem;
    He gathers the outcasts of Israel.

3   He heals the brokenhearted
    And binds up their wounds.

4   He counts the number of the stars;
    He gives names to all of them.

5   Great is our Lord and abundant in strength;
    His understanding is infinite.

6   The Lord supports the afflicted;
    He brings down the wicked to the ground.

7   Sing to the Lord with thanksgiving;
    Sing praises to our God on the lyre,

8   Who covers the heavens with clouds,
    Who provides rain for the earth,
    Who makes grass to grow on the mountains.

9   He gives to the beast its food,
    And to the young ravens which cry.

10   He does not delight in the strength of the horse;
    He does not take pleasure in the legs of a man.

11   The Lord favors those who fear Him,
    Those who wait for His lovingkindness.

12   Praise the Lord, O Jerusalem!
    Praise your God, O Zion!

13   For He has strengthened the bars of your gates;
    He has blessed your sons within you.

14   He makes peace in your borders;
    He satisfies you with the finest of the wheat.

15   He sends forth His command to the earth;
    His word runs very swiftly.

16   He gives snow like wool;
    He scatters the frost like ashes.

Praying Psalm 147

Perhaps the inhabitants of Jerusalem sang this prayer of praise when they celebrated the completion of Jerusalem's walls after the return from the Babylonian captivity (Neh. 12:27–43).

Praise belongs to You, our compassionate Healer and Savior of those who are poor in spirit (vv. 1–6).

Father, thank You for healing the brokenhearted (v. 3).

Lord Jesus, we sing praise for Your preservation of all creation, for favoring those who fear You and who wait upon Your steadfast love (vv. 7–11).

Thank You for providing rain for our land and its crops (v. 8).

Lord, teach me to fear You more and more every day (v. 11).

Father, open the eyes of Your covenant nation to see Your care and sustaining grace in the person of Your Son (vv. 12–20).

I thank You even for the winter with its cold and snow to remind me of Your precious Word that melts cold hearts (vv. 16–19).

Lord, help me to respond quickly to Your Word (v. 15).

17 He casts forth His ice as fragments;
    Who can stand before His cold?
18 He sends forth His word and melts them;
    He causes His wind to blow and the waters to flow.
19 He declares His words to Jacob,
    His statutes and His ordinances to Israel.
20 He has not dealt thus with any nation;
    And as for His ordinances, they have not known them.
    Praise the LORD!

How we praise You, Lord God, for making Your will known to Your people by means of Your spoken and written Word (v. 19).

Thank You for Your grace and mercy to Israel, gracious Father (v. 20).

How Jesus could be interceding for you: You chose Israel and You chose Jerusalem, Almighty Father (Matt. 5:35; Luke 24:45–47). You blessed them with everything beyond any other people (Luke 1:68–75; Rom. 9:4–5). You are worthy of all songs of praise, so increase their praise by fulfilling Your promises to set Me upon the throne of David (Matt. 19:28; Luke 1:32–33).

Psalm 148

The Whole Creation Invoked to Praise the LORD.

1   Praise the LORD!
    Praise the LORD from the heavens;
    Praise Him in the heights!
2   Praise Him, all His angels;
    Praise Him, all His hosts!
3   Praise Him, sun and moon;
    Praise Him, all stars of light!
4   Praise Him, highest heavens,
    And the waters that are above the heavens!
5   Let them praise the name of the LORD,
    For He commanded and they were created.
6   He has also established them forever and ever;
    He has made a decree which will not pass away.

7   Praise the LORD from the earth,
    Sea monsters and all deeps;
8   Fire and hail, snow and clouds;
    Stormy wind, fulfilling His word;
9   Mountains and all hills;
    Fruit trees and all cedars;
10 Beasts and all cattle;
    Creeping things and winged fowl;
11 Kings of the earth and all peoples;
    Princes and all judges of the earth;
12 Both young men and virgins;
    Old men and children.
13 Let them praise the name of the LORD,
    For His name alone is exalted;
    His glory is above earth and heaven.
14 And He has lifted up a horn for His people,
    Praise for all His godly ones;
    Even for the sons of Israel, a people near to Him.
    Praise the LORD!

Praying Psalm 148

This anonymous prayer of praise summons all creation to form a choir with two sections responding to each other—one in the heavens above and one on the earth beneath.

You are worthy, Lord God, Creator of all things. Relieve the anxious groaning of Your creation by revealing the Son and your sons through faith in Him. Let all creation praise You as You deserve (vv. 1–14).

Lord, thank You for allowing me to praise You along with the angels (v. 2).

Praise God! He created everything in the heavens above (v. 5).

I praise You, my Lord and Savior, for everything with which You have filled the earth (vv. 7–10).

Father, I exalt and praise You and You alone (v. 13)!

How Jesus could be interceding for you: Father, You are enthroned upon the praises of Your people (Ps. 22:3). You gave Me Your glory by which I might create all things so that You might be highly exalted (John 1:1–4, 14; 17:5; 2 Cor. 4:6). Stimulate Your people to praise and glorify You (Rom. 11:33–36).

Psalm 149

Israel Invoked to Praise the LORD.

1   Praise the LORD!
    Sing to the LORD a new song,
    And His praise in the congregation of the godly ones.
2   Let Israel be glad in his Maker;
    Let the sons of Zion rejoice in their King.
3   Let them praise His name with dancing;
    Let them sing praises to Him with timbrel and lyre.
4   For the LORD takes pleasure in His people;
    He will beautify the afflicted ones with salvation.

5   Let the godly ones exult in glory;
    Let them sing for joy on their beds.
6   *Let* the high praises of God *be* in their mouth,
    And a two-edged sword in their hand,
7   To execute vengeance on the nations
    And punishment on the peoples,
8   To bind their kings with chains
    And their nobles with fetters of iron,
9   To execute on them the judgment written;
    This is an honor for all His godly ones.
    Praise the LORD!

Praying Psalm 149

This anonymous prayer of praise forms the final prayer of the Psalter since the last psalm acts more like a closing doxology for the entire Psalter.

I look forward to the great day of dancing, singing, and rejoicing with all Your redeemed in the Kingdom. It will be a day of joy and judgment as Your people join You, Lord Jesus, in executing Your just judgment on all who do not love You (vv. 1–9).

⋘⋙

What a joy, Father, to know that You are in control of everything (v. 2)!

⋘⋙

I'm amazed, dear Lord, that You delight in me, an unworthy sinner (v. 4).

⋘⋙

Father, fulfill Your prophetic word to judge the unrighteous (v. 9).

How Jesus could be interceding for you: Glorious Father, fulfill through Me Your covenant promises to David (2 Sam. 7:8–16; Ps. 2:6–12; Rev. 19:11–16). Take delight in Your people (John 14:21; 16:27) as they join Me in establishing Your Kingdom upon the earth (Prov. 8:30–31; 2 Tim. 2:12; Rev. 5:9–10).

Psalm 150

A Psalm of Praise.

1   Praise the LORD!
     Praise God in His sanctuary;
     Praise Him in His mighty expanse.
2   Praise Him for His mighty deeds;
     Praise Him according to His excellent greatness.

3   Praise Him with trumpet sound;
     Praise Him with harp and lyre.
4   Praise Him with timbrel and dancing;
     Praise Him with stringed instruments and pipe.
5   Praise Him with loud cymbals;
     Praise Him with resounding cymbals.
6   Let everything that has breath praise the LORD.
     Praise the LORD!

Praying Psalm 150

This anonymously written doxology closes the Psalter and all of its prayers. Worshippers bringing their offerings of firstfruits to Jerusalem would sing this psalm during their procession.

Yes, Lord. You are worthy of this praise! Come receive the praise of all things in creation. Glorify Yourself (vv. 1–6).

Father, I praise You for all Your mighty deeds (v. 2).

Thank You, Lord Jesus, for all the musical instruments we use to sing Your praise (vv. 3–5).

Hallelujah (v. 6)!

How Jesus could be interceding for you: Father, instill songs of praises in the hearts of Your people each and every day of their lives (Matt. 6:13; Rom. 16:25–27; Gal. 1:3–5; 1 Tim. 6:13–16).